PASSING

PASSING

When People Can't Be Who They Are

Brooke Kroeger

PublicAffairs

New York

Book design by Jane Raese
Text set in 12-point Bulmer

Library of Congress Cataloging-in-Publication Data
Kroeger, Brooke, 1949–
Passing : when people can't be who they are / Brooke Kroeger.
    p. cm.
Includes bibliographical references and index.
ISBN 1-891620-99-1
1. Passing (Identity) 2. Passing (Identity)—Case studies. I. Title.
HM1068.K76 2003
302'.1—dc21   2003046866

FIRST EDITION

10 9 8 7 6 5 4 3 2 1

For my father

Contents

Passing Then, Passing Now

THE IMPETUS FOR THIS BOOK was a stunningly dated melodrama called *Imitation of Life* that has at its center the story of a gorgeous light-skinned black woman who wreaks havoc by passing for white.

I learned a lot about *Imitation* researching the life of its white author, Fannie Hurst, because the treatment of racial themes in the 1934 film adaptation of her novel caused a ruckus among black intellectuals. Not that the controversy diminished the work's appeal in any way. Both the original and its 1959 remake still can jerk a monsoon of tears. I've certainly cried my share.

Peola (Sarah Jane in the later version) is a brash and brazen crosser of the great black–white divide. She risks her dignity and her safety to accept work in a whites-only job. With unflinching resolve, she cuts off her adoring, self-sacrificing mother (*"Let me pass!!"*), and sends the older woman on the fast train to death by heartbreak. In the novel, Peola marries a white man and never tells him that she is not white. To keep her past hidden, she convinces him to move with her to Bolivia. She even has herself sterilized to make sure no dark-hued infant ever exits her womb. It is only in the more sentimentalized Hollywood versions of the story that Peola sees the error of her ways. She returns to New York as her mother's funeral cortege begins its procession. Laden with grief and remorse, Peola flings herself flailing and wailing over her mother's casket.

Despite the different plot twists, the moral in each version of the story is the same. Passing, if not altogether bad, is at least a really bad idea, and society, or life itself, will punish the "passer" for breaking the rules. A "Peola," a passer, in fiction or in real life, has never been a good thing to be.

We judge the Peolas harshly for the lies and deceits they perpetrate, and for the pain and embarrassment they seem so willing to inflict on those they owe the most. We accuse them of duplicity, of cowardice, of not being themselves, of not fighting the good fight. Yet think of Peola's seventy-year-old example through twenty-first-century eyes. Here was a woman reared in a white household in the "sublime democracy of childhood," in an atmosphere of white promise, white hopes, and expectations. She even looked the part. Of life, she asked no more than to hold on to privileges already conferred, privileges sure to be denied in her adult future for reasons that made no sense. And what were these gold-standard "privileges" she so determinedly sought? The chance for nothing more than a job other than housemaid and marriage to someone she loved. Clearly racism, not Peola, was the bad guy in *Imitation*. If we didn't quite grasp this the first few times we saw the movie, we know it now.

Passing: When People Can't Be Who They Are is about the predicament of the modern-day, real-life Peola. It is not about every kind of passing (and I learned that there are myriad kinds), but specifically about people who pass in order to bypass being excluded unjustly in their attempts to achieve ordinary, honorable aims and ambitions. It is about people who pass to be more truly themselves. Sometimes the passers in this book cut through passing's moral and ethical thickets with relative ease. Sometimes not.

For audiences today, *Imitation of Life* is little more than a fraying remnant of the time in which Fannie Hurst wrote it. But the story she told, flawed as it may be, has other ways of remaining useful to us. It (and others like it) provides a sturdy milepost for marking the distance our attitudes have traveled over the past seventy years and assaying how far there is yet to go. The stories of the six present-day passers on whom this book centers do the same. Passing may be commonly characterized as a cop-out, with the passer complicit in the system that made it necessary to pass in the first place. But these stories may move you, as they did me, to see an act of passing as more than a marker, to see it as an effective if slow-moving means of hastening social change. At the very least, these stories help the rest of us assess the validity of the stances we bring to consideration of any number of social issues, from relations across the color line, to class and religious separation, to gay acceptance. These stories are not meant to single out any specific institutions; the settings are in many ways incidental. The point is to clarify our attitudes toward the biases these stories detail, wherever they may appear.

Literary scholar Werner Sollors explains that the very act of passing, the crossing of boundaries that people tend to see as fixed, real, or even natural, makes passers "ideal questioners of the status quo." This is true of the black-for-white passing stories from literature that Sollors examines, and for other passing stories. It is certainly true of the stories in this book.

~

SETTLING ON THE MAIN STORIES that appear in the following pages was less difficult than you might imagine. There were dozens of willing contributors. Everyone I knew seemed to know someone who knew someone who had passed for some length of time.

Confessions even came from some of my friends. I ran into scores of passing permutations along with the ways of passing the term most readily brings to mind: black passing for white, as well as Jew passing for gentile, and gay passing for straight. (Black-for-white passing first brought the Americanism *passing* into use, and, as you will see, passing looks a lot different in our time than it did in the pre–civil rights days of Fannie Hurst.) The prevalence of passing today really shouldn't have surprised me. As scholars tell us, wherever there is prejudice and preconception, there is passing, and of prejudice and preconception we as yet have no lack.

"We pass for rich," a friend whose name appears in the Social Register confided with a conspiratorial giggle. A Swiss friend, a Roman Catholic with a German surname, found it advantageous not to correct colleagues in her class at Columbia Business School who presumed that she was Jewish. I interviewed an ethnic Chinese woman who grew up in Japan, where her family changed its last name to make it Japanese. Now, as a U.S. citizen, she switches among her three identities depending on which identification happens to be the most useful at any given moment, and which government happens to be bashing which.

From the media, I learned about real-life passing stories in America and abroad involving imposters and identity thieves, con artists and hucksters; terrorists who pass as quiet next-door neighbors, and at least one suicide bomber, head wrapped in a kaffiyeh, who turned out to be a girl.

The workforce is rife with gays who pass for straight. Burly major league athletes who disclose their homosexuality—so far, always after retirement—always cause a sensation. The world of big-time Wall Street brokers and financiers is not yet a place where gay people find an easy welcome, nor is the world of organized religion. A devout but tormented Italian Roman Catholic confessed in the *Corriere della sera*, "My superiors don't know that I'm gay; my gay friends don't know I'm a priest."

The Internet turns out to be a borderless godsend for fabulists and fakers and not-so-harmless hoaxers, hustlers, and predators of every description. There's a surfeit of people who aggrandize or flat-out invent their educational background and accomplishments for résumés and privileges or for classroom or party chatter, and we've all heard about the self-proclaimed military heroes who never even put on a uniform.

There is gender passing, class passing, and age passing. One young, androgynous-appearing friend, five-ten and good-looking, told me that in high school, having openly declared herself a lesbian, she often passed for the new boyfriend when she picked up girls for dates. Another, a milk-skinned redhead brought up small-town Texas poor, suppressed her drawl and passed for well-bred East Coast preppy while on a full-ride scholarship at the University of Rochester. A film script writer confessed that she communicates professionally only by e-mail or telephone to stave off screenwriter suicide—being exposed as over forty. Hollywood calls to mind the passing that plastic and reconstructive surgery make possible. There is even what is erroneously termed "reverse passing," as in straight for gay or white for black, along with dozens of acts of racial, ethnic, and national claim or camouflage. ("Passing for Asian: Filipino Americans and Filipino American Studies within Asian American Studies" reads the title of an academic conference paper.) And how about the legions of spouses who lead surreptitious double lives while passing for faithful? I spoke at length with one man who has been married for decades but, unbeknown to his wife, has always had homosexual liaisons on the side.

I learned a lot about the nature of passing from all of these encounters, but the six stories I have chosen to feature best illustrate how passing scenarios play out with our more tolerant age for a backdrop. In these cases, both the main subjects and those who make up their circles were most helpful at articulating what compels a person to make such a drastic life choice. From the start, I knew I wanted to avoid anyone with a high public profile. Celebrity ambushes didn't really interest me, nor did sensational stories from the headlines. The point was to focus on everyday people with everyday lives who would share their stories without the mediation of publicists. The individuals I settled on met all of the criteria. In telling the stories, I have not changed or altered any details, but I have omitted specific references when requested to do so.

These stories are very specific to their settings, but are they representative of passers in other situations and circumstances? Do they represent passing in general? That is my hope, but there is no way to know. The secretive nature of passing makes it impossible to quantify reliably. The only clue to how frequently passing occurs is the unexpected ease with which I was able to identify potential subjects. The only clue to how representative the stories may be is in their common depictions of what it was like to pass, especially given the different circumstances surrounding each case. The result is far from scientific, but the individual accounts are distinct enough for me to venture that taken in the aggregate, cumulatively the stories plus the stories and theories and lay and expert reflections that relate to these experiences provide a reasonably wide account of this kind of passing in our time.

The protagonists of *Passing* are smart, reflective, educated, extremely likeable men and women who range in age from their mid-twenties to their mid-forties. The age range is significant because it gives the stories their contemporary cast. The length of time involved in passing varied in each case, but all of the episodes took place within a delineated period of time during the past ten or fifteen years and then ended, which explains why the passers felt free to tell their stories in detail. The group includes a screen-writer originally from Baltimore, a young teacher in the South, a desktop publishing expert who works on Wall Street, a rabbinical student, a navy careerist, and a very well regarded poet with an en-during passion for teenybopper music. In five of the stories, the passers managed to gain acceptance by presenting themselves as other than who they understood themselves to be. The last story takes a few slightly different turns because of the context in which it takes place. I chose it for reasons that will become clearer in the telling.

The following pages will introduce you to a forthright group of people of good heart and decent purpose who pass or have passed for the reasons people always have passed: for opportunity, safety, adventure, or some combination of the three. They passed in many of the modes of passing we most often associate with the term—black for white, white for black, gay for straight, and so on. They have done it by mistake or they have done it by design. They passed to avoid conflict or personal rejection or to fulfill serious professional aspirations. They passed full-time, part-time, or only on occasion, and all of them coped in different ways with the moral and ethical compromises passing so often exacts.

To proceed, we need a definition for *passing* as this book describes it. In the most general way, it is passing when people effectively present themselves as other than who they understand themselves to be. *Effectively* is key because an ineffectual effort to pass is just that, a failed attempt. Passing means that other people actually see or experience the identity that the passer is projecting, whether the passer is telegraphing that identity by intention or by chance. The somewhat awkward wording is intentional. *Who they understand themselves to be* deliberately sidesteps a more complicated discourse over *Who they are* (and who or what determines who we are anyway?) or even the less complicated *Who others see them as* or even *Who they have become*. Passing never feels natural. It is a second skin that never adheres.

Passing involves erasing details or certain aspects of a given life in order to move past perceived, suspected, or actual barriers to achieve desired ends. These ends take all forms, ranging in impact from the ephemeral to the profound, from the frivolous to the disastrously consequential. Passing is, as the literary scholar Elaine Ginsberg explains, the act of creating, imposing, adopting, or rejecting a given identity and the way society rewards and penalizes people when they do. It is about not only crossing individual boundaries but also the anxiety this provokes. It is about the visible and the invisible, she writes; the seen and the not seen.

With the props of appearance and talent, passers step out of identities dictated by genes, heritage, training, circumstance, or happenstance. They must possess the face, voice, skin color, body type, style, and/or behavior that defies or confounds easy profiling. Passers stay in character no matter what. When the passing is intentional, the passer also needs stealth and gumption, cunning, agility, and social conceit.

Passers curtain off their origins; part-time passers do not own up to the other significant involvements in their lives. Passing, in that sense, takes guile. Keeping secrets, or at least avoiding certain disclosures, is a given in any passing ruse, which means that passing also requires the complicity, safe distance, or death of those who know the passers in their other context. Though passing of-

ten assumes the denial of background and ancestry, it is not always about that. We see this especially in gay stories, where the
inverse is true, where the denial concerns sexual orientation and
current lifestyle rather than heritage.

Passing stories allow us to see which aspects of identity seem
to be fixed and unchangeable—at least at the present time—and
which can shift and gurgle and spill into other identities, those
that are not fixed at all. For the individuals involved, projecting as
"other" can bring into focus what about themselves they are unable to cast off. For those of us looking in, such stories allow us to
gauge where we stand personally and as a society on the wider
subject of identity itself.

The phenomenon of passing also sets up an encounter with
several larger philosophical questions. Must communities put so
many onuses on us? Does authenticity matter? How much information does one person owe another? When is nondisclosure lying? How does lying affect the soul? Even on the plus side,
passing puts us in touch with the wondrous ability each person
has to create and recreate the self.

WHAT I FOUND MOST DIFFICULT in the process of spending
time with the very smart, ordinarily honorable people profiled in
these pages was reliving with them the experiences that compelled them to twist their lives into painful deceit-ridden contortions for reasons that do not hold. This is the territory I set out to
explore. What follows is what I learned along the way.

Brooke Kroeger
March 2003

CHAPTER ONE

Not Some
Social Agenda Struggle

If the jinnee should say,
"I have come to carry out an inexorable command to change you
into a member of another race; make your choice!"
I should answer, probably,
"Make me a Jew."
— JAMES WELDON JOHNSON

HE HAS NO RECOLLECTION OF HIS MOTHER, although he
knows she was Jewish because this much his father told him; that,
and how she took off for Israel while she was pregnant with him,
drawn by the 1967 war. She returned, gave birth, took her infant
son back to Israel, and then returned to Washington again. Not
long after, her soon to be ex-husband relieved her of parental du-
ties. A few cards arrived in the months that followed, and then
nothing. David Matthews never learned his mother's name until
he saw it on a copy of his birth certificate on the way to take his
driver's test at age nineteen.

On his father's side, the heritage is notable, a pedigree, real
yichis, his mother might have said. He is intensely proud to be the
son of Ralph D. Matthews and the grandson of the late Ralph
Matthews Sr., both important journalists and black community

leaders in their day. Both spent a good part of their careers with the Baltimore-based *Afro-American* chain of newspapers.

Life with father, as David Matthews recalls it, meant "a very stoic, very male household in an almost postmodern sense." By the time he was old enough to wonder about his mother's absence, "it seemed such a clichéd movie-of-the-week question to ask" that he didn't bother. "It just seemed too on-the-nose to say, *Well, Dad, where's Mom?* He didn't bring it up so I didn't bring it up." Matthews uses the phrase "Mother's side of the family" to refer to the maternal relatives he has never met and knows next to nothing about.

Sometimes, as they drove together down a street in Washington, D.C., Matthews *père* would suddenly point toward an apartment building and issue forth a statement such as, *That is where you were conceived.* "And that would be the end of the discussion," his son recalled. "We were just tough guys and it just didn't seem like the kind of touchy-feely stuff I needed to know." Matthews *fils* is not impressed by his personal history. He thinks it is just another version of being the child of a single parent, the product of a divorced home. "I'm sure the women I date think that it shows up every once in a while, but I don't have a conscious *Boy, I'd like to know*—I mean, I'd like to know if I'm the heir to a textile fortune, or if there is any congenital illness I need to worry about."

FROM LATE ELEMENTARY SCHOOL until well into his twenties, David Matthews got into the habit of presenting himself to the world as white. Not all of the time, but whenever the need arose. Usually, in these instances, he presented himself as Jewish. Was it passing for this half-Jewish person to present himself as white or Jewish? The short answer is yes, first and foremost, because he experienced the act as passing while he was doing it. Black is how he was brought up to know himself; black is what he understood himself to be. It was passing because he deliberately withheld information about his African American heritage whenever he sensed it would get in his way. Matthews did this despite the fact that very clearly and very early on, he grasped that people in his sphere felt entitled to be told about his African American background. They felt this despite his facial features (his septuagenarian father described them as "Caucasoid"), his wiry auburn hair, his very light olive skin, his dress, his interests, his tastes, his personality, his credible claim to another heritage, and his ability to keep his ties to the black community out of view. His "selective editing" (his phrase)—both in the view of the prevailing culture and in his own mind—was deceptive by design. "Maybe it was a facile thing for me to do; I don't know," was the way he talked about it. "For me, it was always a question of being allowed in. And whatever I had to do to be allowed in wasn't necessarily a bad thing because not being allowed in was so much worse. It seems like it was breathing to me almost."

It was also passing because black is the identity our culture assigns or ascribes to David Matthews without reflection or comment. This automatic response is a throwback, no doubt, to the mind-set that led to cultural artifacts such as the registries of free Negroes of a couple of centuries ago. Had David Matthews lived in the 1800s, his name might well have been inscribed on such a list. He would have been singled out as "mulatto" with a skin color description of "very bright, almost white." In Virginia, for example, up until 1910, one Negro grandparent was enough to classify a person mulatto, and mulatto meant black. From 1910 to

1924, one Negro great-grandparent became enough to warrant the label, and after that, right up until the 1960s, it took no more than a single drop of Negro blood.

Opportunities have opened and attitudes have softened in the years since we stopped measuring blackness in droplets. At least from a legal standpoint, being a lot or a little bit black no longer threatens life or livelihood in Virginia or anywhere else in this country in the way it once did. We don't need David Matthews to rehearse this burdensome history. What his story offers is the whys and wherefores of being someone with an ambiguous personal presence, one that offers the right to float and a shore pass for both sides of the gully between the black identity he has no choice about and the white and Jewish identities he can so ably "perform."

As we know from factual accounts, as well as fiction and film, the practice of black-for-white passing in America has been around a long time. It was common enough in 1945 for the anthropologists St. Clair Drake and Horace R. Cayton to describe it as a kind of process, a natural cycle, that begins unwittingly, inadvertently, with people fully self-identified as black discovering that in some contexts, white people actually see them as white. This inadvertent or unintended passing can lead to passing for convenience, as in the convenience of eating in whites-only restaurants of the time, seeing movies in segregated theaters, staying in segregated hotels, or shopping in segregated stores. Next would come passing "for fun," especially on vacation or in any situation outside a passer's normal routine. From there could come the decision to "pass all the way," meaning part-time, in the way Matthews passed nearly half a century later, or full-time, which often involves drastic measures to erase a tell-tale past—a whole new identity, a move to a new locale, a complete break from family and old friends. This cycle can be broken at any point, with a "return to the fold."

The temptation to pass is perhaps greatest, the anthropologists seemed to suggest, among those who are not "firmly anchored emotionally" in the black community.

～

DAVID MATTHEWS'S FATHER is much lighter than paper-bag tan, with a black identity that is proud and firm. In photographs, David's grandmother, Ralph Matthews's mother, appears white without question. David thinks his father looks a lot like Don Knotts and it's a good description, except that there is nothing even remotely Mayberry about Ralph Matthews. As David says, his father is by far the hippest person he knows. Ralph Mathews has a side interest in jazz and a stunning record album collection that lines one wall of the living room of his home in the Maryland suburbs of Washington, D.C. In 1945 he graduated from Syracuse University on a scholarship that covered full tuition and a train ticket because at that time, the University of Maryland did not admit black in-state residents as undergraduates in journalism but arranged to subsidize their studies at colleges and universities that would. Matthews Sr. has many good stories from his journalism days, the most memorable being his coverage of the historic meeting in September 1960 between Malcolm X and Fidel Castro at the Hotel Theresa in Harlem. Matthews was working for the *New York Citizen-Call* at the time and was one of only two reporters to cover the story from inside Castro's hotel room. A public affairs job with the War on Poverty under Sargent Shriver during the Johnson administration precipitated his move to Washington. Later he worked with the Bicentennial Commission, and while David was a toddler he did a stint at the local public television affiliate, where he craftily succeeded in drafting half the staff as baby-sitters. He and his son lived at a succession of suburban Washington addresses, the kinds of neighborhoods Bill Cosby's television family the Huxtables would have favored. For a couple of years David Matthews had a stepmother, a white woman, but she and Ralph Matthews soon divorced and father and son were on their own once again. Single fathers were very rare in the late 1960s and early 1970s, and Ralph Matthews quickly figured out that life was easier with a woman around, especially since his work often kept him out until well past midnight. Before and after the divorce he had a succession of obliging girlfriends, both black and white. David's grandmother also helped out with child care. An older half sister from his father's first marriage and a younger half brother by the stepmother lived with their respective mothers. They came and went from the Matthews's bachelor pad. The children were not brought up together.

~

DAVID'S GRANDMOTHER GREW UP with a foster family in Rhode Island but actually came from North Carolina. She worked as a school administrator and for a time at the *Baltimore Sun*. David's father said that no one realized she was black or she never would have been hired at the *Sun*. Ralph Matthews got a little testy at the suggestion that his mother had passed to work there. "No, she never passed. She was from Newport," and newly arrived in town at the time she applied for the position at the *Sun*, was his reply. "She didn't know." All of the elder Mrs. Matthews's friendships and associations were in the black community and that was the life she happily lived. Her grandson David adored her, and yet he was always perplexed by the way she would cluck at television reports of local mayhem—rape, robbery, shootings—and hope that the perpetrator *isn't one of us,* cluck again if the perpetrator turned out to be, and then cluck again about the dark-skinned people—"darkies," she called them—who shamed *us* by committing crimes. So who exactly was *us,* the young Matthews wanted to know but never asked. "All I knew was that I didn't want to be one of *them.* And I didn't really view her or my dad as one of *them.* They just said they were."

DAVID MATTHEWS WAS NINE when his father returned to Baltimore to become one of the editors of the *Afro-American* and rented a nice apartment on Mount Royal in a nice mixed neighborhood north of the city center. Not long after, he had the opportunity to purchase for next to nothing a wreck of a row house on Madison Street, a few blocks west of Eutaw Avenue in an all-black ghetto. Shortly before he and his father moved in, the backyard had been the scene of a gangland-style execution. The next-door neighbor, still suffering the posttraumatic effects of his tour in Vietnam, took solace in shooting his AK–47 outside his backdoor. All the same, the house was only a few short blocks from Bolton Hill, with its well-kept townhouses and Gramercy Park–like air. Matthews's plan was to renovate the row house and flip it for a profit as gentrification encroached, but gentrification did not encroach quite fast enough. In the years since he let the house go, there has been substantial redevelopment in the area, enough to make the old row house look that much more forlorn. In March 2002, a slab of whitewashed plywood blocked the entranceway. Stenciled across the plank in red was the number to call "IF ANIMAL TRAPPED."

Life on Madison Street is a recurrent theme in David Matthews's conversation. He found the experience torturous. "I wouldn't walk there until it was dark," he recalled, "because the fewer people who saw me, the fewer chances I had of getting mugged." His father wanted his son to learn to survive in such an environment. "There are protections," Ralph Matthews said. "And if you recognize them, you're twice as strong. I knew all the hoodlums." His son was sometimes threatened, but it was because he did not know "how to give off the right radar," as Matthews Sr. put it. "And giving off *I'm half Jewish* wasn't it." The next-door neighbor with the AK-47 was forever offering to intercede on David's behalf—what Ralph Matthews meant by protection. His son "never stuck around long enough to learn the protections that I think would still stand him in good stead. He was so busy getting out of there that he missed all of that. He's reasonably street smart now, but what Madison could have taught him, he didn't want to know."

Madison Street was David Matthews's first direct exposure to the people his grandmother was forever clucking about, those he too had come to disdain. His only felt connection to his new neighbors was the fact that before the year 2000, a census taker would have checked him off in the same box under the category of race. He also knew that outside the black community, in the world he more closely resembled, the world he sought to inhabit, the sharp and obvious distinctions between him and grandmother's old *them* would be lost entirely. For most white people, Madison Street was synonymous with what it meant to be black. On Madison Street, David Matthews no doubt feared for his safety, but the greater terror, he later acknowledged, was his new and unwelcome physical proximity to a way of life he rejected. Suddenly, *them* lived right next door.

Ralph Matthews did not share David's fear or snobbery. Of his son's itinerant passing, the older man said, "I do wonder about that, about David's trapeze act. In my own life, it's not even a consideration." And in another conversation, he added, "The thing I don't think we could answer is, where did it come from?"

PART OF THE APPEAL of the row house property was its proximity to the Mount Royal Elementary Middle School, one of the city's finest, just a few blocks away on Eutaw's "good side," where David Matthews was enrolled as a fourth grader.

On school days, Matthews walked north two blocks to McMechen and east across Eutaw Avenue's great divide into Bolton Hill. Up and down Bolton Street and Baltimore's own Park Avenue, to the left and to the right, are the townhouses, and then a little further east is the school itself, near the Maryland Institute College of Art. For an inner-city public school, Mount Royal was unique at the time because of its contingent of reasonably affluent white students.

Matthews is not certain if his actions in those first years at Mount Royal qualify as passing "because I hadn't made any conscious decisions yet." But passing, as Drake and Cayton pointed out, does not always start as a conscious act. Matthews found himself gravitating toward a group of Jewish kids and they toward him. He thinks of himself even today as having a certain "Jewish sensibility," apparent in his instinctive preference for Woody Allen over Richard Pryor, or Saul Bellow and J.D. Salinger over Ernest Hemingway or F. Scott Fitzgerald. Lenny Bruce routines really speak to him. "Those things just came my way," Matthews said. "I didn't really even consciously know that they were Jewish." His early friendships seemed to form out of magnetic pull. "It was more like *I look like you and you look like me so we'll be friends.* And I could start to see the different attitudes of those I wanted to be associated with. To me, it was not even a conscious choice. It was an easy choice. Our sensibilities were similar, our sense of humor, our music."

On the subject of musical taste, his father tells the story of a trip to visit relatives in North Carolina with David and David's grandmother, when David was about nine years old. "And so I rented this big, slick—you always do that when you go to visit family, right? I figured my mother would like it. And we were driving down, and we got into North Carolina, or into Virginia, and the music began to change—you know, a lot of country music—and all of a sudden Elvis came on the radio, and I'm driving, and then I said, 'Let me get this crap off of here.' And David said, 'Don't change that! I love Elvis!' And my mother and I both said, 'Oh, my God.' I almost ran off the road. I turned around and said, 'David, where on God's earth could you even develop an ear for this?' Kids have their own secret worlds. Maybe it was from the control booth at WETA when he was twenty months old or less than that. He was deciding something for himself, you know?"

~

IN MIDDLE SCHOOL AND HIGH SCHOOL, David Matthews didn't have friends among the black kids, although his knowledge of their language, its cadences and slang, gave him a certain standing with these classmates. "They considered me the cool white guy, so I got a little bit of a pass on that." His father thought he should be getting more than a pass. Ralph Matthews felt strongly that his son should have black friends as well as white, but his son insists there was no such possibility in the 1980s when this was taking place. "You didn't make friends with both. I didn't know anyone who was friends with both," David Matthews said. "It just didn't work out that way." In high school, he had one friend who was half black, half Norwegian, whose father was a close friend of his father's. And a little cross-pollination occurred when white girls would go out with a black guy for a week or two—but never for prom or anything major. "For something serious it would be, suddenly, back to the kids in their neighborhood," David Matthews said.

As a teenager, Matthews felt he had only two choices: The more difficult one would have been to tell the truth, just to come right out and explain his background to "these people who I feel a kinship with" and risk losing their friendship. This, he reasoned, would have meant losing the friendship of the people with whom he had the most in common. Then he would either find himself totally isolated or have to cultivate friendships with people whose interests he did not share. His solution was to take the first route and omit the information that would have complicated his life. He passed.

I SHARED DAVID MATTHEWS'S STORY with philosopher and scholar Anthony Appiah, a Princeton University professor who has written widely on the subject of identity. I asked him whether he thought Matthews had acted badly. "This is one of those bad situations," he said, "but putting all the blame on the person who was put into that situation seems to be the wrong way to go about it.

"It's one thing to have to hide the fact that you don't have much money or something. But we feel it is just a terrible imposition on someone to have to hide one's identity in the core cases of racial and sexual orientation, gender, nationality, religion, and so on. And even when that person might feel that he would like to answer honestly, a wise person might not in these circumstances because the cost might be too high."

Appiah said it would be nice to think that Matthews's friends eventually would have come around to accepting that he was black. "All friendships involve some disclosures and the timing of disclosures," he said. "But if you're planning never to tell your friends something, isn't there something un-friendlike about that?" Nevertheless, perhaps Matthews's assessment of his circumstances was correct. Perhaps his friends would not have behaved well once they knew the facts. Indeed, perhaps his only choice was no friends or these imperfect friends. "Most of us have these options anyway," Appiah said. "No one has perfect friends.

"So let's stipulate that he was right, that he could not have been their friend in the way he wanted to be their friend if they knew this thing about him. I don't want to blame him because it's not his fault that he was in this situation where he had a hard choice to make. And for him to ruin his life doesn't seem to be much of a choice. *To make a point, I ruined my life. I'll just sit here in the dark.* That doesn't do any good. So what he did was probably the best thing to do."

MATTHEWS NEVER BROUGHT any of his white friends home. He did not introduce them to his father. By the time he was in high school, a few miles away on the hill at the prestigious Baltimore

City College, he had frequent occasion to go to the homes of these high school friends and meet their families. "The Jewish kids were much wealthier," he said, "lot of privilege, you know, kids who were getting cars at age fifteen." They introduced him to the world of adolescent suburbia. By then his look had gotten "a little more exotic"—the epicanthic fold to his eyelids gives his face a slightly Asian cast. "When I would go to kids' houses, I started noticing the first question right after, *Hello, nice to meet you,* was, *What interesting features. Where are you from?* Especially if it was a girl's house. That was the first question—especially the dads asked it right off the bat. And it didn't really make me nervous, per se, but I was aware that there was probably an answer that would make them feel better. I don't think I ever said I was mixed. I just said I was Jewish and when they started to get into *where-do-you-go-to-shul* or something like that I'd say my dad was not practicing. I'd say that we didn't have any religious anything in my house. Christmas was a perfunctory commercial holiday, but there was never any church or any praying or anything like that. And I always got brownie points that Mom went to fight in the Israeli war. That always made them think I was more Jewish than perhaps I am."

~

ALTHOUGH HE CERTAINLY DID NOT KNOW IT at the time, David Matthews was plenty Jewish already, as Jewish as it is possible to be. One of the supreme ironies of his story is the role his absent mother plays, quite apart from the preference for Jewish girlfriends she seems to have stimulated in him. Although he may not know his mother or have much interest in knowing her, and although he may never have studied Judaism or attempted to practice it in any way, the fact that his mother was born a Jew makes *Jewish* an identity that would not be questioned from inside the faith under even the most rigorous religious scrutiny. In the opinion of Jewish educator Rabbi Avi Weinstein, who is Orthodox, the Jewish identity of David Matthews is not only firm, it's immutable. It cannot be cast off. Like any Jew who does not observe the commandments, he is in a kind of "outlaw" position from the perspective of the most observant, but he is still a bona fide Jew.

This is how the rabbi explained it: If a Jew is not observing the commandments, he is in breach of Jewish laws. And in Jewish law, just as under the laws of any society, to be in breach of the laws can mean some sort of censure, or punishment. The censure in this case, the shunning, takes the form of being banned from partaking in certain religious honors and privileges, mostly involving rites of group worship. This censure applies to all lapsed or nonobservant Jews, but it does not mean that Matthews or anyone else in his religious position has been excommunicated or expelled from the faith in any way. If at any point a lapsed or never practicing Jew decides to engage with the prayer and ritual life the religion prescribes, he or she is not only free but encouraged to do so. All that is required is to start doing it. Judaism has no special entry or reentry procedure for those born into the religion. Of Matthews's situation, Weinstein reasons, "If there is no formal procedure to bring him back, on the most fundamental level, he hasn't ever left. He can't leave." As it is written in the Babylonian Talmud, "Israel, even when sinning, is still Israel."

The same can be said of being black, at least it has been said, in an examination of the black-for-white passing of Anatole Broyard, the esteemed *New York Times* literary critic who died in 1990 at the age of seventy. Broyard never told his children about his background, let alone his employers. A profile of Broyard by Henry Louis Gates Jr. appeared in the *New Yorker* in 1996:

> Broyard passed not because he thought that race wasn't impor-tant but because he knew that it was. The durable social facts of race were beyond reason . . . Anatole Broyard lived in a world where race had, indeed, become a trope for indelibility, for per-manence. "All I *have* to do," a black folk saying has it, "is stay black and die."
>
> . . . But the ideologies of modernity have a kicker, which is that they permit no exit. Racial recusal is a forlorn hope. In a system where whiteness is the default, racelessness is never a possibility. You cannot opt out; you can only opt in.

To me, it is remarkable that David Matthews's situation has so many parallels to that of his illustrious passing predecessor. Matthews was born nearly half a century after Broyard, into the aftermath of dramatic improvement in conditions for African Americans in this country. Unlike Broyard, Matthews came of age when almost all of the ill-considered attempts to define blackness in law had been struck down. And yet identifying as black in the 1980s and 1990s seemed to constrict Matthews in much the same way it constricted Broyard so many years earlier. The black David Matthews seems to have been unable to muster any more social flexibility than the black Anatole Broyard.

Despite the many parallels in their two stories, they resonate for different reasons. What is most fascinating about Broyard's case is who he was, the position in the world of letters his act of passing helped him attain, how elegantly he pulled it off, and the personal price he paid for his actions. What is stunning about Matthews's story is why the act of hiding one's blackness was so advantageous in the years in which he was doing it. And yet it was. At the end of the twentieth century, his hat trick of "authentic" black, white, and Jewish identities should have given him a range of options in the way he could comfortably present himself in the world, options that by this point should be thoroughly unremarkable, even for the purposes of a book such as this one.

~

WHEN PARENTS OF MATTHEWS'S FRIENDS would ask about his father's occupation, he always said "journalist" but never mentioned where Ralph Matthews actually worked. "Saying the word *Afro-American*—I didn't have the intestinal fortitude to do that yet. And it was a total cop-out. It was just that I could see the way the wind blew, and I just wasn't up for my life being some social agenda struggle. If this is how people viewed me and accepted me, then it was just much easier. You know?"

Matthews thought about his actions in terms of coming up with "the right password," of having the right answer to that second question, "because in that beat, I had to make a decision: I'm either going to be in the club or I'm going to be out."

Later on, if a relationship with a girl got serious, Matthews sometimes would bring her home to meet his father. He would acknowledge how light-skinned his father was, but would quickly add that it wasn't something he was comfortable talking about. Or he would say that his father had a mixed background but had been raised very openly. The latter part of the statement was true, of course, but Ralph Matthews's parents both identified as black and he too was comfortable with this identification. He absolutely never would have described his background as mixed—miscegnated, maybe, meaning that the mixing occurred much earlier in a black ancestral continuum, but never more than that. His father thinks back on this period in David's life with some amusement. At the time, he imagined his son telling white girlfriends how he was a white child abandoned at birth and taken in by these well-meaning poor black people, or how his father did mysterious journalism at a place he could not disclose. "We sort of laughed at David," Ralph Matthews said, "and watched him go around."

The friends of David Matthews came from families a lot wealthier than his, always off to London for the summer and such, but even then he was keenly aware of how much richer his own household was culturally. "Mind-boggling," is the way he talks about it. "You leave our house hearing this stuff you can't hear anyplace else. My dad is a national treasure, but I didn't want anyone back then to know that."

David Matthews's story is a perfect illustration of how passing upends all our tidy little methods of recognizing and categorizing human beings, how it "blurs the carefully marked lines of race . . . and class, calling attention to the ways in which identity categories intersect, overlap, construct and deconstruct one another." Passing is subversive and amusingly mischievous as it undermines injustices built into the established social order. If revealed, an act of passing can force those in the passer's wake to rethink what made the passing necessary in the first place, and for that reason, I think, it's not too much of a stretch to begin to see passing as an instrument of positive social change.

What better present-day example of a social order in need of upset than our antiquated but entrenched system of categorizing human beings by skin color. A perfect case in point is the triangulated saga of the descendants of the slave Sally Hemings, the DNA they share with Thomas Jefferson (not to mention Jefferson's wife, Martha, who was Hemings's half sister), and the brouhaha this has caused among Jefferson's previously anointed white heirs. To appreciate the sheer folly of dividing up human beings by how they happen to look, you need only see film clips or photographs of a Hemings family reunion. Many of Sally Hemings's direct descendants who have lived as black for the last couple of centuries strongly resemble those who have lived as white.

The issue of race mattered enough on the threshold of the twenty-first century for two Hemings descendants to crisscross the country on the lecture circuit talking about why it shouldn't. One has lived as white all her life and the other as black. Race mattered no less in David Matthews's life. And as it did for Sally Hemings's son Eston, six generations earlier, passing provided the way to get around race, to operate as if it did not matter. Passing is a way "of trying to gain control," as Sander Gilman writes about the passing that the work of aesthetic surgeons makes possible. "It is a means of restoring not 'happiness' but a sense of order in the world. We 'pass' in order to regain control of ourselves and to efface that which is seen (we believe) as different, which marks us as visible in the world." It is, writes Gilman, about "passing as human."

~

A COWORKER OUTED DAVID MATTHEWS ONCE, at a Baltimore hotel restaurant where he was working as a waiter. This was not because his appearance gave him up, but because a young black woman on staff happened to know a friend of Matthews's father. "She would always make jokes—in front of people. *Are you sure you're not black because you look* . . . And I would be like, *I don't know what you're talking about* and walk away, which I'm totally ashamed of now."

The fact is, the girl was part of the restaurant's bus staff. All known people of color on the staff bussed. Matthews quickly surmised that getting hired as a waiter was not some token bow to equal opportunity. He had once again managed to pass. And continuing to pass, he said, "just made perfect mathematical sense." The year was 1985 or 1986, not 1930 or even 1950, so it did not cost Matthews his job when other members of the staff picked up the busser's taunts. But it did cost him the friendship of another waiter, a "red-necky guy who was definitely the person I did not want my cover blown to more than anyone. And he was a little pissed. He played it off like it was a joke, but things definitely cooled off after that in terms of our friendship. I don't know if he actually hated black people, but from a working-class part of Baltimore, if you're white, the word *nigger* just flows. There's no political correctness there. It's back to the days of AC-DC, guys who feathered their hair and put blond streaks in it. Very red-necky."

The busser's insistence on outing Matthews is atypical in passing lore. More usual is the response of Matthews's father—not to give his son up, even while disagreeing with his choices. It is not customary for African Americans to expose the African ancestry of those who decline to acknowledge it. The artist Adrien Piper is profoundly black-identified but, like Matthews, is usually "read" as white. Although neither she nor any members of her immediate family has ever passed, many of her near relatives do. Pointedly, Piper declines to expose them because it is not in her culture to do so. She cites several reasons: self-respect, the vicarious pleasure of watching an infiltration, fear of retaliation, the impulse to protect a fellow traveler, and the desire to refrain from inflicting

further pain on people who surely have suffered enough in sever-
ing their ties to family and root community, which the act of passing often demands.

MATTHEWS RECOUNTED two other experiences of being outed.
"Once on a bus, a crazy black woman just came up and started
talking to me," he said. She came up to him as he was getting off
the bus and said, "That's okay. I know you're black." Then she
pushed him off the bus. "The door was open and I was getting off
anyway and I was trying to ignore her because she was crazy, but
for her to say that, that was a little weird." In another instance, he
was in Baltimore to show his hometown to a new girlfriend. As
they walked by a hospice, Matthews spotted an elderly woman
looking out the window, saying the rosary. The sweetness of the
scene struck him and his glance lingered just long enough to see
the old woman lift her index finger to her neck and make a swift
knife-like motion across her throat. He was sure she thought he
was black with a white girl. Both of these incidents were more disturbing to Matthews than what happened with the busser, who
had inside information about his background. The way the old
women reacted to him meant that he was vulnerable to exposure
because of the very thing that had consistently provided cover
and a range of options—his looks. "That stuff doesn't happen to
me," he said. "That's what they make jokes about with other people. It freaked me out. It totally freaked me out."

During this period in his life, Matthews was never one to struggle with racist remarks made in his presence; he responded by
laughing them off. "Luckily," he said, his experiences in the black
and white worlds "bred in me an astute sense of political incor-

rectness. Even to this day, I'm pretty well aware of what I was doing and why I was doing it and I don't disavow it," he said. "Malcolm X had a famous line that he loved black people but hated
niggers. That's sort of where my head is at, at this point. Because
of my dad's involvement with the civil rights movement, he has
made it personal for me. And to me, it's one of the richest things
that I could possibly have. On the other hand, having been a little
bit in both worlds, I also have the eyes to see that there's a huge
population of black people—just like there's a huge population of
people in Kansas—that I probably don't want to know. And I'm
not saying that it's their fault or anything—there's a culture—O.J.
and Tupac—that I don't want to know. I think that I'm a little
more able to cut through the party line and see what is actual. I
don't have an automatic response about black issues."

LOOKING BACK TO, SAY, 1896, the time of the New Orleans case
Plessy v. Ferguson, it doesn't take much to grasp why someone
deemed Negro, who also had the possibility of getting around it,
might be inclined to do so at least some of the time. Homer A.
Plessy, a white-looking man who was in fact seven-eighths white,
challenged the strict racial segregation of railroad cars. The case
went to the Supreme Court, which upheld the legitimacy of "separate but equal" for the nation's black and white residents, regardless of how black the black people happened to be. Separate,
as we know, was never equal. It would be arrogant to pass judgment on the light-skinned, white-looking people of some or much
African ancestry who passed to slip through a system both designed and bound to deny opportunity. Passing provided the
chance to live their lives in the present, not as "some social

agenda struggle," as Matthews, living more than one hundred years later, described making a similar choice. It was about availing themselves of alternatives that otherwise would not have existed. Black-for-white passing mocks the practice of making racial distinctions. It does an end run around the criteria still in place that stuff unique individuals into fixed social castes mostly because of how they happen to look. As an act of infiltration, passing certainly gets around that. But on the downside, it can be seen as a way of buying into that same oppressive social order and, in the process, helping legitimate and perpetuate it.

~

ALL THIS LEADS TO A QUESTION: Why, in the case of David Matthews's biracial black-Jewish identity, is he not free to choose between the identity options his birth provided? The answer is that he cannot just choose because cultural identity is never solely a matter of choice. A given identity can be embraced, but that embrace often affirms what would be difficult if not impossible to escape anyway, what has already been assigned, or ascribed. As the young ethnographer David Vine put it so aptly, ours is a world of social inequalities with very real material effects, a world of arbitrary social divisions in which identities are ascribed to people that they do not get to choose, identities that have a dramatic impact on their life course and daily experience. For Vine, there is no more compelling example than this most classic one—the passing of anyone designated African American to circumvent a system with racism embedded in its every institution, even, as David Matthews's story suggests, the institution of making and keeping friends.

And yet we recognize the awkwardness in David Matthews's choice to pass whenever it suited him. We might see his actions as those of a young black man willfully engaged in a hurtful insult to his black heritage. Or we might stand amused at the way he draws on his tenuous Jewish connection to play the old stereotype of the "Jewish chameleon," as Daniel Itzkovitz has written about it, passing as is "the Jew's natural place." By passing, perhaps David Matthews simply embraced, as if in a time warp, what is now a very "dated emblem of change or transition, an emblem of decreasing urgency and frequency in a new modern context" as the literary scholar Thadious Davis talks about black-for-white passing today. Are we uncomfortable with David Matthews's omissions and finesses? His evasions and outright lies? Had he been found out, would he have been condemned or punished for his transgressions, as his fictional predecessors so often were censured or punished? Or does his story help us understand why the decision to embark on an act of passing of this kind is still viable, and not only for Matthews in the 1980s and 1990s. Check out the angst-ridden discussion posts about passing on Internet websites such as Multiracial Voice ("Transcend race consciousness!") or My Shoes, where a clinical psychologist hosts a site "for multiracial children, adolescents and adults who have a white appearance."

~

DAVID MATTHEWS WRITES SCREENPLAYS. He thinks his personal passing scenario is too quaint and anachronistic to be grist for the blockbusters he hopes to write. The screenplays he crafts are always "plot-driven" not "character-driven," because plot-driven stories have blockbuster potential and character-driven stories do not. At least that is the advice of the Hollywood manager and agent who represent him. The black-passing-for-white theme is too dated an idea for the realm of big budget productions, too evocative of those tear-at-your-insides tragic mulatto story lines of the early twentieth century like *Imitation of Life, Showboat,* or *Band of Angels*—even *Pinky*, with its 1949 exclamatory promotional tagline: *"The love story of a girl who passed for white!"* Philip Roth explored the subject of passing with contemporary vigor in his 2000 novel, *The Human Stain*, by setting it during the Clinton impeachment scandal of 1998. And it was indeed snapped up for a film version. But Roth's protagonist, the classics professor Coleman Silk, begins passing in a time when it seemed to make more sense, before World War II, in the era of Jim Crow. Silk passes for opportunity, to wrestle competitively, for placement in the military, for marriage, for life in the academy. We see the logic in the decision, the pragmatism, and the wrenching pain for the devoted family that his life choices force him to leave behind.

For the strongest dramatic appeal, the subject needs to be considered against a pre–civil rights backdrop. That was when passing was audacious, dangerous—riveting theater for audiences black and white, as viewer response to those earlier films amply attests.

Matthews started passing long before a number of real-life black-for-white passing revelations captured public attention in the 1990s. One was Broyard's. The others were the members of Shirlee Taylor Haizlipp's family who passed into whiteness in *The Sweeter the Juice* and Gregory Williams's own story in *Life on the Color Line: The True Story of a White Boy Who Discovered He Was Black*. In late 2002, the actress Carol Channing disclosed that her father was half black, a fact her parents never mentioned to her until she was a young adult, and she in turn did not reveal until the publication of her memoirs at the age of eighty-one.

None of these stories provides a good parallel to Matthews's. Like Philip Roth's novel, the real-life Broyard, Haizlipp, and

Channing stories all begin in the time of separate but equal. And although Williams begins life a generation later, he lives his formative first ten years before *Brown v. Board of Education*. Young Matthews, by contrast, with his origins in the sophisticated black upper middle class, was born thirteen years after 1954 into the time of black pride, Panthers, power, and affirmative action. To the mainstream African American community, black-for-white passing before the 1960s might have been the stuff of cultural tragedy, but passing after the mid-1960s was more like cultural treason.

In the years when Matthews passed, the notion of black-for-white passing had become so passé that it had to shift genres to have any standing even as an entertainment vehicle: out with melodrama, in with farce. For confirmation, rent the "White Like Me" sketches Eddie Murphy performed for *Saturday Night Live*. Matthews passed straight through our national obsession with political correctness, multiculturalism, and the politics of identity. He was passing when to do so had become something of a national joke.

Matthews was sixteen when the Eddie Murphy sketches first appeared in 1984. They depict the actor in a business suit and white face going undercover à la John Howard Griffin in *Black Like Me*, the novelist's classic recounting of his actual experiences with dyed skin, living as a black man in the South. In the sketch, Murphy's "white" character gets an insider's view of the more subtle privileges that whiteness confers. He obtains a bank loan without collateral and enjoys free cocktails on a public bus as soon as the last black person gets off. Appearance and style give Murphy access and entry, just as appearance and style give Matthews access and entry. He doesn't need an identity card or a VIP pass to be welcome. He looks the part. The bouncer steps aside.

Matthews's passing story is neither comic nor tragic. Passing was a simple expedient, a way to grease his way through adolescence and early adulthood. Unlike many passing stories from the pre–civil rights era, Matthews's actions had no real debilitating costs. Passing allowed him to get beyond the barricades and connect with his Jewish brethren, those with whom he felt a cultural affinity. It did not stop him from staying tight with his family. His black identity remained firm. No one felt particularly betrayed by his actions; no one hunted him down. In the act of passing, David Matthews may have been deceptive. He may have engineered his encounters in ways that enabled him to be mistaken for other than who he understood himself to be. But in several important ways, passing also allowed him to be, well, himself.

Comparing Matthews's tale, as well as other latter-day passing stories, to those of the pre–civil rights era provides a way to trace the evolution of our own attitudes. What we find is that the old tragic mulatto story line so common in the fiction of passing no longer works. To be compelling, passing stories need a much more complicated structure. The moment of unmasking does not necessarily provide high drama anymore. It no longer carries a guaranteed reaction of shock, accusation, revulsion, or even violence from the deceived. It usually provokes some surprise, no doubt some gossip, but then what ordinarily follows is a big "So what?" And even in those tragic instances when the reaction is more vociferous, when the unmasking triggers an extreme or even violent reaction, it is not the passer whom we are likely to judge harshly. We judge the haters and we judge the institution, environment, or social situation that made the passing necessary in the first place.

Considering the choices that David Matthews faced brings to mind the words of W. E. B. Du Bois in a 1929 review he wrote of the Nella Larsen novel, *Passing*. He rightly described black-for-white passing as a matter "of great moral import." But he also foresaw a time when passing would be seen for what it really was: "a petty, silly matter of no real importance which another generation will comprehend with great difficulty." Hasten the day.

~

MATTHEWS BEGAN TO CLIMB DOWN from the trapeze platform in his second or third year of college, around 1990. He pegs the moment to when Professor Griff—Richard Griff, choreographer of the hip-hop group Public Enemy—was blaming Jews for most of the world's wickedness and Chuck D was taking heat for "Fight the Power," his confrontational rap theme for Spike Lee's movie *Do the Right Thing*:

> Elvis was a hero to most
> But he never meant shit to me you see
> Straight up racist that sucker was
> Simple and plain
> Mother fuck him and John Wayne
> Cause I'm black and I'm proud
> I'm ready and hyped plus I'm amped
> Most of my heroes don't appear on no stamps . . .

Matthews was drawn to the extremism and the polemics that such hip-hop lyrics poeticized, lyrics that "challenged mainstream notions of racial justice and rallied for self-empowerment," in a publicist's depiction.

"Do you remember when Spike Lee came out and said, 'Black people can't be racist'? I don't know why it clicked with me or resonated with me," Matthews said, "but it did." "Fight the Power" and all that it represented offered the first popular discourse on race that Matthews felt he could get behind. It made him feel like a revolutionary even though he never attended a single demonstration. "This was a new cultural thing in which music and movies were taking a stand, as it were," he said. He was drawn to its forcefulness, its oppositional stance, its arguments—even when he found the arguments wrongheaded. Until that point, winning his father's approval had been his only real point of connection to anything "black." For the first time, his grandmother's old *them* started to feel a lot more like *us*.

Still, Matthews kept his own counsel. His past experiences enabled him to straddle all the worlds he inhabited with an independent spirit. He still had no interest in spouting any group's party line. He argued bitterly with his father over the O. J. Simpson acquittal when his father supported the verdict on grounds that for once in four hundred years, a brother had triumphed over the racism in American justice. He was just as quick to quarrel with a Jewish girlfriend when she insisted that the anti-Semitic views of Louis Farrakhan, the Black Muslim leader, make anything else he says irrelevant. Matthews said he would never care what the "right" response of the black or Jewish community might be to any given controversy. He would always call things as he saw them. "I'm able to do that," he said. "It doesn't matter to me what's politically correct. It matters to me more what the actual results of something are."

~

LONG ABOUT 1998 came the next in David Matthews's succession of Jewish girlfriends, a woman he met in Washington while she was a National Public Radio producer. "Coming out of Barnard and Columbia in the 1990s as I had," she said, "every hip Jewish kid I knew was rocking the black thing and I instantly thought David was one of those kids. Hip-hop, black films, hat tilted in his driver's license picture." There was a Malcolm X poster over his bed and he wore a "Make Black Films" T-shirt. "He said he was black and I wondered if it was a pose for the first twenty-four hours—it was so like every Jewish kid at Columbia, so like myself, protesting the university's plans for the Audubon Ballroom, doing black studies; that was my frame of reference. Black kids I knew were not into James Baldwin and Miles Davis. They were into hip-hop. David had the black culture that the white intelligentsia gravitated toward, and he didn't look black. So I didn't believe him. I had met so many posers at Columbia."

She found it amusing the way people were forever trying to figure out David's background. At the restaurant where he worked there was actually an informal guessing contest. "Half French? Half Chinese? That's what they got to," she said.

At a certain point in her relationship with Matthews, he read a review of the Danny Senza novel *Caucasia* (1999) and recognized the parallels to his own story. "That was a revelation for him," she said, "something he talked about for weeks and then couldn't talk about anymore." Toi Derricote's *Black Notebooks* (1997) might have been similarly affecting, or even Rebecca Walker's *Black, White, and Jewish: Autobiography of a Shifting Self* (2001).

David Matthews took his first public race stand in 2001 at the age of thirty-four. It happened during the daily staff meeting at the restaurant. One of the chefs announced a change in the menu, eliminating a dish that happened to be the favorite of one of the black waitresses. A colleague remarked that the black waitress would be sorry to see the dish go because she liked it so much.

The chef responded, "Well, she can always eat fried chicken," and walked away.

"No one said anything," Matthews recalled. "I was eating dinner and my fork just . . . I'm like . . . *Did I just hear that? Do people still . . . ?* So I said something to the general manager." The manager in turn confronted the chef, who then burst into tears and said it wasn't what she meant at all. "Well, what other kind of synaptic connection can you make?" Matthews said. "She didn't say, 'She'll have to go eat sea urchin.' It's like one step away from watermelon."

"And that surprised me," he said. "In the middle of a very politically correct, hip New York restaurant with a bunch of artists [New York waiters are often also actors and artists] and nobody said anything. Nobody was really that bothered. They thought I was making a big deal out of it."

It pleased Ralph Matthews that his son was moved to take action. "It was a step," Ralph Matthews said. "But he should have punched her."

By 2002 David Matthews still had no black friends, aside from his work colleagues. "I wish I did, but it's literally a function of demographics for me. I would have to go hang out at the Nuyorican Poets Café or go uptown. I'd have to make a pilgrimage to a place where there were intellectual black people. Because I was raised in the ghetto for a couple of years in that house, I don't have any romantic ideas about hanging out with people who didn't graduate high school."

There was another Jewish girlfriend in the summer of 2001, an aspiring actor. The Jewish mother in Matthews's background makes him acceptable to her parents, but not so acceptable that they could refrain from trying from time to time to fix her up with other men, especially those with advanced professional degrees.

That may have more to do with their view of Matthews's economic prospects than his Matthews half. "I feel like she is sort of waiting for me to be a doctor or a lawyer or to sell something for ten million dollars right now."

"It's very weird," he mused. "I meet a lot of black kids who are like her. They have the safety net. If they don't make rent, there's always a phone call they can make and things will be okay. It makes me wonder if it is even race anymore, or if it's all class."

Class certainly figures, but it is not, we can tell him with some assurance, only about class.

CHAPTER TWO

Passing, Virginia

"Tell me, sir, do you really think that
a white could look the negro so?
For one, I should call it pretty good acting."
"Not much better than any other man acts."
   —HERMAN MELVILLE

WHEN IT CAME TIME FOR COLLEGE, her father laid out a map and put the point of a compass on the dot that signified their small town. His pencil circled an approved portion of the country, a radius that expressly excluded New York City, which he declared absolutely off-limits. Within the designated boundary, his daughter chose a university that put her no farther than a commuter train ride to Manhattan. That way she could still get into the city for night life or shopping whenever she wanted and she could say she went to college in New York and be telling the truth.

During the months she prepared to move away from home, her biggest fear was that she might end up with a black roommate. Two decades later, she finds this particularly embarrassing to admit. She affects an operatic stage whisper to explain why the prospect of an African American roommate frightened her back then, when such fears were far more common: *Because they're different from us.* As an eighteen-year-old born in the mid-1960s, she did not know a single person of African American heritage. Her hometown is predominantly white, Protestant, and Catholic. The Jews live one town over and everyone else lives in the larger city that borders on both of these towns. Of the 380 students in her high school graduating class, she cannot recall anyone of color, at least no one she knew personally. Growing up she heard whispers about the time a black family bought a house in town. Neighbors apparently pooled funds to buy the house back from the people and they quietly moved on. That was the way it was.

~

SHE IS A BEAUTY, slender and seductive with small, alluring features and delicate hands. The heritage is half blue-eyed, blond Yankee WASP, half Italian. Even though the summer is short where she now lives, her soft, even tan in early June appears to have required no effort at all. The tan works especially well against her dark brown hair, as does the tight black sleeveless cotton shift she wears hemmed a couple of inches above her knees. Without chemical intervention, her hair is as straight and fine as silk thread, but she perms it into loose kinks that fall gently to her shoulders. It takes a perm to give her hair any volume, height, or curl, so she has been perming it religiously since she was seventeen. All through college and beyond, it was jet black and styled the way all the women in her circle styled their hair, big. Now she is a much subtler presence, not at all bookish despite her two master's degrees and the Ph.D. work nearing completion. She is a very entertaining conversationalist, honest, funny, a delight to get to know. "I would be more than interested in talking to you," she charmingly responded to an e-mailed request to meet. "I love to talk about myself."

It is difficult to picture her heavy, but she confides that she weighed more than two hundred pounds until she turned twenty-one. The extra weight started coming off during her sophomore year in college and kept coming off during her junior semester abroad. By the time she returned to campus for the fall of her senior year, she was Cinderella out the door of the pumpkin-turned-golden-coach. Her mother exclaimed that she had lost half of herself, which was true on another level as well because this was when she met her boyfriend and lost some of herself in that too. He was only a sophomore but was so incredibly handsome she didn't think it mattered a bit. Even better, it was obvious from the moment they met that he really liked her back. They started "dating, whatever, hanging out twenty-four hours a day." Her boyfriend thought she was a showpiece. No one had ever seen her as a showpiece before—"*Ev*-er. This is something that a woman aspires to be," she said. "And I thought it was just wonderful."

It was also very, very heady for the fat girl still directing traffic from inside her head. Being with her boyfriend led to all manner of new experiences—fun, exciting, fantastic experiences for the most part. They made a very striking couple and she reveled in the way people responded to their appearance together. Bouncers never blocked their way at the ropes outside the nightclubs and they got the same welcome approval inside. "I still like to be the center of attention. I'm not going to lie to you," she said. "But I think I liked it more then."

Her boyfriend was from the Bronx, the adopted son of a beloved Puerto Rican mother. He wasn't sure of his blood parentage—maybe half Puerto Rican, half African American; it wasn't clear. But he was noticeably dark-complexioned. She felt sure this was why her parents seemed to dislike him so intensely, although her mother still insists her only objection was the way he treated their daughter. "They handled it because they didn't have a choice," she said. "They had a lot of negative things to say about him, and now, as an adult, I think they might be right on many, if not all, of the things they were saying. But at the time, all I could think was it was *because you think he's black*—and I would hear nothing of it."

Never mind that the relationship "was never healthy, never good for me in any way, shape, or form." For one thing, right from the start, he stepped out with other girls on the side. She tolerated his indiscretions because on some level she was prepared to tolerate them and because she wanted to reserve permission to do the same. She also didn't think the behavior was altogether his fault. He worked out and had modeled a bit. Women just fell all over him. In her presence, other girls did not hesitate to slip their telephone numbers into his pocket. Of course, she minded. But being with him, and being seen with him as a couple, mattered more.

After graduation, the university made her a very appealing offer to stay on and complete her master's degree. This was convenient because it allowed her to remain on campus until her boyfriend graduated too. When he was accepted by a graduate school in another town, she decided not to follow. She wanted to be with him and eventually marry him, but there was something she had to do first.

FOR A DECADE IT HAD BEEN HER DREAM to move to Richmond, Virginia. The idea came into her head on a road trip her family took to Disney World to celebrate her thirteenth birthday. She slept through most of the drive but happened to wake up just as the car passed through Richmond and that most gorgeous of American boulevards, Monument Avenue. It left her breathless. "And I'm moving here," she summarily announced.

But the fall after graduation, there were no openings for a newly minted teacher in the Richmond school district so she settled for an offer from the Essex County Intermediate School in Tappahannock, Virginia, a good forty-five minutes from Richmond to the north and east, on the banks of the Rappahannock River. Washington, D.C., is a hundred miles north and Norfolk, a hundred miles south.

When she got to town, Tappahannock had a population of about fifteen hundred, a figure that swells to about nine thousand people with the surrounding countryside of Essex County. You have to count the countryside. The hamlets of Essex County are little more than clearings for clusters of neatly maintained double wides on groomed half-acre plots. Double wides, for the uninitiated, are jumbo mobile homes that rest on solid concrete or even brick-faced foundations, often with stunningly elaborate entrances, additions, and carports with corrugated aluminum canopies. Each little settlement has, perhaps, several other houses, a farmstead or two, maybe a convenience shack or a mechanic's garage, and almost always a church. During church hours on a Sunday, the roads are empty. The cars and trucks that do pass by get to Battery, Beazley, Beverly, Sparta, Occupacia, Passing, Hustle, and all the other hamlets in the immediate area over picturesque two-lane country roads that bear these names as often as not. The intersection of Passing and Hustle makes for the most intriguing road sign. All of the county's schools are in Tappahannock, as is shopping for anything more than a bag of potato chips and an orange soda. Since the young teacher's time in

Tappahannock, the town has expanded considerably, though you can still canvass every street by car in about four minutes flat. There are many more businesses now but back in the late 1980s, the only local commercial establishments she had reason to frequent were the fast-food stops, the legendary Lowery's Seafood Restaurant ("known throughout Virginia and beyond" since 1938), the only grocery store for probably thirty minutes, and the little shop where she earned an extra seven dollars an hour working Saturdays. That plus her $21,000 annual salary and no debts made her feel really flush.

The school board arranged housing for the teacher, with another white teacher as roommate, in a row of neat, two-story, three-bedroom townhouses "south on US 17, take a right at the Dairy Queen." The very agreeable rent was $395 a month, and the back windows gave on what are now the playing fields of the ubiquitous low-rise red-brick school building where she taught the county's early adolescents.

Tappahannock was welcoming and friendly, "the kind of place where people brought a casserole," especially for a new teacher in town. Her boyfriend drove down with her to help her settle in. He visited often on weekends, so people got accustomed to seeing them together. Her townhouse complex happened to be integrated, which, she quickly learned, was unusual for Tappahannock. She made friends with neighbors who happened to be African American and through them she met other African Americans, and her social life in Tappahannock took off from there. Her black friends avoided Lowery's with a reticence not universally shared, but one that lingered from the restaurant's whites-only era prior to 1964. Her new crowd partied in private homes, not in bars, because there were no bars. The county is dry. Organized social and political life emanated from the churches, which were segregated—still are, local people say, except for the Catholic and Seventh-Day Adventist—as the social clubs continue to be. Everyone seems to agree that the public schools were and are still the major point of social intersection between the blacks and whites of Essex County. Even that didn't happen until the beginning of the 1970s—a long and seething seventeen years after *Brown v. Board of Education* and a full seven years after the Civil Rights Act of 1964—and then only under threat of a loss of federal funds. In that period of desegregation, the movie house started letting in black patrons and there were black cashiers in the county for the first time.

Sandy and Ken Pounsberry came to the area in 1990 to set up a bed and breakfast on the Linden House Plantation, not actually a plantation but a restored 1750s planter's home in Champlain, about five minutes north of Tappahannock on US 17. Sandy Pounsberry remembers how stunned she was when a black person ahead of her in line at the local general store stepped aside to offer her precedence. This was in 1990, mind you. Nothing like that happens any longer. By the turn of the new century, the county even had its first black sheriff.

Then as now, to meet federal assistance requirements under the 1964 Civil Rights Act, the Virginia Department of Education required the state's schools to perform annual civil rights audits. In Tappahannock, teachers were obliged to tally the number of students by racial classifications. The purpose was reasonable enough: to monitor student success by the various census categories. The young teacher found it appalling to make such distinctions out loud. "You have to count: how many white boys, how many white girls, how many black boys, and I remember having a conversation about it with the principal and I said, 'How do you know?' and he said, 'You ask.' They raise their hands!

I would have died sooner than ask, *All the black boys raise their hands. Okay, great. All the white boys? Okay. Any boy who didn't raise his hand?* I refused to do it. Somebody else had to come and do it because I refused to do it. I was a troublemaker anyway."

~

THE SOCIAL LIFE IN TAPPAHANNOCK WAS FANTASTIC. "I had a car. And I was from New York—even though I wasn't really, I was to them—and right from the get-go, I caused quite a stir. I dressed very much like a product of New York in the '80s. Big shoulders. Big hair. I was a little bit more on the freaky side than the non-freaky side. In Virginia, all my clothes were too short; my clothes were too tight. Men would show up at my door to ask me out that I had never met." On weeks when her boyfriend wasn't visiting, men who wanted to date her just seemed to emerge from the ether. Her roommate called them swamp monsters. "You'd be at a party and it would be outside and men would just come out of nowhere and surround me," she said. "I had never in my life experienced anything like that, anywhere else at any other time."

At school, however, fellow teachers from that year remember her ability as well as her beauty, and considered her a teacher who added real value during her brief time in the community. She was one of the few in a long line of starting teachers, one-year-contract, in-and-out teachers who made any impression at all and a really good one at that. In addition to her regular course load, she volunteered to teach a high school equivalency course at night. She even joined forces with another teacher to help the students start a student council. She kept her private life as separate as she could in a town of that size.

As it happened, most of the men she dated in Tappahannock

were black. "The men that I dated would have me meet more people and you know, your networking starts," she explained. She attributes her popularity in part to being a white woman who was open to dating black men. She liked being seen as a white woman who dated black men because it set her apart, even though interracial dating was by no means unheard of in the town and its environs, especially in the more remote countryside. In the hamlet of Central Point, for example, twenty minutes west of Tappahannock, the population is so commingled that many of Central Point's black residents are white enough to pass—and have done so for generations. Local lore has it that this is the reason the crossing only a half mile from Central Point is called Passing. Several former Tappahannock residents now in their early forties recalled that while they were in high school, during the tense early years of school integration, blacks and whites sometimes dated each other.

There was another "cultural piece" to the African American social milieu in which the young teacher happily found herself. Tappahannock offered a social life without variety or gradation, cultural options that were distinctly black-white, either-or. "There is white music and black music in Tappahannock, Virginia, and you can just believe me on that; you don't want to listen to either. But I certainly wasn't going to listen to the white music. Do you know what I mean? So I guess there were all these things that you did if you were black," she said. "And I did them."

IN A NEAT LITTLE RANCH-STYLE HOUSE just a few doors down Marsh Street from the Essex County Intermediate School lives Lillian H. McGuire, an expert in local African American history.

Lillian McGuire is the widow of the Reverend Charles Edward McGuire, a respected Baptist minister and county civil rights leader, and for twenty-three of her thirty-six years as an educator, she taught in the county schools. Mrs. McGuire's retirement created the faculty opening at Essex County Intermediate that brought the young teacher to town.

In 1945 Lillian McGuire graduated from the historic Rappahannock Industrial Academy. This was a black private school established by the black churches of Essex County in 1902 because the county refused to provide more than an elementary school public education for its black children. Thirty-two years after that, the county relented. The white high school students got a brand-new building, and the dilapidated pile they vacated became the black school. Another seventeen years passed before the county's black children got a decent facility and twenty more years passed after that for the very belated arrival of integration in 1971. At that point there was one public high school for black and white students and what had been the black high school on Marsh Street became the integrated Essex County Intermediate. Of course, a couple of "white flight" private schools immediately appeared too.

Never during her Tappahannock days did the young teacher hear the full extent of this history, but she did know that the building where she taught had once been the black school because people made a point of mentioning it.

~

MRS. McGUIRE began doing documentary research into the history of Essex County's African Americans in 1982. She was enlisted to help young Jimmy Slaughter, a product of the Essex

County public school system, except for fifth grade, the year after integration, when his parents sent him briefly to private school. Between graduating from Yale and being admitted to Columbia University Law School, he applied for and received a commission to write the county's official history for its tricentennial. The county board of supervisors had it published. Mrs. McGuire also went to work on a book of her own, published in 1999 under a mouthful of a title: *Uprooted and Transplanted: From Africa to America, Focus on African-Americans in Essex County, Virginia, Oppressions, Achievements, Contributions, the 1600s–1900s.*

Locally produced county histories must please many factions, and yet both publications endeavored to be forthright about racism in Essex County into the modern era. Clearly, both authors sought to tell the story whole. Slaughter's introduction describes the county as "distinctly Southern," "distinguished yet tragically flawed" by slavery's damaging imprint. "A God-fearing people struggled with a great moral dilemma in their midst until it overwhelmed them," he wrote. He is proud of his work and equally proud of the county board of supervisors for "letting the chips fall." Slaughter thinks he was able to stretch his leeway to "talk about issues" in the book by devoting ample space to the Confederacy and by tracking Essex County's troops through the Civil War, "which the Conservatives love." Now he is a partner in a Washington, D.C., law firm. As a 1978 graduate of Essex High School, he is not too young to have missed the eerie ghost of a sign marked "COLORED" above a restroom at the back of his family's furniture store. Mrs. McGuire would have been well into her thirties before the layers of paint meant to obliterate the sign started to be applied.

As Slaughter circulated early drafts of his manuscript among county leaders, he found the touchiest subject was miscegenation, or racial mixing, the sexual union of black and white, especially in master-slave relations in the period before the Civil War. "I remember somebody being upset about it, about soiling the illustrious gentry," he recalled. Mrs. McGuire's book also skirts the subject. She reports and documents that 75 percent of the free Negroes in antebellum Essex County were "dark mulatto," "mulatto," "high mulatto," "bright mulatto," "very bright mulatto," or, like David Matthews, "very bright, almost white." But she does not explain or explore how they got that way. Neither the word *miscegenation* nor any of its synonyms appears in either index.

Curiously, neither book refers to *Loving v. Virginia*, the 1967 U.S. Supreme Court decision hailed by civil libertarians for eliminating slavery's last legal vestiges, the decision that affirmed the right of any person of any color to marry any other person of any color in any state in the land. It is a monumental decision that the Virginia legal scholar Philip T. Nash described twenty-five years later as "a judicial recognition of the sanctity of marriage and the ability of people irrespective of race to enjoy the protections of the Constitution in their choice of mates." *Loving*, in the opinion of Harvard legal scholar and author Randall Kennedy, "is a story of unambiguous triumph for those who march under the banner of Freedom to Choose, who believe that . . . government should play no part in regulating the contractual decisions of private parties, and who grant a virtually indefeasible presumption of authenticity and voluntariness to the actual choices people make." In the late 1960s, *Loving v. Virginia* forced all remaining antimiscegenation statutes off the books in Virginia and the fifteen other states that maintained them. The events that brought the case to the high court's attention occurred twenty miles west of Tappahannock, just past the intersection of the Sparta and Passing roads.

~

ROBERT ANTONIO PRATT, known at home as Tony, comes from Essex County, rural Battery to be precise. He is now a professor of history at the University of Georgia, specializing in African American history and the history of the South. Pratt knows Jimmy Slaughter because they went to Essex High School just a couple of years apart and he knows Mrs. McGuire because she taught Pratt fifth grade. He also knows *Loving v. Virginia* because he has studied it and written about it, and because as a boy growing up in Battery, he watched part of the story unfold from his grandfather's front porch.

In 1958, seven miles from Battery, in the hamlet of Central Point, the county sheriff and his deputies rousted Mildred and Richard Loving from their beds with blinding flashlights at two o'clock in the morning to haul them off to jail. Childhood sweethearts, the Lovings grew up together in Central Point and had married five weeks earlier in Washington, D.C., returning to their birthplace right after their wedding to live with Mrs. Loving's parents. Richard Loving was white, a bricklayer and drag racer of English and Irish ancestry, and the former Mildred Jeter was part Cherokee and part-black. After the arrest, the couple waived their right to a jury trial and pleaded guilty to charges of violating Virginia's ban on interracial marriages, specifically its Racial Integrity Act of 1924. One state court appeal failed. Judge Leon M. Bazile's written rebuttal to their case contained the statement that God had separated the races by placing them on different continents, "And but for the interference with his arrangement, there would be no cause for such marriages. The fact that he separated the races shows that he did not intend for the races to mix." The court sentenced the Lovings to exile, which they spent in Washington, D.C., forbidden to return to Virginia to live as a couple, forbidden to return to the state together as visitors for the next quarter of a century.

The banishment lasted nine long years until the Supreme Court ruling reversed it. During that period, Mildred Loving, who hated urban life, often brought her children to Essex County for long visits with her sister, Garnet Hill. The Hills lived in Battery and rented rooms in a big wooden boardinghouse that Pratt's great-uncle owned. And well after dark from his grandfather's porch, Pratt would see Richard Loving's car make its way quietly down the dirt road to the boardinghouse on clandestine visits to his own family.

Chief Justice Earl Warren delivered the high court's unanimous opinion on June 12, 1967, rejecting the state's arguments and the legal precedents that spawned them. The ruling struck down Virginia's Racial Integrity Act, since its obvious purpose was to "maintain White Supremacy," apparent because the only interracial marriages it expressly prohibited were those involving white people. A state's "invidious racial discriminations," Warren concluded, cannot restrict the freedom to marry, which resides with the individual and is guaranteed by the Fourteenth Amendment.

Not long after the young teacher departed Tappahannock for good, reporters from the *New York Times,* the *Washington Post,* and other major newspapers converged on Central Point to write stories commemorating the twenty-fifth anniversary of the landmark Supreme Court decision. They found what the teacher had found: that attitudes had not changed much in the intervening quarter century. Robert D. McIlawin III, one of the assistants to the Virginia attorney general who had argued the case, told David Margolik of the *Times* that *Loving v. Virginia* was no more than "a footnote to history" that no one even remembered. McIlawin, in his argument before the high court, asserted that Virginia's antimiscegenation laws served the public interest in the way that laws against polygamy, incest, and marriage between retarded persons served the public interest. Garnet Brooks, the sheriff who arrested the Lovings, told the reporter that he was still against interracial marriage and thought the antimiscegenation laws should remain in force. He had never given the Lovings another thought. "If they'd been outstanding people I would have thought something about it," he said. "But with the caliber of those people, it didn't matter. They were both low class."

~

JIMMY SLAUGHTER AND LILLIAN MCGUIRE, in their otherwise diligent county histories, both (perhaps understandably) went weak on the subject of racial mixing in a general way. But how could they leave out *Loving v. Virginia* entirely? The same way a young teacher could spend a year teaching the children of Essex County, socializing on both sides of the color line, and never hear a word about the case. Separately, both Slaughter and Mrs. McGuire were asked why they had not mentioned the case in their books of local history. Both the white, Ivy League–educated child of the 1970s and the local elder African American stalwart found the question rather surprising, and the same matter-of-fact reply came from each of them: "That was Caroline County."

And that is the fact. All the legal developments in *Loving v. Virginia* occurred in Caroline County. But then so did a lynching case from the early 1800s that Slaughter used in his book when he couldn't document one in Essex. Once the question was put, Slaughter himself pointed this out while sifting through his own recollections as to what he might have been thinking two decades earlier. Neither he nor Mrs. McGuire thought to seize on the significant role the Essex County town of Battery had played in the *Loving* drama. In retrospect, Slaughter regrets leaving out mention of *Loving v. Virginia* in his book, especially since his legal training has enlarged his understanding and appreciation of the case's significance. Aside from that, the Caroline County hamlet of Central Point, where the Loving story begins and where the Lovings quietly returned as soon as they could legally, is a nearly imperceptible three and a half miles over the county line. Tappahannock is where the folks of Central Point often go to shop.

The omission was as conspicuous from the black author as from the white. It demonstrates how submerged the subject of interracial unions remains in Essex County. Pratt said the *Loving v. Virginia* case is still very touchy for people in that area: "You talk to people about it thirty-five years after the fact and you still get a range of opinions. There certainly is unease, touchiness about delving into it." His comment gave currency to quotations in a scholarly piece he wrote about the Loving case, culled from a Simeon Booker story in *Ebony* magazine, published at the time of the Supreme Court ruling. Booker quoted an unnamed local farmer who acknowledged the prevalence of illicit racial commingling in the area, particularly in Central Point, long before Richard Loving married Mildred Jeter. "There's been plenty mingling among races for years and nobody griped or tried to legalize it," the farmer said. "Negroes got kind of slick and passed and fooled outsiders. Rich [Loving] wasn't the type. What he wanted, he wanted on paper—and legal. As a result, he broke up the system." And another local leader said, "You can bet there was a lot of pressure on this couple. Both of them believed and worked for what they wanted. A lot of whites in the county would have done everything to knock this case out, but they couldn't find the couple and they couldn't use any more rough stuff since it was in the courts, so some just got angry. The power boys in the county despised Rich because he ended the white man's moon-lighting in romance. Now they got to cut out this jive of dating Negro women at night, and these 'high yaller' Negroes got to face up to the facts of life. They don't have to pass anymore."

The touchiness helps explain the conscious and unconscious editorial choices of two self-styled county historians and what that says about relations between blacks and whites in Essex County, Virginia, and no doubt elsewhere. It also helps explain an incident that left the young teacher more unsettled—*horrified* was the word she used—than anything else that happened to her before or since.

$\sim$

THE DIAMOND ENGAGEMENT RING her boyfriend presented at Christmastime was a shade under two carats, large by any stan-dard, "but in Tappahanock, Virginia," she enthused, "it was posi-tively Prudential. All these other girls were getting engaged and I had this *rock and a half,* and if they had a quarter of a carat they were like all shades of happy."

She cannot remember exactly when, but at some point in the spring, toward the end of the school year, she decided to move nearer to where she had come from, to be closer to her fiancé while he completed graduate school. Before she left town, the mother of one of her students approached her and asked if she would be willing to serve as master of ceremonies for a charity fashion show and awards presentation to be sponsored by a local group; she does not recall which. She was told she was being se-lected because of all the fine things she had done for the school.

Naturally, she readily accepted. "Originally I said yes because I thought, *Omigod, this is such a big honor. I can wear something really, really outlandish.*"

She went to the planning meetings whenever asked, and in time she began to realize that all of the organizers were black and that the membership of the organization was all black. This in itself did not faze her. By then she was well accustomed to being the only white. But several times the women mentioned the kind of role model she was and "all of the sudden it became very evident to me that the reason they wanted me to do it was because I was a young black woman who was doing good things in the community." She did not find this amusing. "I'm like *Holy Shit! I'm a role model, yes I am, but I'm not the role model you think I am!* I was horrified because, I'm like, *What do I do now???*"

She realized that she had been passing inadvertently. Once that was clear, her first instinct was to continue passing, to get through the event without disclosing what the organizers did not know about her. It seemed like the simplest way out of an extremely awkward situation. She called her fiancé for guidance. "He got mad at me," she recalled. "He got angry either because I was trying to take some kind of honor away from the downtrodden poor black women who deserve it or because I was trying to pass." She heard him out. "It was easy for me to just dip into that world and if it got uncomfortable or touchy, I could say, *Oops, I'm white!* and go back to the white world. I didn't have to deal with the problems. I could just go for the good parts. I could go when there was some kind of honor. I could go when I wanted to be a role model. I could go when it made me feel happy. But when there was a problem, I could leave." Over the next several weeks, her boyfriend kept working her over. She went to a couple more planning sessions, keeping her silence, no longer passing inadvertently. But she kept thinking about her fiancé's reaction to her decision.

"And the more I thought about it, the more I realized he might be right." Finally she called the woman who initially contacted her and arranged for them to meet privately.

The words came out straight. "I don't know if you know this," she began, "but I'm *white*." The encounter made her desperately uncomfortable. She avoided making eye contact and cannot remember the woman's reaction, probably, she said, because she blocked it out. "I don't remember what her reaction was other than anger. She was definitely angry with me. And I don't know if it was anger because she had thought I was black and found out I was white or she was angry because, *Who is this little bitch coming to me and saying, 'I'm white'?*"

Somehow a happy excuse was concocted about the young teacher being too busy with wedding plans and getting ready to move to be able to emcee the event after all. Soon the school year ended, and all the young teacher could think was, thank God this happened close to the time of her planned departure. "And I had a lot of really good friends there and I really disconnected with them when I left. I was *so* uncomfortable with what had happened." She slipped out of town quietly, and that was the end of the story, except in her good conscience.

AS SHE ANALYZES HER BLISTERING DISCOMFORT with the incident, she knows her relationship with her fiancé was a factor. She was devoted to him, much as her mother doted on her father. He felt strongly that racial discrimination was at the root of any suffering that he or his family experienced. "If he got a C on a test, it was because he was black, not because he didn't study," she said. The racial tension his presence caused in her family intensified those feelings, as did the personal identity struggles he was undergoing at the time. When they first met, he identified himself as Puerto Rican but went through a stage when he identified himself as black. "And then he went through the whole Malcolm X thing—that was really funny—always with a white girlfriend.

"The thing is," she went on, "the reason blacks and whites were not together was because they just didn't want to be together. And I did. I would go many places with him and I would be the only white. So what was the problem?"

She answered her own question. The problem was all the baggage that came with that choice, baggage heavy enough to be an issue in her relationship with the man she wanted to spend the rest of her life with, baggage awkward enough to rob *Loving v. Virginia* of its rightful place in local lore and history; baggage messy enough to keep the rate of black-white marriages at the start of the twenty-first century, our time of widest spread ethnic and racial blending, the lowest of all mixed-marriage rates nationally. It is why the young teacher, who saw herself as the great-looking white chick who dated black men, could pass for black without trying to, without wanting to; without even realizing she was doing so, in Tappahannock, Virginia.

All along, she said, her fiancé made her feel as if the problems in their relationship stemmed from her not being good enough. "I wasn't thin enough, I wasn't pretty enough, and I couldn't wear the right clothes. He couldn't bring me places because I wouldn't blend in, because I would stick out," she said. It embarrassed him when she met people for the first time and automatically shook hands to greet. "When I meet people, I shake their hand. I've always done it. And he was just mortified that I would go to some party and shake someone's hand. That's not what you do. And I was this big sore thumb and I always stuck out.

"And then, all of the sudden, this was proof for him that I could fit in," she said, and paused to let the idea sink in before she expressed the next thought. "And that maybe he could not really fit in with my family." Another pause. "And I think that is a lot of the reason that the issue was so sensitive."

~

THEIR ENGAGEMENT LASTED THREE YEARS, surviving moves to three different cities. Finally a wedding date was set and then the wedding date was canceled and then they broke up for good.

Though she has had plenty of training in psychology, it fails her when she looks back on the incident in Tappahannock. She cannot say for certain why it caused her and continues to cause her such deep distress. "That's the thing," she said quietly. "I really don't know." All she can really say for certain is that "it was horrible, really horrible, one of the most uncomfortable moments of my life." As she reluctantly admits, the likelihood is, despite all the energy she put into erasing color as a consideration in her personal life, "I'm embarrassed to say that I think it [the discomfort] was because somebody thought I *was* black. At *that* time. In *my* life."

Here a passage from an essay by Adrien Pipers starts to resonate: "The ultimate test of a person's repudiation of racism is not what she can contemplate *doing* for or on behalf of black people, but whether she herself can contemplate calmly the likelihood of *being* black."

~

IN THE END, the young teacher presumes the incident happened because her student's mother related to her as someone of her own social class. She saw the big diamond and the fine-looking educated young black man who had placed it on the young teacher's finger, and the woman assumed the teacher was black because the man was not white. "People have ways to identify black," the young teacher said, "and I guess association is good enough."

After the relationship ended, she took a studio apartment on her own in New York, not in the Bronx, which the fiancé had taught her to know and navigate, but at 78th and York Avenue on the Upper East Side of Manhattan, which she had learned from him to refer to as the "Upper White Side." Later she earned another degree and met and married a wonderful man—not a professional with advanced degrees like her former boyfriend, she couldn't care less about that—and yes, he happens to be white. But far more significantly, the relationship is healthy. He treats her wonderfully, accepts her as she is, and makes her very happy.

Hearing her story read back to her more than a decade later, all the pain and embarrassment of those last months in Tappahannock came flooding back. This was a white woman who had done far more work on teaching herself to be color-blind than most people ever consider, let alone attempt. And yet her reaction was to insist that all identifying details in the story be removed. She didn't know Adrien Piper's essay but responded as if she did: "Does this chapter have a title? I feel like it should be called 'The Day I Found Out I Was a Racist.' Or, 'The Day I Knew I Was a Racist.' Coming to the realization that I am/was a racist was and is not easy," she wrote in a subsequent e-mail. "Having others find out does not make me feel a sense of pride. Actually it produces feelings of dread, embarrassment, discomfort."

Dread, embarrassment, discomfort—these are all very familiar feelings to another young woman. Her name is Vivian Sanchez and she has passed deliberately to avoid those feelings, first at school and then later both at work and in her religious life.

CHAPTER THREE

That's Not Me

Whiteness in Latino communities (as in others) typically signifies
a range of individual traits that perpetuates social and sometimes
economic dominance; morality, gentility, intelligence, and wealth. . . .
Whiteness operates as symbolic shorthand for genealogical
connection to imperial Spain and its colonizing projects.

—MARIA CARLA SANCHEZ

THOUGH HER PARENTS WERE BORN IN PUERTO RICO, Vivian
Sanchez is quick to report that she traces her ancestry to Spain.
She always refers to herself as Spanish.

Her father has been making bangle bracelets and repairing all
kinds of jewelry since he arrived in New York as a teenager. Her
mother, who came to New York at age nine, was a secretary until
computers outdated her skills set. In her last job, before she went
on disability for a repetitive stress injury, she did piecework in a
clothing factory. Though Vivian's parents always speak their native language to each other, they encouraged their two daughters
to speak English. Sanchez guesses that they were "proud to be
raising two English-speaking kids who would do better in American society without Spanish accents."

Until Vivian Sanchez turned four in 1976, home was a public
housing project near Lincoln Center on New York's West Side.
When the family's economic situation improved, they moved

seventy-five miles north of the city to a little house in Middletown, New York, an Orange County commuter town of twenty-five thousand people. Sanchez grew up Catholic in a once-a-year-to-church kind of way. Nevertheless, she always felt very spiritual.

She was also a very good student. In the Middletown public school she fit in so well that by sixth grade, the administration moved her onto the AT (academically talented) track. She thinks this would have happened earlier in her schooling had she been Caucasian (that is how she differentiates) because in all those years of elementary school, she never had a mark lower than the equivalent of A.

Her troubles in gifted classes were social, never academic. With her medium-brown hair and light skin, Sanchez could have been related to the young teacher or David Matthews. There was no one else of her background in the gifted group, but it wasn't appearance that set her apart. Physically, she looked like the other kids. Her difficulties stemmed from a combination of economic circumstance and class. Her recollection is that the majority of her fellow students came from professional homes. "You'd go to their houses and they're talking about different brands and different toys and gadgets and you don't have these things. That's when you start to stand out," she recalls. "I remember just always feeling 'less than.' They always had brand-new clothes, all the new styles, and I had my sister's hand-me-downs from seven years before. I was in butterfly collars and bell-bottom pants when they had Oshkosh and Jordache and Hello Kitty things." In sixth and seventh grades, many of her gifted classmates had bar and bat mitzvah celebrations. She longed to be invited to one but never was. "They didn't exactly reach out to talk to me in class. We just didn't click. My only friends really were these two Indian people, as in from India, one girl and one guy. They were the only ones who even bothered to talk to me or anything like that." She described her situation as "almost a cliché. You could take some-one out of the ghetto, but take the ghetto out of them?"

These experiences were so painful that she said she deliber-ately began doing poor work in some of her subjects so that she could be retracked into classes where she would not have to feel so isolated, "so I could feel as if I belonged. I succeeded in doing that in every class except math." She found ready acceptance in a group of mostly disadvantaged African Americans and a few Lati-nos and whites from poorer families, who spent a lot of time get-ting into trouble. She met a few of these friends at school, but most she befriended at parties, going dancing, hanging out in the mall, or working at part-time jobs. She tended, she said, "to gravi-tate toward people who are of a similar economic background to my own."

At every turn, it seemed, she was reminded that she was differ-ent. She told the story of being assigned alphabetically to a high school guidance counselor, like the majority of the other stu-dents. Repeatedly she tried to make an appointment to see him as required and repeatedly he ignored her requests. "Finally I went to his office and I said, 'I'm trying to make an appointment with you.' And he said, 'Well, aren't you with so-and-so? Because you're Spanish.'" There was a designated Spanish-speaking guid-ance counselor for students with issues in English. This was not a problem she had. In fact, her Hispanic classmates never thought she was Hispanic enough. She didn't speak the language and she was much lighter skinned than they were. From her earliest recol-lections, her life always seemed uncomfortably split up.

Although she did not want to be in classes with the richer kids, she did want to succeed in school, something she pointedly did not disclose to her street friends. Very early on, her older sister had clued her that her best chance for getting ahead was college, and her only shot at college was a scholarship. For a scholarship, she needed good grades. She managed to graduate with a rank of thirty-second in a class of 320. And at home she never caused trouble. She created the impression of perfect obedience, doing whatever her parents asked. Little did they know that almost every night she was climbing out her bedroom window to meet with her friends.

"I needed a release," she said, "and that is how I got my release. I was in National Honor Society, and I had to be one way, but when I was with my friends, I felt that that was really who I was, releasing the pressures of home, of being in a very strict family environment with a very hot-tempered father, and that was how I got my release. I hung out with people who could understand me. I didn't have to explain myself. I didn't have to be ashamed of who I was."

Her father may have had some idea about the company she was keeping because he would admonish her from time to time to stay away from blacks and Hispanics and cultivate white friends. "He told me I was only to have white friends because that's the only way I'll succeed in life. And I would say that I didn't see the point of looking at color. A friend is a friend. But he was very, very concerned about me succeeding and what the neighbors would think and things like that. I wasn't very happy about that." She never talked to her family about the people she hung out with and she never brought any of them home.

Sanchez applied to Marist College in nearby Poughkeepsie and was awarded a scholarship and enough financial aid to cover tuition and board. "That semester was a big rude awakening as to just how poor my family was," she recalled. She didn't even have enough money to cover the cost of her books, nor could her parents help her at all. The contrast with her roommate, a stockbroker's daughter from Long Island, was acute. The roommate not only received all the support she needed from her family, but saved money for college from her summer vacation jobs. Sanchez too had been working for extra money since she was fourteen. But as the first person in her family ever to go to college, she had no preparatory guidance. She hadn't figured out that she should have been putting some of that money away for this purpose. "Girls were calling their parents and saying, 'I can't live without my Diet Coke' and getting care packages," she said. Little things like that made the differences very real.

Social life during that term was a holdover boyfriend from high school who lived thirty miles away in Kingston. He sent her five dollars for the bus so that she could visit him every weekend. There was never anything but cereal in the cupboard at his parents' house. "We were terrible," she said. "We would break into cars to try to find money or anything we could cash in to be able to go and buy food. And we'd hang out with other kids who were just as crazy and there'd be riots in the streets and things like that. And I was on a Presidential Scholarship. It was just bizarre."

As the semester progressed, it became harder and harder to cope financially as well as emotionally. Her weight dropped to ninety pounds. She managed to complete the term, but it left her spent. She went through the motions of trying to line up a work-study job for the spring, applying for a position in every academic department and office on campus. But the effort yielded nothing. Worst of all, she said, was the exacerbation of those leftover feelings from elementary school and high school, the sense of living a "dual life." She couldn't handle it anymore. It was a relief to quit.

BACK IN MIDDLETOWN, Sanchez returned to her parents' home and took a job as a receptionist in a kitchen sales company for several months until a better opportunity came along. She managed to save enough money to buy a car and then got a better-paying position in northern New Jersey. The commute was an hour each way but she never minded the drive.

She wanted her own apartment and quickly understood that the only way to make enough money to have one would be to find work in New York City, with its higher pay scale. This she did. Ultimately she ended up in the desktop publishing department of a major Wall Street firm, where she has built a career. Her work puts her in regular contact with the company's complement of young analysts and associates, a group of very self-assured mostly Ivy League graduates. They are not, for the most part, minorities, like the secretaries, receptionists, and other administrative personnel that form her circle of close friends at work. She finds the presence of the Ivy Leaguers inhibiting, off-putting. They bring the old feelings of inadequacy, of "less than," thundering back, both for being from a disadvantaged background and for not finishing college. A few years ago, at a supervisor's suggestion, she enrolled in the Division of General Studies at Columbia University and managed to complete two semesters of study. She did well in her courses and it buoyed her self-confidence. At an Ivy League level, she could do the work. "It was the proof I needed for myself and to the world that I'm not an idiot," she said. But again the costs overwhelmed her. "It was so much money and I was having heart palpitations about student loans," she said, and again she withdrew.

Then another long-standing interest began to come to the fore, an idea that had intrigued her since a classroom epiphany she had when she was about seven. It was Christmastime in Middletown and two of her little classmates demonstrated how to spin a drei-del. Watching their fascination with the little Hanukkah top en-chanted her. It gave her chills and she started to cry. "I've never stopped feeling that," she said. But for the longest time, she thought the only way to be a Jew was to be born one.

~

SANCHEZ KNEW SECULAR JEWISH KIDS from her elementary and high school days and was accustomed to seeing members of the Hassidic community shopping in the mall on Sundays. There are two large Hassidic groups in the Middletown area, so the men in their black coats and hats and side curls and the women with their covered hair and modest dress, always surrounded by chil-dren, were a familiar sight. Sanchez began reading up on Judaism, and once she found out about the possibility of conver-sion, she began studying in earnest.

Her mother was fine with the decision. "Just as long as I was following God," she said, "she didn't care." Her mother even bought Sanchez a menorah while she was still living at home. Her father was not particularly aware of what she was up to. "In our household, it was kind of like, you live your life and you tell every-body after the fact. So he didn't quite know what was going on."

After moving to her own apartment, she began to attend Torah study classes and to think seriously about committing to the rig-orous Orthodox Jewish path. "I was always nervous about it," she said, "because a lot of people would say, *Oh! The Orthodox will never accept you!* But Orthodox was the path I preferred. She was twenty-seven when she asked the leader of her study group for a referral to a conversion class. That was in the spring of 2000, around Passover time, and the conversion process, with its intensive study and immersion in Jewish observance and ritual life, took a full year.

~

ABOUT TWO MONTHS after the completion of her conversion, she gave a full account of her experiences, exploring at length her decision to put herself in yet another situation in which a sense of belonging was going to be difficult if not impossible to achieve. No doubt Sanchez already had developed a certain comfort level with being cast in the role of outsider. But as much as the literature of the Orthodox extols loving the convert, a Puerto Rican named Sanchez presenting herself as an Orthodox Jew was bound to have her tussles.

At first she just rationalized all the awkward, hurtful moments away. "I guess I could do this because I'm so used to never really truly fitting in with my Caucasian friends or with my Spanish friends. Growing up, I hung out mostly with black people. I was just so used to not really quite fitting in that this really didn't faze me." Here was a community of people focused on ritual life, learning, and mutual nurture, a ready-made answer to her spiritual longing as well as her social and intellectual needs, a situation in which her background and educational level, at least in principle, were finally irrelevant among members of the educated white upper middle class. Had becoming Jewish and living among active, very observant Jews finally provided her with a way to feel a true sense of community on some basis other than common class origins?

Not exactly. "I've met a number of very warm and open families that I can go to with anything at any time," she said. "When it comes to friendships, that's where I still have a struggle, because

I'm still more comfortable with people from my background." Even as her involvement with the Orthodox community deepened, she still preferred the company of her coworkers, a group of law-abiding minorities who accepted her decision to convert. They didn't seem to be put off by the restrictions an Orthodox life imposes on its adherents—strictly kosher food, restrictive holiday observances—and continued to hang out with her. "They know the gist of things because I explained it to them," she said. "They're totally understanding." All the same, she never asked them to call her by the unusual Hebrew name she had assumed to signify her new life: Adaya.

Shortly after her conversion was complete, she left her apartment in New Jersey to live on the Upper West Side of Manhattan, not far from the public housing project where she spent her early childhood. At the suggestion of her religious instructor, she moved into an apartment with two other religious girls. Being on the Upper West Side meant a constant stream of invitations to join other women at synagogue, attend Sabbath dinners, and participate in various holiday observances and celebrations. All of that was fine. Her dance card was full. But the roommates were standoffish and, more often than not, she found herself feeling more set apart than part of. For the longest while, she swept those feelings aside, unwilling on the other side of so many sacrifices to let a few offensive, unthinking slights deter her. But there was no denying how discomfiting it was. "Moving to the West Side was a real eye-opener," she said.

The roommates, for example, immediately made it clear that their interest was in a third person to share the rent, not in making another friend. The three of them had barely been introduced when one of the girls asked Sanchez if she kept kosher. Keeping kosher is so basic to Orthodox observance that the question was just plain offensive, like asking a physician if she had really gone to medical school. "She knew that I had fully converted as an Orthodox Jew," Sanchez huffed. "She would never have asked that of anyone else. I felt like I was being watched, to see whether I was really observant, and that bothered me."

At Sabbath gatherings, the endless games of Jewish geography became so very tiresome. *Where did you go to yeshiva? Where did you grow up?* Sanchez would say that she was from Middletown and the automatic next question was, *Is there a religious community there?* She would answer no and prepare for the inevitable question, *Where did you go to school?* "And I'd tell them and they'd say, *Oh.* And suddenly they wouldn't want to talk to you anymore because you are not the same as they are."

There were exceptions, of course, mostly among fellow converts or Jews who had come late to the religious life. "But there were a lot of instances where people would ask me my last name and I would just try to avoid the question or change the subject or say I had to go to the bathroom. You know, that is ridiculous. When I told a matchmaker what my last name was, she said, 'Oh! We'll have to get rid of that name.' It was little things like that."

The background issue was so tricky she started finding it easier just to lie about it. Sanchez invented a story about having a Sephardic, or Mediterranean-Spanish Jewish, background. Once on a hiking trip with a Jewish outdoors club, someone in the car on the ride back to the city made disparaging comments about blacks and Hispanics. In any other context, Sanchez would have taken the idiot on immediately, but in this setting, she found herself tongue-tied. Another woman in the car then compounded Sanchez's discomfort by asking about her exotic Hebrew name. "All I could think was why didn't I pick a simple name like Esther, instead of picking something that was going to make people ask questions. And the girl said, 'Oh, whose name was that in your family?' and I'm thinking, *Crap!* And I say, 'It's original. My parents wanted to be different.' And here I am making believe my parents are Jewish and that they named me!"

Deception and lying can make passing much harder on the passer than on the people the passer has to dupe. Anthony Appiah explained that the source of the anxiety is both ethical and moral in nature. The ethical anxiety is about authenticity, about the deception of presenting yourself as other than who you understand yourself to be, and the moral anxiety is about lying. Lying is troubling because it is about betraying others, and inauthenticity is troubling because it is about betraying the self.

Sanchez felt miserable about deceiving this new acquaintance but couldn't do otherwise in the moment. Once at home, she e-mailed her an apology. She admitted being a convert and explained that she had been made to feel awkward about her background, which inhibited her from telling the truth. The woman expressed understanding. She e-mailed back for Sanchez not to worry about it. It was no big deal. Yet Sanchez never saw her after that.

~

SANCHEZ EXPERIENCED another upsetting incident. She was walking down the street with a group of religious acquaintances and they began talking about how Latino men treat women. "Really?" Sanchez asked them. "How do you know this?" She said she decided not to reveal her origins. She was getting tired of having to tell her story over and over again and of watching the way people reacted to the story, always in exactly the same way. "All of the sudden they get quiet or they're not sure what to say next," she said. "They don't want to hurt my feelings so they're very, very cautious. I feel that. What I also notice is that prior to their finding out, I'm treated as if I know what I should know about Orthodox Judaism. And then once they find out, suddenly, it's like, *Oh, do you know why we use hallah on Shabbat?* And I'm like, *I didn't study for a year for nuthin'! Give me some credit, here!* Sometimes I just feel like when the questions start happening, like, *Where's your family from? Where are you from?* I would just like to be treated like everybody else. Instead, it seems like for the rest of my life, I will be telling my story, even if it's just during a simple meal at someone's house. And once the questions start popping up, I have a panic attack. I want to run out the door. It just happens a lot. It happens a lot."

FOR SINGLE ORTHODOX JEWISH WOMEN in their twenties, matrimony is a primary objective. The subtext of much of their relentless socializing is the quest for a permanent mate. Because of the religious restrictions on premarital sex, courtships tend to be short and intense. They either lead directly to an engagement announcement or end summarily. Right after her conversion, Sanchez began seeing a young aspiring lawyer who was studying for the bar. He was from an observant family, despite the general feeling that converts do better with other converts. He had a deeply spiritual side. "A lot of the Modern Orthodox guys tend not to be in that direction," she explained. They have what she sees as an "outward expression of a religion without much depth." She liked this about him especially. Sanchez said she felt quite comfortable with him. She said she was able to be "somewhat myself" but was "nervous to unleash my full self." And yet she understood that in her journey into Judaism, a relationship with a Jewish man was going to be the point of reckoning, the time when some of the either-or choices she had successfully put off for so long would have to be made. That left her feeling especially nervous.

"Up until this point, I'd been able to maintain my two separate lives," she explained. "The friends I have today—my minority friends, my non-Jewish friends—we have music in common, and movies. R & B, hip-hop, freestyle, which not too many people are exactly fond of in the Orthodox community." She feared her cultural tastes were going to be a "stumbling block" with the boyfriend.

"I don't know how else to phrase this. I don't want this to sound wrong," she said, "but most Orthodox Jews don't listen to that kind of music, at least on the West Side or in Monsey," the heavily Orthodox community in Rockland County, New York, where she was also spending a lot of time. She hadn't shared these cultural passions with the boyfriend, even though the two of them already were talking about marriage, at least in general terms. And she acknowledged that most of the Modern Orthodox people she associated with were "pretty open."

She used the metaphor of language to talk about her ambivalence, the experience of her different voices. On the one hand is her "professional voice," the one she uses at work, with her Orthodox friends, and in our discussions—the one she calls her "how to succeed in life" voice. On the other hand is the slang that kicks in when she's with her closest pals, even on the sly at work, when she is not within earshot of her bosses or the Ivy League brigade. That language, she said, "is just very 'street,'" but declined to offer a demonstration because "it doesn't come out naturally to talk like that with people who aren't from that type of background." Her automatic pattern is to switch back and forth, depending on the company in which she finds herself. Asked how she thought the Orthodox boyfriend might react to hearing her lapse into ghetto-speak, she said, "I'm afraid he'd run in the opposite direction and I'd never see him again."

She went on. "When I'm with my friends, I'm like, *Oh! I'm this!* But I know I can't talk to my boss like that. I can't talk to my rabbi like that. And I can't talk with a lot of my Jewish friends on the West Side like that either. They'd think I was crazy." It's not that they're close-minded or particularly rigid, she said; some of them even go to clubs and bars. But the street language signifies her otherness, interests she cherishes that she feared her Orthodox friends would find alien, objectionable.

Still, eight weeks into her relationship with the young lawyer, she held on to the hope that he would accept her "street" side. "I was telling my friends that after the bar exam, we have to plan an event. We have to get him to come out to dinner with us or something, because he's got to see this side of me, because if he doesn't like it, it's not going to work. I don't want to surprise him. Like, one day he comes home early from work and I'm on the phone with a friend and I'm talking the way I'm talking, and he's like, *This is who I married?* But I'm dreading this because I know it's very difficult, and I know I'm not going to find a black Orthodox guy. There are very few. That's obvious. So, that's what I'm struggling with right now. It's just followed me throughout life and now it's getting to a point where both worlds are finally looking at each other. Before, I could always keep them separate."

⌒

EVERYONE PUTS ON MASKS or adopts different personas from time to time, often short-term, to achieve a variety of reasonable aims. We are forever modulating our voices and adjusting our styles to manipulate outcomes, to get the best result. People are forever feigning interest in other people's lives in order to soften requests for help in unrelated ways. The art of sweet-talking a contractor who is exasperatingly over deadline, when we really would like to bludgeon him, is a common strategy to keep the work going. These are ordinary performances, mundane practices, acceptable acts of deception that sociologist Erving Goffman examines in detail in *The Presentation of Self in Everyday Life*. But when we perform in this way, we are not assuming a false identity; generally speaking, we are choosing among aspects of an identity we recognize as our own. It is not, then, an act of passing. What Sanchez describes is something different. It is passing because she does not recognize the persona she assumes as her own. She feels it is outside of herself. Her experience is distinct from cases where the shifting back and forth feels natural, where the various aspects of self are reconciled. Using her own metaphor of language, consider the Argentinian writer Hector Bianciotti and his description of abandoning his native Spanish to write in French. He already was enamored of France's influence on his favorite Spanish-speaking poets by age twelve or thirteen. Like many South Americans, he considered France the cultural center of the Western world. His interviewer, Jason Weiss, compares Bianciotti's zeal in embracing the French language to that of the religious convert. Even his later biographical writings on Argentinian themes were written in French. In fact, he is so successful in his adopted language that the Académie Française inducted him into membership in 1997.

By contrast, Sanchez was unable to meld her two experiences. She does not think of herself as ambidextrous. In her professional and Orthodox guise at this time, she experienced herself as passing. Even though she has been assuming this persona for years, when she described herself at work or among the Orthodox, she used the words, *That's not me.*

Despite her evident ambivalence, a year into her life as a Jew, Sanchez was adamant about the seriousness of her commitment and her unwillingness, even given the obstacles, to veer from her chosen path. Give it up? "Not with what I had to go through to get to this point! And I'm at the point right now in my life where I'm realizing that dating is for marriage and I'm Orthodox. And there are major sacrifices that come into play. Never to eat my mom's cooking again—there's just a lot involved. And for me to go through that and for me to turn away from it would be ridiculous."

～

AS IT TURNED OUT, there were other issues in the relationship with the Orthodox boyfriend, issues of a more ordinary nature. "He didn't like the shoes I wore. He didn't like the way I looked, thought I didn't do enough with appearance. He needed me to be the most beautiful thing on his arm when we went out in public." Once at the library he was describing an Orthodox wedding (and using the personal plural pronoun freely), when he openly ogled another woman. Sanchez called him on it and he snapped back, "Well, it's not as if you're drop-dead gorgeous."

This really stunned her. "I'm not saying anybody ever told me I was drop-dead gorgeous but no one has ever put me down like that in my life!" And to make things worse, he mentioned in passing that if they did marry, he was hoping they could change the wording on the traditional marriage contract, the Ketubah, so it wouldn't reveal that she was a convert. For Sanchez, that was it. She waited until after he got through the bar exam at the end of

July and then ended the relationship. He didn't understand what the problem was. He thought maybe they needed premarital counseling.

~

OVER THE COURSE OF THE NEXT SIX MONTHS, it became more and more clear to Sanchez that her experience of life in the Orthodox community was probably not going to change. All those big Sabbath meals with ten, twenty or twenty-five people at the table, all the explaining, all of the asking about her background, the *What's your name?* "It's great if you're one of them," she said, "but it didn't quite work out that way for me." She was quick to acknowledge that she had made some friends, that there actually were some people with whom she did "click"—that grade school word again. But most of what she experienced was a struggle to fit in. "How is this happiness?" she started to wonder. "How is this living? That's what was hurting me. Here I was, making all these sacrifices, and then this is what I got in return? I was just like, 'Forget it!' I started to get really fed up."

~

AT A SABBATH TABLE a few months into her life as a Jew, in June 2001, one of her new friends brought up the subject of passing. It started Sanchez thinking about her experiences in just those terms. Sensing a sympathetic ear, she sent her friend a long e-mail. This is what she wrote:

There was something you brought up that I wanted to talk to you about, but I didn't feel comfortable doing so in front of everyone else on Shabbos. The subject was passing and I believe I am still doing it until this very day.

I have been living two distinctly separate lives for as long as I can remember. In school I was a member of the National Honor Society and was in the academically talented track. At home, I was the dutiful daughter who could do nothing wrong. My parents knew that I was doing well in school, but they had no clue as to what it was to succeed academically or in the true career world. Unbeknownst to my classmates, teachers, and parents, my friends were primarily black and Hispanic dropouts who spoke only slang, smoked weed, were alcoholics, in trouble with the law, and they definitely did not know that I was in the top 10 percent of my class. My boyfriends were drug dealers and wanted for selling illegal weapons. My female friends have children from different fathers, which didn't hold them back from having sex with any man they wanted. All of my friends loved to fight in the streets and we all carried weapons for protection. If my friends found out that I was a goody two-shoes in school and at home, I would've been beaten and left on the curb. If my classmates and teachers found out what kind of company I kept and how I lived outside of school, I would've been rejected, kicked out of the NHS for breaking the "character" oath, and treated like a stereotypical Hispanic. After all, I was the only Hispanic in their classes. My father would've beaten the daylights out of me if he found out. My classmates knew my parents weren't wealthy. Although their parents were the doctors, lawyers, and political figures of the area, they accepted me because of my intellectual abilities and because I acted like one of them.

Because of this long-term charade, I still do not know where I stand. I have always felt more comfortable with my dropout friends because we share common backgrounds and struggles,

THAT'S NOT ME   83

but then I have always feared intellectual regression. It happened to me once. I picked up the *New York Times* after a year of working in a noncorporate environment with less educated coworkers and I could not understand any of the articles. I nearly passed out from fear and shock and immediately ran back to the rat race, purchased a slew of books, and enrolled in classes to become articulate again. Although I enjoy intelligent conversations and learning, I do not feel fully comfortable with those who cannot relate "to the streets." I have difficulty relating to them as I'm sure they have difficulty relating to me. Unless, of course, I pass so well that they do not suspect a colorful background. Basically, I know where I feel at home but I know that I will never succeed or reach my full potential if I remain there. Thus, the struggle continues. I must continue to pass in order to survive.

SHE ALSO TALKED ABOUT HER EXPERIENCE of passing in terms of her name, how she identifies herself and how others identify her. "When I'm with my minority friends, my hang-out friends, that's Vivian. When I'm at work, I'm Vivian, but that's not me. When I'm at synagogue, that's the spiritual side of me, but that's not my total being, unless I'm with certain friends whom I can be myself with. I feel that I'm passing when it comes to everything outside of my social life. With my family now, I can be myself. With my friends, I can be myself. But when it comes to work and being an Orthodox Jew, as much as I love being an Orthodox Jew, I feel that I'm passing. Lately, I've been having some of my friends over to my new apartment and that was a shocker. It was probably the first time my two Orthodox female roommates have probably ever had a black guy in the apartment. One of them walked in and saw him before she saw me. She said hi to him and hi to me. But if she had run into me on the street, she would have said something like, 'Hey, howyadoin'?' Her reaction was not the norm."

Bringing her black friend home, she said, was one of her concrete attempts to reconcile her two worlds, to end the passing. "Well, that's the thing," she said. "I'm trying to bring it home. I'm trying to be me." So who is she? Vivian? Adaya?

"With my Orthodox friends, when I'm with them, I want them to call me Adaya. The Orthodox friends who knew me from the beginning of the process still call me Vivian. They feel more comfortable like that. My friends when I'm hanging out, I'm Vivian. My family? I'm Vivian. When I talk to myself, I'm like, *Viv, what are ya doin'?* I'm Vivian to myself. And any new Orthodox people I meet when I go to Brooklyn or to Queens or to Monsey, I'm Adaya."

~

FROM HER JOURNAL (JULY 2001):

How do people of extremely different cultures do it? Why do I have two sides? Why can't I click with people of my own religion? No matter what, I am still just passing—pretending to belong to a social class and culture different from my own. It's an act that I don't want to bring home with me. It's fine at work or at school, but I want to be me at home. I want to put an end to the show.

I read a commentary today about Ruth and Naomi's other daughter-in-law, Arpah. Arpah's problem was that she was unable to separate herself from her Moabite culture and fully join herself to the Jewish people the way Ruth did. Ruth was rewarded and

Arpah was raped on her way back to Moab and was never able to conceive. Is this my situation? Am I afraid to leave Moab?

I picked up a highly recommended book entitled *Mixed Matches: How to Create Successful Interracial, Interethnic, and Interfaith Relationships.* I really hope it will provide some insight.

The next six months for Sanchez were a period of deep introspection about the choices she had made, trying to determine what she really wanted. So who was she on the other side of her grappling?

"Vivian," she said firmly.

"At first I thought maybe I needed to go to a more Israeli-type synagogue, that maybe I would be able to connect better with that culture." With its Sephardic cultural influences, she thought, an Israeli-style environment might be closer to her own than the Ashkenazi, or European-based Judaism, that dominates Orthodox Jewish life on the Upper West Side. Moving to the neighborhood, she felt, had been a mistake. She hated "people making me feel insecure because of my last name, making me always feel as if I had to disguise who I really was, making me feel inferior because I was a convert. Too often in her West Side experience, she heard racist remarks, often targeted at Hispanics. "I thought moving to a community would make me feel more immersed and part of something," she said. "And if anything, I felt more and more alienated." And to think she had picked the Orthodox community of the West Side of Manhattan because it is considered the youngest and the most open and welcoming.

The change of heart coincided with a developing friendship Sanchez had with a former coworker, a non-Jew, a black-white-Cherokee who accepted her Judaism but didn't hesitate to challenge her beliefs and assumptions. "Basically," she said, "he helped me to realize that I was miserable with the decision I had made for myself. I couldn't eat with my own family. I wasn't allowed to attend my sister's wedding. And I could only eat in certain restaurants, which made it difficult for me to hang out with my nonreligious friends. I couldn't dress the way I wanted to dress. In the heat of summer, I wanted to wear shorts and a T-shirt, you know? I couldn't live where I wanted to live.

"The things I was used to doing growing up, I couldn't do any more. The reality of the decision I had made really hit me hard. Was this truly how I wanted to live the rest of my life?

"And there were things I never fully agreed with. I never fully, truly, fully believed the entire oral law. I couldn't stand the fact that I couldn't shower on Shabbat or on the holidays. Things that just irked me continued to irk me even more over time. And I started reading books about who wrote the Bible and one called *The History of God.* I read some books by Reform Jewish authors and even one by Alan Dershowitz, just trying to get all different perspectives on Judaism, on religion. On God. It just really challenged me and led me to question a lot of things that I had just always blindly accepted.

"In the beginning, Orthodox Judaism was, to me, the ultimate-sacrifice-to-God kind of thing," she said. "But when you don't feel any more that the stuff really is from God, it just doesn't take on nearly so much meaning.

"And then, of course, came September 11. That was pivotal. And I recall going to synagogue and I couldn't even pray. I saw the words "God is compassionate" and "there are those who love him and follow him" and I just felt it was all hypocrisy and I couldn't— I stopped going. Or, I would go with my friends because they asked me to, but I wouldn't pray while I was there. I would just sit there. And as a result of all that, I made a decision that life is too short and I didn't want to bog myself down with a lot of manmade rules that only left me irritated, angry, and depressed. And I actually started dating the guy I was hanging out with."

~

AFTER THE ATTACKS on New York and Washington, D.C., on September 11, 2001, Sanchez began to distance herself from her West Side surroundings. "I still had to respect my roommates and my community because I still lived there. So on Shabbat, I would just stay in my bedroom and do forbidden things, like write. I just wouldn't do it flagrantly in front of my roommates. For holidays, I would stay at my boyfriend's apartment. I would just get away from there so that I didn't feel confined and so they wouldn't sense the tension. And then it got to the point where I asked myself, 'Why am I making myself so unhappy?' Why am I deliberately keeping myself in an apartment with two girls that I really don't get along with in a part of town where I don't want to live?' I'm moving back to New Jersey!

"So I can say now that I feel free to be who I am. I feel so elated that I'm with someone with whom I can totally be myself. I don't have to put on an act for anybody anymore." Her boyfriend, who became her fiancé within a year, has helped a great deal with the transition. He is someone very much like herself, deeply engaged with the world of ideas but does not have a college degree. "We can get into intelligent discussions with each other about topics we are passionate about because we know that neither of us will turn around say, *You sound white*, as so many minorities do," she said.

She still feels proud to be a Jew, but "more on the Reform-secular side, where I am proud to be a Jew, but I don't believe in religion telling me how I should live my life. There's a place for it, but I don't ever want it to come between me and my family again or make me feel uncomfortable, unhappy, or not proud of who I am or where my family comes from. That was the big thing that I didn't like."

The break from the ritual life was difficult. "Even to go eat bread, I had to tell myself not to wash. I had to remind myself not to do the things that I would do automatically. And then it just got to the point where it was just so freeing not to have to be bogged down with all those little details."

Over lunch, Sanchez did confide in one Orthodox friend, a smart and understanding woman whose first name is Sarah. She has an Orthodox background and works for a nonprofit organization that does Orthodox outreach. She met Sanchez at synagogue during the year of Sanchez's conversion and they have remained friends. They sometimes walked together in Central Park on long Sabbath afternoons. She tried to convince Sanchez to give her Orthodox friends a chance. "I tried to convince her that it was not her Orthodox friends who have turned away from her, but she who has turned her back on them," Sarah said. "She gave up a lot of friends under an assumption or fear that her religious Jewish friends wouldn't accept the changes in her. I remember trying to communicate to her that it's not up to her to decide what their reaction will be. Sure, if she divulges to them, some of them might not be able to handle it. That's a real risk. But there are many, many who would want to be her friend anyway, who are confused and hurt that she disappeared to New Jersey and hasn't been in contact with people who had grown to care about her. If she takes the risk, she might lose a few friends. But if she continues to be out of touch, she will definitely lose all her friends." Sarah reported that an Orthodox middle-aged woman, who had supported Sanchez during her conversion, figured out for herself what was happening. To Sarah, the woman acknowledged that she herself had done "all sorts of things that would surprise you" when she was younger, and that it saddened her that Adaya had not been in touch.

Sarah's reaction was much like the middle-aged woman's. "I think Adaya is a really good, sincere person with a great sense of humor. I would never turn my back on her just because of the spiritual struggles she's going through. I think I am relatively okay with it because it's not like she has decided to start practicing another religion. If she had decided, say, that she believes in Catholicism after all, that would have been more of a slap in the face to my beliefs, and I would have a harder time with it.

"But what I see in Adaya is not someone who has drawn conclusions, but someone who is struggling a lot to figure out who she is and what she believes and who she feels comfortable with. And within different parameters, I've gone through struggles like that too. I think all people who are introspective and have intellectual honesty go through that to one extent or another. So I'm able to appreciate Adaya's many good qualities, and respect her struggle, even though I'm personally disappointed that she's not practicing Judaism anymore. I'm not disappointed in her; I guess I'm disappointed that she doesn't see Judaism the way I do, and that she doesn't have a relationship with God that allows her to see Him even in events like 9/11. But I know that this isn't my struggle to go through; it's hers. And the only thing I can do is be here for her and listen and make sure she knows that if she ever wants to come back to the Orthodox community, there will be a lot of people who will be so happy to see her. And if she never comes back, of course I'll feel sad about it, but I still respect her for all her great qualities and I hope she finds a way to be happy."

~

THE FIANCÉ OF VIVIAN SANCHEZ has no interest in becoming Jewish, but he enjoys their theological discussions and would not stand in the way of her practicing Judaism full-time if she decided to once again. As it happens, she hasn't prayed since 9/11. Almost a year had passed when she reported the fact. "I haven't totally gotten over that one yet," she said. But she lights candles on the Sabbath and lights the menorah her mother gave her on Hanukkah. She refused to have a Christmas tree in the New Jersey apartment that she and the new boyfriend now share. "And I love hearing the shofar. There are certain symbols of Judaism I love and will always love and that's why that's the religion that I will always associate myself with," she said.

A corporate merger has helped reconcile her duality at work. "I'm sitting with my new group and we're all different nationalities, so it's a nice blend. I can be myself at work now," she said. "We're one big publishing department and the associates and analysts are all on the other side of the building."

Only one new problem has arisen and Sanchez feels sure it will work itself out. Her most recent choices have upset her mother, who became a born-again Christian following her daughter's spiritual lead.

"She's not happy that I'm shacking up," Sanchez said. "And she's not happy that I'm not religious anymore."

~

WHAT FREED VIVIAN SANCHEZ of the need to pass was her decision to abandon a religious aspiration that ended up being too entangled with a community that, in the end, did not provide the succor that attracted her to it in the first place. To survive in its midst, she felt forced to edit too much of herself out. And yet without the community, this style of Jewish observance didn't really seem possible. Stepping away from being observant made the problem go away. At about the same time, she found a guy who was intellectually compelling, not Jewish, of her own social class, who liked her just the way she was. The passing, at last, evaporated.

Sanchez was able to remove her observant mantle but sometimes this is not an option. Sometimes the religious life has an urgent, irresistible pull. Sometimes it takes the form of a very specific vocational calling that cannot be ignored, reassessed, or cast off, a force so powerful that it has to be pursued, even as it demands the negation of significant aspects of the self.

CHAPTER FOUR

Leviticus 18:22

I can define my identity only against
the background of things that matter.
—CHARLES TAYLOR

JOEL ALTER STILL TALKS ABOUT the jarring zigzag that disrupted his otherwise placid childhood. When he was a month into third grade, his family left Minneapolis for Tel Aviv and then repatriated to Philadelphia ten months later, before the next school year began. After that he started Jewish day school, building fluency in Hebrew and Jewish law that his parents reinforced at home and with pricey religious sleep-away camps each summer. There was the Sabbath table every Friday evening, synagogue every Saturday morning, and all the holiday rituals his large and loving family faithfully observed. Judaism for the youngest Alter had full and welcome expression right from birth.

At camp and in middle school and high school, at Philadelphia's Akiba Hebrew Academy, where his mother became the secretary, he starred in all the plays and musicals—Oliver in *Oliver Twist*, Lysander in *Midsummer Night's Dream.* For years thereafter, he adorned his walls with posters from *The Wizard of Oz* and *Cabaret.* Hours were spent in ninth-grade philosophical discussion with his girlfriend Amy over whether it was right for them to kiss. When high school friends compared notes on girls

93

hot and hotter, casually, he added his assessments, feigning an enthusiasm like their own. He found it mystifying the way one guy
after the other could get all gooey and romantic over this girl or
that, eye each other in the morning, be fooling around by after-
noon, and move on to the next a day later. He was adept at ratio-
nalizing his own disinterest. Physical attraction was never going
to be enough to push him into any short-lived involvement. He
was waiting to connect emotionally, to fall in love; to celebrate and
be celebrated at his own wedding; to be a father; to complete the
circle his three older brothers and older sister had begun, taking
his place in "the chain of generations" of his American Jewish
family. His day too would come.

Even in high school, when he thought about girls, he let those
same underlying assumptions guide him. That Jews marry and
have children. That family life is central. That fulfillment finds expression in the confluence of family and synagogue, in prayer and
ritual observance, in Jewish community life.

His memory records no childhood or teenaged upsets outside
the ordinary. He was not a troubled child. The report card word
"well-adjusted" comes to mind. He is smart, thoughtful, cen-
tered, without neurotic affect; always well liked in school. Friends
describe him as happy-go-lucky, someone who feels safe in the
world. In appearance, he is appealing in the way nice Jewish boys
can be appealing, lean, not a heart-stopper. He doesn't really look
like Rob Lowe but Rob Lowe could play him in the movie, or
Chris O'Donnell with darker hair. It is easy to imagine observant
Jewish girls fantasizing about the perfect husband this son of a
neuro-epidemiologist would make, especially given his love for
the Jewish family ideal as he had lived and understood it.

For college in September 1985, he chose Columbia University,
where he declared a major in history with a concentration in Jewish history. At the north end of campus sits the imposing block-

long neo-Georgian building with the words "The Jewish Theo-logical Seminary" above the portico. "The seminary," as it prefers *not* to be called, JTS, *la perla* of Conservative Judaism. He hoped to study there one day, not in the graduate school programs, where seminarians trained to be scholars, but in the rabbinical school, where the chancellor, the revered Gerson Cohen ("You gotta love the seminary. The head of the seminary is still called The Chancellor"), had recently installed as dean his dynamic, progressive young protégé, Gordon Tucker.

⌇

THE SPRING BEFORE ALTER ARRIVED on the Columbia cam-pus, graduation ceremonies at the seminary drew national atten-tion. On May 11, 1985, Amy Eilberg became the first woman rabbi in the one-hundred-year history of Conservative Judaism. Her or-dination culminated a long, contentious political struggle within the movement that Tucker, who had been ordained a decade ear-lier, had championed as head of a committee on the status of women. Agitation to admit women to the Conservative rabbinate started in 1972, when Congress passed the Equal Rights Amend-ment and the Reform movement ordained its first woman rabbi. And yet at 122nd and Broadway, the only noteworthy event in the struggle for women's advancement was the rabbinical school's re-jection of Susannah Heschel's application. At the time, she and the entire Judaic universe were mourning the death of her father, Abraham Joshua Heschel, the seminary's own exalted philoso-pher, ethicist, social activist, and theologian, who had encouraged her to apply.

For the seminary admission's office, the thirteen years it took to allow the ordination of a rabbi named Amy created a consider-able backlog of women hopefuls. The entering class in the fall of

1984 was one-third female, a topographical shift dramatic enough to cause "frayed feelings," in Tucker's polite phrase, but no real upheaval. Still, he said, "people felt their world was changing and people don't like their world to change." The move prompted the resignation of Rabbi José Faur, a professor of rabbinics who filed suit against the seminary in New York Supreme Court, charging religious discrimination and breach of contract. He hadn't signed on to teach women. But Faur's response was the exception. Tucker saw the move to admit women not as a liberalizing of the tradition, not as a "watering down," but as an "opening up," in the best sense of the phrase. It concretely indicated a new willingness in the movement to hear different voices and different perspectives, an openness to what was going on in the field and in the congregations, where up to that point it had been considered unseemly to ask some of the questions that were starting to be raised regularly.

DOWN THE BLOCK in the Columbia quadrangle, Joel Alter was adjusting to undergraduate university life. He remembers a student representative from one of the gay organizations on campus giving a talk on his dormitory floor, the kind of diversity-sensitivity training that was becoming common on liberal college campuses. The speaker made the unfortunate tactical error of opening the session by asking for questions instead of setting the agenda. One of Alter's suite mates, a son of Turkish Catholics who was struggling mightily with his own identity issues, blurted out, "Well, don't you think it's a little sick?" The words reverberated in Alter's head.

Looking back at his date book for 1982, age fifteen, he now

finds a snip of coded language. "Are you 'happy'?" the entry reads, a thought he let lie dormant. There was one "quasi-relationship" with a male classmate and a confidence passed to his best friend, phrased in the manner of, *What if I'm gay?* Or, *I think I might be gay*, but nothing he acted on. By then AIDS was enough of a scourge in the gay community to make the cover of *Time*, and that was his only gay frame of reference. He didn't know anyone who was gay in high school, or if he did, he didn't know that he did and wouldn't have understood what it was all about if he had. It's not as if the rabbi at synagogue or his teachers at day school ever sermonized or lectured about Leviticus 18:22 or Leviticus 20:13, the "abomination passages" in the Bible that cause all the trouble, the ones that state so unequivocally, "Do not lie with a man as one lies with a woman; it is an abomination." And "If a man lies with a male as one lies with a woman; the two of them have done an abhorrent thing they shall be put to death—their bloodguilt is upon them." The authority figures in his life gave their share of lectures about, say, the perils of drug use. But no one mentioned homosexuality—not among friends, not at home, at least not that he remembered. The subject was invisible, simply not on the scope. For him as a high school kid in the 1980s, gay was, he said, "a notion without reality."

And what could gay possibly have meant for a boy so well steeped in Jewish law and tradition, the way the Movement for Conservative Judaism gave form to it. The name Conservative, in the context of the denominations of American Judaism, means liberal, or at least more liberal than Orthodox, but not so liberal as Reform or Reconstructionist. Conservative Jews see themselves as those who conserve Jewish tradition by honoring its laws and customs while remaining open (or at least more open than the Orthodox but less than the Reform) to a wider interpretation of the faith's multitudinous pronouncements on living a Jewish life.

In college he remained as sexually illiterate—his phrase—as he had been in high school. He had plenty of friends, but the girlfriend thing remained elusive. He thought of himself as physically unappealing, too scrawny.

He also was becoming more and more conscious of the attraction he felt to men, but he walled it off. What deterred him was the way "gay" did not fit "Jewishly." Living a Jewish life meant marriage to a woman; it meant children; it meant living in Jewish circles like the ones in which he grew up. Wanting to live a Jewish life kept the idea of "gay" at a distance. He gave no thought to the stern admonitions in Leviticus or if God had strong opinions on the subject. He never pondered whether God would hate him if he acted on his feelings, the way this fear tormented some religious gay people he later came to know.

$\sim$

AT THE SEMINARY, and in the Conservative movement at large, progressive momentum was building. In 1987 Chancellor Cohen's successor, Ismar Schorsch, gave permission by fiat to allow women to become cantors, and the entire Rabbinical Assembly passed a pro-gay resolution at its May 1990 convention. It made a point of affirming the "Jewish prescription for heterosexuality," but at the same time deplored violence against gays and lesbians and supported their rights to civil equality. It also affirmed their welcome as members in synagogues and affiliated organizations and noted the concerns of parents in the movement over the safety and acceptance of their gay and lesbian children.

This mood of acceptance and tolerance, however, in no way

extended to the seminary, and most assuredly not to the rabbinical school, where the climate was "just so homophobic and totally ignorant." This was in the view of Dawn Rose, a rabbinical student at the time who had taken up the cause of gay awareness. Her efforts proceeded without incident until the fall of 1989, when she invited a noontime speaker from the gay congregation downtown, Beth Simchat Torah, and the Student Life office stepped in to object.

This set off a petition drive spearheaded by Rose, who helped collect 150 signatures to protest the position of the Student Life office. The organizers ended up in the office of the chancellor, who, in Rose's recounting, waved the matter off as a misunderstanding and said the speaker could indeed appear. At the same time, however, Chancellor Schorsch reminded the protesters that Jewish law forbade the practice of homosexuality. Rose recalled that she asked him if the prohibition against male homosexuality extended to women and he answered yes.

Later in the school year, in the spring of 1990, rumors about Rose's private life reached the chancellor's office—something about her living openly in a romantic relationship with another woman. In the words of one former administrator, on the seminary's scale of offenses, for an unmarried girl to be living with a guy was a parking ticket; with a girl, a capital crime. If true, it was grounds for expulsion.

The chancellor ordered Gordon Tucker, in his capacity as dean, to confront Dawn Rose. Reluctantly he called her into his office. No one in authority asked such questions around the seminary and certainly no dean had ever been obliged to do so. "He said he didn't want to ask me this and had fought against it, but it was not an issue over which he felt he could go to the mat," she recalled. And so Tucker put the question. Was she a lesbian?

"And I said I wouldn't answer. I refused. I refused on grounds that I wouldn't engage in a witch-hunt," Rose said years later. For Tucker, that was the end of the matter. Then, more timidly, Rose asked him if she would be expelled. Tucker told her he didn't know but advised her to keep her head down and her mouth shut. In Rose's view, "There's an old boy's promise that, *We'll look the other way if you don't make waves*. Some sink. Some get through."

She considered Tucker's advice and at first thought she would try to stick it out. She had already been at the seminary for some time, having arrived with her partner from the University of Judaism in Los Angeles in 1986. They both enrolled, Rose in the rabbinical school and her partner in the graduate program. All that time they had worked at staying undercover, like the Jews who converted to Christianity to survive the Spanish Inquisition, careful never to socialize with fellow seminarians, never inviting anyone home. But, as she later wrote:

> On the one side I was tortured by the realization I was becoming someone I could no longer respect. On the other, I lived with the constant fear that one day there would be another call from the dean's office—perhaps three years later and $30,000 more in debt. It would be all over. I would have nothing, be nothing. Nothing but silent, permanently compromised.

Rose kept her head down long enough to complete the midway mark in the program, her master's degree in rabbinics. This was minus her longtime study partner and several other school colleagues who distanced themselves from her, fearing guilt by association. She could have moved to the Reform movement, which changed its policy on homosexuals in the rabbinate in June 1990, or to the Reconstructionist, which affirmed gay ordination as far back as 1984. Instead, she transferred quietly into the JTS graduate school, reasoning that by sticking around the seminary she might still be able to "do some good." The graduate school, in part thanks to its receipt of federal funding, had no official policy of discrimination on the basis of sexual preference.

In the fall of 1991, Rose and her partner formed the Incognito Club, with only their names listed on its membership roster. They welcomed all other gay and lesbian seminarians to join, incognito, obviously, if they preferred, and "Oh," she said, "indeed they were."

⁓

ALTER RECEIVED HIS B.A. FROM COLUMBIA in the spring of 1989 and remained in New York, working one year at the Hebrew Immigrant Aid Society and the next, the 1990–1991 school year, as an assistant to the fourth-grade teacher at Ramaz, a Jewish day school. Having more private time, he allowed himself to wander mentally where he had never gone before in the way he fantasized about men and in the way he looked at them. In one extremely anxious moment, he furtively bought a gay magazine.

During this period a friend, in casual conversation, reeled out a list of a "good handful" of women who wanted to date Alter in college. He never had a clue. "The real revelation," he said, "was that I was attractive." And very soon thereafter, at his roommate's suggestion, he began seeing one particular woman, his first and only liaison with "any plausibility to it, that had any life to it." And remarkably, there was progress, kissing and all (well, not all), but he was able to say convincingly to himself, "Oh, look at that. A relationship."

"And then, within a few months, I don't remember how long, it just hit a wall. And the wall was very much tied up with sexual intimacy—that this just, it could go this far, but it wasn't going any further. And I started to be very conscious that it wasn't going any further because I didn't want it to go any further. And I started to think about men when I was with her.

"And over the course of that relationship—as it started to really hit a wall—I had a conversation with a friend of mine and I was telling her about the difficulties in this relationship, and she asked me the question that no one in my entire life had ever asked me. She said, 'Well, Joel, do you ever find that you're attracted to men?' I'd been asked a direct question. I always answer the questions that people ask me, and I said, 'Yes.' And I really feel that that was the critical moment. Again, there had been this transformation over the course of these two years as I was increasingly open to what I was feeling. But that question was very much a watershed, and my answer to the question.

"So I remember in that year, I really allowed myself to acknowledge the attractions to men that I felt. I would do things like notice ads, like the Calvin Klein underwear ads. This was during the time of the whole explosion in homoerotic advertising. And I allowed myself to look at that and to notice it and to acknowledge what I was noticing. I would do things like verbalize to myself what I found attractive. To say the words, so I could hear myself say them."

It was the beginning of the process of coming out to himself, "very much in the stage of *am probably, it seems clear . . . clearer that*, you know, lots of tentative statements." He was at the threshold of understanding that being Jewish and being gay were both inextricably part of who he understood himself to be. His Jewishness was fully formed, but the gay, he said, was still "hibernating." "At the same time," he said, "I am applying to rabbinical school."

〜

ANYONE COULD SEE that Joel Alter had the right stuff to become a rabbi, the kind of rabbi the Jewish Theological Seminary would be proud to ordain. He knew it too. In his freshman dormitory room at Columbia, he remembers sitting bolt upright in bed one night and proclaiming to his roommate, "I have to become a rabbi." Not that the very typical "package of ambivalences" didn't crowd in on him as soon as he sat down to fill out the application six years later. What was his belief system? How rigorously observant was he really prepared to be? Could he really commit to praying three times a day every day for the rest of his life? There was no doubt in his mind that he wanted a rabbinic education, rabbinic training; he was dead set on that, even though his goal always was to be a Jewish educator of some sort, not the head of a congregation. The reason, he said later, was "a desire to serve, a sense that the Jewish world needed people who 'get it'"—he meant being Jewish in the traditional Conservative framework— "and I 'get it.' And I can speak to it. And I can help lead and teach. It was a real identification with a community that needed help," he said. "And I sensed that I could be that person."

Right up front in the interview and after, the deans encouraged open discussion of all these matters, or at least they seemed to encourage it. At the time, Alter was well aware of the "gay piece" of his ambivalence, but he also knew how inappropriate it would be to raise it. Instinctively, he understood "this was a place I couldn't go, a conversation I couldn't have with them." Looking back on that time, he has trouble articulating or even recalling how he got through the discomforts of the application period. There was a strategy, however unconsciously he applied it, and it was omission. He withheld the information that could have damaged his prospects. It provided a layer of protective coloration.

At the time, this was possible for him because he was only beginning to come out to himself: "The full reality of being gay was
not there for me yet." Nowhere on the application or in interviews
was the subject raised directly or indirectly, as it used to be on ap-
plications to join the military, before "Don't Ask, Don't Tell." As
an applicant, Alter was not required to make a direct statement.
"That's exactly the point," he said. "The invisibility of it." It just
didn't feel like a lie.

What Alter did know was that as a committed Conservative
Jew, he wanted the rabbinic education the Conservative movement offered and the only place to get it was the Jewish Theological Seminary. Already two years out of college, he could not delay
the decision to undertake a five-year course of study much longer.
Squelching his vocational aspirations when he was not entirely
sure he was gay anyway seemed extreme; and even if he really
were gay, it wasn't obvious. Taking the gay piece out of the package was not only possible as he worked through his options; it
made the most sense.

The behaviorists would call Alter's plan "disclosure management" with "assimilation" as the primary strategy. Put simply, it is
passing. It is presenting the self as other than who one understands oneself to be. It is a decision made by all passers, however
honorable, nefarious, or benign their intent. Like Matthews and
the young teacher and Sanchez, they do it to bypass the preconceptions of others, especially those preconceptions that get in the
way of reasonable, desired ends. In deliberate acts of passing, not
only must passers withhold or camouflage revealing personal information that could damage or destroy their prospects, but they
also must take deliberate steps to stop outside sources from
telling on them. The point is to blend in with the surroundings.
Passers make an art of appearing in all respects—speech, ges-

tures, attitudes, conversation, mannerisms, expression, associations, interests, apparent lifestyle, and dress—to be bona fide members of the group or situation in which they seek admittance or acceptance. Alter, without much stealth and despite (or perhaps because of) his background and his naturally trusting nature would prove masterful at this.

~

PASSING, IN THIS SENSE, fits the dictionary definition for deception. (*"Deceive: implies deliberate misrepresentation of facts by words, actions, etc. generally to further one's ends. Deception: the act or practice of deceiving."*) Sissela Bok, the author of a classic work on lying, considers Alter's dilemma a matter of protecting his right to privacy. Although Alter is clear that his actions involved deception, he sees them as an attempt to accommodate the feelings of others. To explain why the accommodation is necessary, he cites what he considers the gross and recurrent misconception that sexuality is a totally private matter. He is especially critical of the argument often put forth in straight circles that it is inappropriate for all people, gay or straight, to discuss their personal sex life in public. The fallacy in that statement is that heterosexuals do it all the time—unconsciously, perhaps, because they are so accustomed to seeing their own behavior as the norm. "You put on a wedding ring and you're inviting the question, *Oh, you're married? Tell me about your family. Tell me about your wife. Tell me about your children.* The pictures on the desk at work." He went through the list. "I mean it is utterly normal and appropriate conversation to discuss one's spouse and children. The question about where you're going on vacation is utterly normal. Appropriate." And that's where the only choice for gay passers is to be silent or to dematerialize. Passing enforces the silence, but it also accommodates the discomfort of others.

At the same time, passing is about accommodating the self. Alter talked about the lie the gay person tells himself to rationalize keeping his homosexuality secret. *Oh, I don't want to get into it; I don't want to make them uncomfortable.* This is one typical explanation gays and lesbians give for not coming out. "And I think behind that," Alter said, "is that the presumption is heterosexuality." People automatically presume a person is heterosexual—and part of the dominant group—unless they have other suspicions or information. "And certainly, if you've grown up under the presumption that you are heterosexual, the whole world knows you as straight. They like you as straight. They accept you as straight. And so the question you hold because of the fear of bias is, *Will they like me? Will they accept me if they know that I'm not who they think I am?*" For someone whose core experiences and core values were as mainstream as Alter's, this was especially true. "That's the other side of accommodating yourself to other people's discomfort," he said. "You're not accommodating yourself; you're protecting yourself." Passing, in this sense, is not only about creating or preserving opportunity. It is about safety.

To pass effectively, lots of things in Alter's life would have to change. He would have to be extremely careful about exploring his evolving feelings openly with close friends. And in his new life, he would have to be really careful in determining whom, if anyone, to trust. One possibility: Because rabbinical school was bound to be an oppressive structural deterrent to gay expression, it occurred to Alter that he might "come out of this labyrinth" in a place he could not yet imagine. At that point, there was still the vague but fast-fading prospect he might fall in love with a woman and find a way to fence off his gayness for good. Maybe the force of seminary culture was powerful enough to lock that gate permanently, what with its scholarly intensity, its gossipy halls, its close quarters, its tight bonds, not to mention the overt, relentless pressure exerted on every young prospective rabbi to marry and start a family yesterday. *Are you seeing anyone? Is it serious? Can I introduce you to this young woman I know?* As Rabbi Tucker explained it, this happens in part because bachelor rabbis are considered "undomesticated." They raise *what's-he-doing* kinds of questions. "A rabbi is supposed to be married or supposed to have a girlfriend he's about to marry or he's supposed to be actively looking," Tucker said. "There's a lot of pressure for this. It's the norm."

At the same time, Alter was well aware of the near radical changes occurring in the Conservative movement. Women were reading from Torah scrolls, singing the liturgy, taking part in prayer minyans, and serving as rabbis, all unthinkable images only a generation earlier. The Rabbinical Assembly's pro-gay resolution of May 1990 came within a few months of the Reform movement's decision to go ten steps further and sanction gay ordination. Perhaps this was a prelude to more changes in the offing. Perhaps Conservatives again would follow the lead of Reform, as they had on the women's issue, even if the Conservative debate would have to rage intensely for nearly a decade and a half before consensus emerged. In the December 1990 issue of *Atlantic Monthly*, Paul Wilkes devoted a whole section of his report on the state of American theological seminaries to the issue of gay and lesbian clergy of all persuasions. Yale's Ellen Charry was quoted as saying, "Homosexuality sits there as a question and a powder keg in all denominations." As Alter thinks back on that period, what gave him the courage to proceed with his application was not only his own sense, but the prevailing sense that the gay issue was on the table; somehow it would all work out.

~

GORDON TUCKER WAS A BOYISH THIRTY-SIX when he assumed the post of rabbinical school dean in 1984, a lightly freckled child of the sixties with a bushy mustache and long, mussed red hair. Nearly twenty years later, he was boyish still. At six-four and a half, there is no missing him standing. He wears good jeans and manages to appear neither imposing nor gangly. The nonchalance he exudes is hard to reconcile with the high nerd quotient in his résumé: Yeshiva of Soloveitchik. Bronx Science. Harvard at sixteen. A doctorate in philosophy with a dissertation on mathematical logic slipped in at Princeton during his years of rabbinic preparation at JTS. But three years after joining the seminary's philosophy faculty in 1976, he took a two-year leave of absence to serve the Carter administration as special assistant and speechwriter to Attorney General Benjamin R. Civiletti and then helped in the transition to the Reagan administration. He's a hiker who loves the outdoors. Married, one son; divorced, remarried, a daughter, another son. To students, he was never "Dean" or "Rabbi Tucker" but Gordon, always Gordon, first names, the way it had been among the otherwise intimidating behemoths who taught philosophy to the doctoral candidates at Princeton. Tucker was accessible, always, and a willing listener, but he never pried into the details of his students' private lives. "The dean is always supposed to be stressing the importance of family, of being married," he said. "This is not my style, not my own background. I never got into that." As rabbinical school dean in the freewheeling 1980s, Tucker was an inspired choice.

Back in the fall of 1977, Tucker headed up the Rabbinical Assembly's special interdisciplinary commission on women's ordination. Six years later, in one of his early responsibilities as dean, he took special satisfaction in both the actual and the symbolic roles he played in ordaining the first women rabbis in the Conservative movement. In terms of seminary politics, a period of relative calm followed until Tucker's contretemps with the chancellor over Dawn Rose in the spring of 1990, presaging where the Conservative movement's new battle lines were being drawn.

～

JOEL ALTER'S ARRIVAL at JTS coincided with the 1991–1992 session of the Rabbinical Assembly's Committee on Jewish Law and Standards, also known as the Law Committee. This is the Conservative movement's most authoritative advisory body on Halakha, as Jewish law is referred to in Hebrew, the oral interpretation of the Scriptures. The Law Committee's twenty-five voting members—all rabbis—and its numerous nonvoting lay members gather at the seminary several times each year for one- or two-day sessions. When faced with sticky religious or ethical issues, local congregational rabbis and representatives of the movement's various institutions often turn to the committee for counsel, even though final authority always rests with the local clergy. The committee's job is to "offer parameters," to serve as a kind of collective Dear Abby for the halakhically committed, but an Abby with real authority. At times, when something significant in the broader Jewish or secular culture invites official comment, the committee offers opinions preemptively. It is not unusual for the approved positions to cover a range of approaches and ideas, sometimes even contradictory ones. The answers come in the form of religious position papers known as *teshuvot,* or *responsa,* complete with citations and footnotes. The committee debates them one by one and then votes to accept or reject. With six votes in favor—

a quarter of the voting committee—a given *response* becomes an official opinion.

Ordinarily the committee holds its sessions in a large seminar room with a handful of students and faculty sitting around the perimeter as observers. But that autumn, the decision to take up the issue of Judaism and homosexuality brought out so many spectators that the location shifted first to the second-floor synagogue and then to Feinberg Auditorium, the building's largest public space. Nothing quite like it had ever happened at the seminary. "A class unto itself," said Tucker, who had been a voting member of the committee since 1984. The movement's very institutions seemed to be undergoing "somewhat of a trial."

"I was taking it all in deeply rather than personally," Tucker said. "I wished it weren't happening because it was clear what the outcome would be." Alter, of course, took it deeply and personally. He had barely adjusted to his class schedule when all anyone could talk about it in the halls and dorms and cafeteria was the gay *responsa* being drafted in advance of the committee's first meeting December 11. With an ironic half laugh, Alter recalls that time as "my welcome-to-JTS year."

~

ALTER COULD NOT KNOW at the outset how a sustained passing experience was going to affect him, especially in a setting like the seminary. He had no way to anticipate the impact of five years or more spent editing out whole parts of his thinking process; whole parts of his preparation for a consuming vocation; whole parts of his future and past experiences; whole parts of himself. Anyone who chooses to pass in a school or work setting must devise and deploy an entire arsenal of subterfuges just to get through the day.

It can mean avoiding friendships or personal conversations with seemingly compatible persons. It can mean laughing at personally offensive and hurtful jokes (or brushing them off, like Matthews, or keeping silent, as Sanchez did) or feigning deep involvement in activities or interests that avert suspicion; it means dressing to fit in. Sometimes it can mean inventing fictitious romantic interests as decoys. Alter never went that far, but he knows plenty of people who have; and he certainly did his share of deflecting well-meant but nosy inquiries about his romantic life.

No doubt it would be excruciatingly difficult to try to pull this off in, say, a major-league ball club. As late as 2003, locker-room machismo and fear of public rejection meant that the few gay major-league athletes to reveal their homosexuality only dared to do so after they retired. Nevertheless, as oppressive as the antigay atmosphere in the major leagues may have been over the years, no central authority enforces the bias and federal laws are supposed to protect against it. The distant roots of this antigay bias may be biblical, but the hurtful, exclusionary behavior stems from run-of-the-mill hatred and intolerance. "Right," if you will, is on the side of the gay athlete. By contrast, Alter elected to pass in an institution where the Bible directly supplies the ethos and the law, and discrimination takes its authority from a very specific biblical prohibition. In this case, "right," for better or worse, is on the side of the institution. Not only that, but in rabbinical school the basic curriculum compels students to examine their personal values and ideals and to debate the theological and social issues that shape their personal religious development. It directs each prospective rabbi to declare a personal theology. Spiritual transformation rates parity with academic and professional training and ideally infuses the other two. At its best, the seminary experience is about conflating the personal with the communal. It encourages an intellectual and spiritual struggle among the religious texts, the community, and the individual soul. In this context passing is unbelievably complicated. Even so, Alter could see no reason to forgo a calling because of a treacherous proving ground, any more than a talented gay athlete would forgo his shot at a major-league career.

TUCKER THOUGHT the law committee's gay debate brought out the worst in everyone. Even though committee members were their customarily decorous selves in tone and demeanor, the atmosphere was anything but. People "were really speaking very viscerally, and so the arguments were not very rational," Tucker recalled. "They were dressed up as rational arguments." It was hard not to sense a "primal fear" among those who opposed change, "but one you could not really put your finger on because you can't get people to really be that honest about what they're so exercised about." The real problem, he said, was that the committee members were being asked to deal with matters "that there was almost no way to ferret out."

In trying to explain why this happened, Tucker drew a parallel between two male behavior models that contradict the married Jewish ideal: the gay Jew and the confirmed Jewish bachelor. Only the former triggers a visceral reaction because the Bible never decries bachelorhood as an abomination. But perhaps more significantly, he explained, "seeing bachelors around doesn't raise any questions about the fragility of sexual identity. Having gays around does. It makes you think about the—maybe fragility is the wrong word—the variability and the diversity of sexual identity and orientation. And that spooks people out. I don't know how else to explain it."

Furthermore, Tucker said, Judaism is filled with cultural assumptions about separation: light from dark, Israel from Gentiles, the Sabbath from weekdays, meat from milk. He cited Mary Douglas in *Purity and Danger* discussing the prohibition in the Jewish dietary laws against eating amphibians. As creatures of both land and sea, amphibians are "out of category." They threaten order and they are without separation. Imagine, then, how threatening it is to challenge something as culturally basic as the difference between male and female. Tucker thinks this may be part of the Bible's "hang-up" with homosexuality. "Gay males are male," he said. "But they are also a kind of exception to the divine order. They're out of category. They're male but they're not doing what males are supposed to do, which is to make love to females. It disturbs the order. It disturbs the sense of order which makes other things possible."

Tucker thought the paucity of firsthand gay testimony also hurt the Law Committee's deliberations. By way of analogy, he recalled how much personal information his committee on the status of women had been able to amass. "We knew a lot of things about women's religious aspirations, religious frustrations, all of that, because no one was ever inhibited about admitting they had women in their family. People would talk about their daughters, their wives, their mothers and things that they could do, wanted to do, would never think of doing, were frustrated about not being able to do. People would even talk about women's spirituality and whether there is such a thing. But if people aren't going to talk about their own or their child's or their brother's sexual identity, how do you get information about this? So it was an automatic kind of hindrance," especially in the early 1990s. One notable exception was a poignant letter to the committee from Dawn Rose and her partner, detailing the plight of the gay seminarian.

For Alter, the entire enterprise was infuriating. He described it as "this parade of rabbis at each of the meetings making horrible, hateful comments, ignorant comments, stupid comments along the lines that the only possibility for holiness in sexual relations is in the heterosexual relationship.

"You can assert that," Alter went on, "but when you try to demonstrate that, either you sound like a mystic from another century or you sound like an idiot. You can assert that as a theological position, but when you try to bring science into it, it just is not compelling, to say the least." He also complained about repeated assertions during the Law Committee's deliberations that being gay is a matter of choice, about whether or not one chooses to be gay.

Coincidentally, that very fall, two respected scientific journals published the first studies to indicate a biological basis for homosexuality, and news reports about both turned up in the committee's packet of materials. There was also a particularly prickly missive from Chancellor Schorsch, urging the committee to drop the issue entirely. Tucker protested that one vocally as a violation of the separation of powers in the movement. He likened the pressure from the chancellor to the president of the United States deciding to tell the Supreme Court what it should or should not consider. "It reminded me of something I had read long ago about some of Galileo's contemporaries not wanting to look through his telescope for fear of what they might see," Tucker said.

As for Alter, he had cover to attend the sessions because everyone was attending the sessions, and he could be relatively vocal in support of the gay position because the student population had a large and outspoken liberal wing. In those early days on campus, he had met and befriended Roderick Young, a gay graduate student who was totally out. "So he was cover for me, right? Everybody loved Roderick." Alter even felt safe enough to attend a meeting of the Incognito Club as well as an AIDS education workshop. Still, he watched his comments very carefully, conscious that if he appeared too interested in gay issues, too personally interested, if he said too much, it could have real and unwanted consequences. Everyone knew what had happened to Dawn Rose.

There was no containing Alter after the Law Committee meeting at which members discussed the *responsum* of Rabbi Joel Roth, the committee chairman, the paper that most insistently upheld the status quo. Alter was even more incensed at what he considered the arrogance and the biased, insulting tone of Norman Krivosha, retired chief justice of the Nebraska Supreme Court, who led the session. Roth had relinquished the chair to Krivosha, one of the committee's lay nonvoting members, because Roth's own paper was under consideration.

As Krivosha left the auditorium, Alter accosted him in an explosion of indignation. He accused the judge of stupidity and bias and said he sincerely hoped that as an officer of the Nebraska court he displayed "some modicum of the professionalism" that in this setting he sorely lacked. Alter said the judge smiled calmly in response, put on his coat, and said something like, *Oh, I'm sorry you feel that way*. No one thought a thing of Alter's outburst. Tempers were flaring all over the place.

SUE FENDRICK LIKES TO THINK OF HERSELF as "an old lefty from way back," even though her transfer route to JTS was from the far more liberal Reconstructionist Rabbinical College. Still, compared to Alter, she was far less steeped in the "life of the halakhic Jew." The two of them clicked immediately. They still like to joke that they were sure God had given each of them half of the same personality until they realized they both had too much. In seminary, they were close enough friends for Fendrick to move into Alter's dormitory living room when mice invaded her own suite. For two whole weeks, they stayed up talking half the night. Mutual friends were sure the mice story was a pretext to hide a budding romance. That story still makes Fendrick chuckle.

The truth was, she did have a huge crush on Alter. She "felt a charge" between them whenever they were together and couldn't quite figure out why he didn't try to court her. She considered telling him how she felt but didn't want to be the first to admit to having special feelings.

The evening after Alter's confrontation with Judge Krivosha, he went to Fendrick's room for solace. He knocked on her door and said he needed to talk. At first he sat down in the little living room of her suite but then suggested they might be more comfortable on her bed. It was obvious he wanted to tell her something important. There was silence and then he muttered something to the effect of *Well, these conversations are always hard for me.* Fendrick was sure he was about to follow that up with a declaration of intentions. "So I'm gay," he blurted suddenly. Of course, she realized, by *these kinds of conversations*, he had meant what was happening in the Law Committee. "You know," she laughed, "I was in my own little world."

Remarkably, in all the months she had known Alter at such close range, Fendrick's well-calibrated "gay-dar" hadn't beeped once. She was six years older than he and over the years had made dozens of gay and lesbian friends and acquaintances. Many of them had come out to her, going back to her college days at Brown. In all that time, not one of these disclosures had ever caught her by surprise. "*This*," she said, "was surprising."

All through seminary, Fendrick steadfastly kept Alter's secret.

Slyly, she redirected the interests of women who inquired about his availability and she also took it upon herself to help educate him as a gay person. He was so "mainstream," she recalled, so devoid of any gay frame of reference. "I was able to hold out the model of saying: Yes, you will have a life because people do have a life and people do all sorts of hiding and closeting for a time in their lives because that's how they get by, and you will get by. And if you decide it's too hard, you will leave. But you don't need to decide that it's too hard based on your vision of what's going to be out there, because it's going to be okay. And you are going to have lovers and you are going to have a partner." All of this was especially difficult for Alter, she said. Although he faced the challenge of figuring out how he was going to survive as a Conservative rabbi, he also had to figure out "how he was going to get from point A to point B."

"It was all about envisioning this world beyond the walls of the world that he already knew and meeting the people who lived in this other country and adopting this other citizenship and how was that all going to happen," she said. So his friend Sue Fendrick helped him with all of that. Eventually she even introduced him to his first gay connection.

THE DAY BEFORE THANKSGIVING 1991, shortly before the first formal meeting of the Law Committee that term, Chancellor Schorsch stunned Gordon Tucker by asking him to step down as rabbinical school dean, effective at the end of the school year. The reason he gave was a simple wish to relieve Tucker of his administrative burden after eight years of service. Tucker had not sought relief from his workload; he loved being dean. He considered his deanship a rabbinate. He asked who would be replacing him and the chancellor said he did not yet know.

When the decision was announced sometime later, news shot through the halls and cafeteria. The gossip held that the chancellor thought Tucker was too liberal in general and certainly too liberal on the gay issue. Students started circulating petitions, but Tucker urged them to stop and they did.

Despite the rumors, Tucker has no evidence that there was any reason for the chancellor's move other than what he was told. All the same, it was curious that the chancellor did not say whom he had in mind as Tucker's replacement when he delivered the news to him.

At the time, Tucker said, he was certainly "no banner carrier" for gay rights. The Law Committee debate over the coming months "radicalized" him (if such a word can apply in this instance), and the deliberations had not yet begun. But over the coming months as the debate progressed, Tucker said, "I saw a certain circularity, a certain illogic, and then, to some extent, a certain meanness of spirit. And at that point, you begin to say to yourself, 'What the hell is going on here?'" Still, Tucker cast one of the votes that helped soundly defeat the most pro-gay position paper because he did not support the way the argument had been framed. But he also voted against all of the papers that upheld the status quo, including Chairman Joel Roth's, which passed on a fourteen-to-seven vote with three abstentions. Tucker further opposed the "Consensus Statement on Homosexuality," which the committee issued at its third and final meeting on the subject on March 25:

We will not perform commitment ceremonies for gays and lesbians.

We will not knowingly admit avowed homosexuals to our rabbinical or cantorial schools or to the Rabbinical Assembly or the

Cantors' Assembly. At the same time, we will not instigate witch-hunts against those who are already members or students.

Whether homosexuals may function as teachers or youth leaders in our congregations and schools will be left to the rabbi authorized to make halakhic decisions for a given institution with the Conservative movement. Presumably, in this as in all other matters, the rabbi will make such decisions taking into account the sensitivities of the people of his or her particular congregation or school. The rabbi's own reading of Jewish law on these issues, informed by the *responsa* written for the Committee on Jewish Law and Standards to date, will also be a determinative factor in these decisions.

Similarly, the rabbi of each Conservative institution, in consultation with its lay leaders, will be intrusted [sic] to formulate policies regarding the eligibility of homosexuals for honors within worship and for lay leadership positions.

In any case, in accordance with The Rabbinical Assembly and United Synagogue resolutions we are hereby affirming, gays and lesbians are welcome in our congregations, youth groups, camps, and schools.

The gay initiative had been soundly defeated. As dean of the rabbinical school in Tucker's stead, the chancellor appointed the man who had preceded him in the post, the most insistent supporter of existing policy on the subject of gay ordination, Rabbi Joel Roth.

∼

TWO PLACARDS FULL OF STUDENT WELL-WISHES are "important artifacts" for Tucker, a memento from a surprise farewell party the students gave in his honor at the end of the 1991–1992 school year, his last as a full-time faculty member at the seminary. The chancellor had offered him a two-year leave of absence, which he took, and during that period he accepted the post of senior rabbi of a large, important suburban congregation in White Plains, New York. He continues to teach philosophy at the seminary in an adjunct capacity, slipping into the city from his Westchester County home only long enough to conduct his weekly class. Ten years later, the two posters still hang next to the computer in his home office.

Among the inscriptions is one from Alter. "Gordon," it begins. "I have been positioned opposite your smiling face in a few crucial situations" and ends "it's very important to me that I face you as a student in the future." Tucker thought Alter must have meant to write, *I look forward to being your student in the future*, but didn't read much into the awkward phrasing. Alter had impressed him, like everyone else at the seminary, as a "model student; extremely well liked." Tucker admits to being stunningly oblivious in such matters, but he had not picked up the slightest intimation of Alter's personal struggles at the time. It was only years later, when they chanced to meet at the wedding of a mutual friend, that Tucker figured it out, but his reaction was without any sense of *ohhhh-that-explains-a-lot*, the way it had been in so many other such moments.

"There was not a sign," said Tucker. The encounter immediately brought Alter's curious farewell inscription back to mind. Finally, it made sense. Alter must have suspected Tucker would be sympathetic but may have had his own reasons for not wanting to open the conversation. "I think to some extent out of his goodness and kindness, he spared me knowing," Tucker mused, "knowing what I might have had to go through."

ON SEPTEMBER 16, 1992, the seminary offered a service in memory of its formidable chancellor emeritus, Gerson Cohen, on the first anniversary of his death. Tucker's leave had barely begun, but he returned to the seminary to deliver the eulogy for his beloved mentor. He spoke movingly of his personal loss, describing Cohen as a scholar, rabbi, and historian of extraordinary depth and insight, a man who, in Tucker's pointed depiction, "utterly rejected, as a first principle, and a methodological postulate, the facile discontinuities on which fundamentalisms thrive. He would have said, 'If those who preceded us were as angels, then we too can be angels!' And he would have believed it passionately. . . ."

For Alter, the speech was inordinately powerful, "a gorgeous talk in a very emotional gathering." He was particularly struck by the way Tucker described what it meant to have such a mentor and by the integration of Dr. Cohen's entire existence—his Judaism, his scholarship, his personal life—"how all the pieces came together for him in a beautiful seamless whole." Alter left the room weeping and went directly to see Sue Fendrick. "I think one of the reasons I was crying was that it had been a beautiful talk, in the same way you cry in a movie or when you witness grief. It was beautiful and affecting that way. But I think it also touched a chord in me of *How am I going to put the pieces of my life together?* And one of Sue's tasks in those first two years was to constantly reassure me that I would find a man, that I could have a life, that I could have a family, that I could be Jewish, that it could all work out for me. Because what was hard to imagine was that I had a future, that I could bring the pieces of my life together and have what I want."

BY THE MIDDLE OF ALTER'S SECOND YEAR at seminary, he carefully began bringing more friends into his ring of confidence and even took the risk of coming out to a sympathetic visiting faculty member. "There was going to be zero pressure on him and that was perfectly clear from who he is," Alter said, adding that "it was a very difficult conversation to have, but I knew it would be okay." His reason for risking exposure is a classic one. At some point the passer begins to feel "totally invisible in the silence," in Alter's phrase. Studies bear this out. It is certainly safer, more expedient, and freer of surface complications for the passer to maintain total secrecy. But it also rules out such workaday commonplaces as the celebration of happy events or support during painful breakups or the illnesses and deaths of friends and loved ones. To separate public and private life so drastically often causes unbearable strain and conflict in the passer, not to mention depression and hostility, anxiety, low self-esteem, high rates of substance abuse, and bouts of ill health. In the words of sociologist Erving Goffman, with selective confessions the passer "retains his standing as someone who relates honorably."

Letting confidantes in on the secret, Alter said, is "about wanting to be normal." Among his papers is the list he kept from the spring of 1991 to August 1994, in chronological order, of everyone he told and when. "Ostensibly, it's the record of my attempt to control the information. I had to remember whom I had told, and I wanted them to know about each other so they could talk to each other, I suppose. I was conscious of the burden of silence and secrecy I was imposing on them." He kept the list short for his parents' sake, so they wouldn't be "the very last people in my world to know."

Alter explained that he was still trying to settle into the identity. "There were lots of conversations about it with people like

Sue. I think I already had the sense that this would work out, that life is complicated." There were a couple of gay relationships, earnest but short-lived, and a discreet but concerted effort to find a partner who would last. And yet, he said, not a day went by without his thinking, *Why am I doing this? Why am I passing?* "That's my memory," he said. "Five years. My memory of it is that this was a constant. This was constantly present in my mind. *What am I doing? This is crazy!* I went around feeling like I was walking off a gangplank."

Alter also reports that his seminary experience was by no means torturous all of the time. He was basically happy during those five years and fit in well. Wedding and engagement announcements came as often as bar and bat mitzvah invitations to a seventh grader in Jewish day school, and on each occasion, the entire community would erupt in celebration. "A Jewish wedding ceremony is not just an event for the two people or for their families and friends," Alter explained. "It's an event for the whole world—that changes the world. I believe that." He had long been conditioned to share in this happiness and both the desire to celebrate and the act of celebrating came easily in every instance. But bundled with the impulse to embrace the joy came "this terrible sadness of *What about me?*"

There was also the increasingly stressful ordeal of passing in the presence of family members, the torment of the inevitable third degree: *Are you dating anyone? Are you seeing anyone?* and the repeated need quickly and deftly to cut those conversations short.

At about this time, he accepted a dinner invitation from two apartment mates, a man and a woman, not a couple, whom he had recently met through Sue Fendrick. The woman was a Reform rabbi and the man was a gay activist who had put aside rabbinic aspirations because of his homosexuality. Alter liked him a lot.

After the meal, with music playing on the stereo, all three of them got up to dance. The woman turned to Alter. Over the music, she asked, *Are you gay?*

Flabbergasted, he thought fast. "I had to accomplish three things. The first was not to fall over," he recalled, and the second and third were to answer her question with a *no*, but a *no* that actually said *yes* to him. So he looked at her and shook his head from side to side. Later he called the man and told him otherwise. That was how they got together. A decade later, they remain friends.

That was his closest call. He speaks of "lots of tears" during those years, yet when I pressed him for examples of what caused them, circling back to do so a number of times, I made almost no headway. There was a vague, flat affect to his recollections and few were very specific beyond the ones he readily and no doubt repeatedly shares.

He remembered fending off gay jokes and other offensive remarks under the guise of being "on the left," like so many of his seminary peers. But he said this happened rarely. Often likeminded fellow seminarians would wage the daily minibattles, allowing him to remain silent without feeling thoroughly compromised. It was a great relief and helped him get by.

In year number three, the one he spent in Israel, he told his family. Before his departure he sat down with each of his siblings and saved the more difficult conversation with his parents until his return from overseas. His siblings took it well. Both his mother and his father are very supportive now, but it has taken time. The initial conversations were difficult, even disorienting. The date of the first encounter—August 1, 1994—is the last notation on his secret who's-been-told list.

He told his parents at the table in the evening and then they moved to the library to talk about it more. His mother then went to her room but had difficulty sleeping. When she encountered her son at the kitchen counter in the morning, she tried to speak but broke into sobs. "It was straight out of the textbooks," he recalled quietly. "She is a very reticent person in terms of speaking her feelings, but she shows them on her face. She was grieving for the son she had just lost." As for his father, he took a clinical tack that left Alter "screaming angry."

"I felt he neither totally acknowledged where I was emotionally or where he was emotionally," Alter said. "I felt he masked his sense of loss with what he dressed up as ostensibly sound advice." He wanted dearly for his youngest son to be a father, and in working through the ways that might be possible, even suggested that his son might find a suitable wife. "It was as if there was no air in the room," Alter said of his own reaction to the idea, though he understood it came out of his father's love and desperation over his son's future, not out of callous indifference to the woman who would have been involved. Since surrogacy and coparenting were not so common then, what his father was proposing in the abstract seemed to be the most reasonable solution. "And he wanted me to be safe," Alter said. "Being in a gay relationship was socially"—not to mention medically—"unsafe."

~

IF ANYTHING, the Law Committee's rulings exacerbated the foment over gay issues in the Conservative movement leadership. Rabbis and theologians, in both lay and scholarly journals, churned out essays and papers and responses to essays and papers and responses to essays and papers on both sides of the issue. There were even tremors among the Orthodox, sparked by a pseudonymous article by a gay Orthodox rabbi in the magazine

Tikkun. If any doubt remained about which position JTS would back, Chancellor Schorsch quashed it in a speech to the Rabbinical Assembly convention in March 1993: "The ash heap of history is cluttered with proposals for reform rejected by our movement despite the fact that they were bathed in the bathos of ethical imperatives," he declared. In Judaism's rabbinic tradition, he said, ethical imperatives are "subjective, arbitrary and impermanent, a prescription for anarchy." The Law Committee, he said, had made it clear "that the community is not ready for gay or lesbian rabbis." Moreover, he personally opposed the Law Committee's affirmation of a proposal to establish a commission on human sexuality to study the issue further. The committee, in fact, was formed anyway.

In the May 1993 issue of the magazine *Tikkun*, the theologian Judith Plaskow decried the fact that Joel Roth's rigid *responsum* remained in force, especially since the issue so deeply divided students and faculty at the seminary as well as the Rabbinical Assembly. Roth, she noted, had already resigned as rabbinical school dean. She saw a parallel between the confident assertion in Roth's paper of the *verboten* place of homosexuals in Judaism with the belief of students she once taught in Wichita, Kansas, "the buckle of the Bible belt," who warned her out of genuine concern and kindness to accept Christ or burn in hell.

By June, Gordon Tucker was quoted in *Moment* magazine saying it was conceivable that the prohibitions of Leviticus 18:22 should be overturned. Although an argument for doing so was not yet fully in place, it was "beginning to emerge."

In the same period, Rabbi J. B. Sacks-Rosen, ordained by the seminary back in 1986, summoned the courage to reveal that he was gay to his Jersey City congregation. He took the step because his partner was dying of AIDS. He was the first Conservative rabbi ever to do so and there were no apparent repercussions from the disclosure. Furthermore, the Rabbinical Assembly did not stand in the way of his accepting a subsequent pulpit in Southern California even though he presented himself to the congregation and its board of directors as openly gay. Like Alter, Sacks-Rosen is a "product of the Conservative movement" and was reported as saying his long mainstream history might account in some measure for his continued good standing. Of the Rabbinical Assembly's uninterrupted support, he told the *Forward* in 1999, "It's unclear to me if they placed me because they like me . . . [or] because I'm soft-spoken and easier for them to deal with." Among the various *responsa* on the homosexual issue, there was acceptance for the idea of "grandfathering in" current members of the Rabbinical Assembly who, it emerged only later, were gay.

All of these developments appeared to put Chancellor Schorsch on the offensive against liberal Jewish politics. A town meeting was called over Roth's resignation as dean, at which a number of students expressed concern over the seminary's increasingly antileft atmosphere. Alter too stood up to speak. His notes from those remarks show that he began by thanking the chancellor for being a great teacher and then implored him not to invalidate the left, which had advocated for women as rabbis and was advocating now for other kinds of access and inclusion. "The ordination of women as rabbis is one of the very proudest moments in the history of the movement," Alter said. "The current debates are the logical next step in that proud tradition. Don't cut us off. This will not lead to an undifferentiated mass of liberal Judaism; this is not a slippery slope. Rather, this controversy is an example of the movement living its convictions. We don't want to live out our convictions in ethical violation of Halakha as it stands; we want to live our convictions with the full support of Halakha as the living word of God."

Fendrick was stunned at how far her friend seemed prepared to go "and to hear Joel identify himself as someone on the left, I think, was a revelation for him. . . . And he was in tears, not sobbing, but very emotional and in tears." She saw it as a defining moment for Alter in terms of how he was beginning to state things for himself. Until that point, he did not participate in marches or any sort of public advocacy. And there he was, advocating. Because Joel Alter was the one speaking, no one else read anything particular into it. No one except Fendrick picked up on his use of *the left* as code for *those of us who are gay*.

ALTER LIKES TO JOKE that God saved the most savory ironies for his fifth and final year on the seminary campus. The publicity office put out a new "come to the seminary" brochure with Alter on its cover. When the admissions office needed a recruitment speaker to appear at congregations, camps, universities, and day schools, Alter was considered top talent. Fendrick wasn't exaggerating when she described her friend as "the poster boy for the seminary," and Tucker confirmed it was everyone's impression. For the mandatory "senior sermon," every rabbinical student drew by lot the biblical passage that would form the basis of his or her exhortation. Need you ask? Alter picked Leviticus 16–20, inclusive. How he managed to skirt the key abomination passages and still give a compelling discourse was a virtual miracle, but he did. Afterward, as is customary, he hosted a luncheon. Among his ninety guests was his boyfriend at the time.

Shortly before graduation, Alter's third and last dean, Rabbi

William Lebeau, led a role-playing exercise in senior seminar, the professional studies class. He asked his students to pose difficult questions that he in turn would attempt to answer honestly.

"I have a scenario," offered one student, who happened to be Alter's best friend from day school days and one of his seminary confidantes. The young prospective rabbi walked to the front of the classroom and sat down before the dean. He said he would be portraying a rabbinical student within a few months of ordination.

"Rabbi Lebeau," his character said. "I feel that before leaving this institution, I need to be honest with you, and I need to tell you that I'm gay."

Transfixed, Alter listened for Rabbi Lebeau's reply. Calmly and without hesitation, the dean said, "Then I can't ordain you."

"The fact that my heart was leaping out of my chest didn't change the fact that I kind of knew that it was going to go that way," Alter recalled. That didn't stop the scene from replaying repeatedly in his head as ordination day approached. He was in the first month of his first significant romance, one that would last another five years. The boyfriend was also a "product of the movement," a son and grandson of rabbis. Alter was still living in the JTS dorm when the two men got together. He remembers being so fearful of discovery that that whenever they entered the building at the same time, if his partner took the elevator, Alter took the stairs. Alter invited him to the luncheon following his senior sermon but, as a precaution, seated him at a different table and never introduced him to his family. The boyfriend stormed out.

None of this behavior was paranoid. Alter had every reason to fear a Dawn Rose redux. His prescient assessment was that if he were found out, he was not going to be "publicly hanged or tarred and feathered or anything." But he was certain the repercussions were bound to be "pretty awful," as they were for a fellow seminarian, Benay Lappe, not long after. The dreaded call to the dean's office came a mere three days before her 1997 ordination. An anonymous telephone caller had outed her to the administration. In her two-hour confrontation with the dean, she steadfastly refused to answer the "central question," as he put it. Ultimately, however, she decided to "act in self-defense and lie in order to do what was right."

GRADUATION DAY, MAY 1996, Joel Alter's ordination proceeded without incident. Afterward, however, there was what seemed to be an inexplicably long wait for his actual diplomas, one in Hebrew and one in English, in elegant suitable-for-framing calligraphy. All of his classmates seemed to have received theirs, but, strangely, his did not arrive.

Before graduation, Alter fantasized about telling Rabbi Lebeau the truth on the day after his ordination. He checked that desire, thinking that the timing would be a terrible slap in the face for a man he admired. He got a job offer from a Jewish day school in suburban Maryland and decided to wait a year to tell his former dean. The feeling of deceitfulness lingered and he wanted to expunge it, straightforwardly for once. Still, he was cautious enough to want the documentation proving his ordination first safely in hand. So he chose as the appropriate time a planned weekend visit to New York. The reason for the diploma delay turned out to be bureaucratic, but that did not make the waiting less anxious. Rabbi Lebeau had agreed to see him that Sunday.

By telephone, Alter negotiated with the registrar, urging her to have the diploma signed before the planned appointment. She assured him she would take care of it. He went to see Lebeau and told his story, wanting very much to know from the dean if he thought his student had betrayed the institution. Alter said the dean assured him this was not the case, adding that it upset him to hear the seminary accused of forcing gay students into secrecy. Alter replied that he never felt forced into secrecy by the seminary. He was fully aware of seminary policy before he ever applied for admission. No one forced the secrecy on him. He chose it.

AS TUCKER SEES IT, the act of a homosexual passing for straight in the seminary context is a difficult and complicated choice, to be sure. But in his view, it is neither an act of betrayal nor an act of deceit. In the seminary environment, he said, the Rose and Lappe episodes were absolute aberrations. The seminary is not an environment where such questions are bandied about. "No one was going around asking, *Are you gay?*" Tucker said. "No one was asking these questions. So there was no occasion where you had to tell an outright lie." In his view, if the rabbinical school wants to have a policy of not knowingly accepting or ordaining gay and lesbian students, the burden is on the institution, not the applicant, to ascertain the information—and without engaging in witch-hunts, as even the Law Committee's policy statement prohibits. Is it a lie if the applicant knowingly omits the information? "Not if the institution isn't asking the question," Tucker countered. "And if the institution doesn't know, it is not knowingly accepting you." Alter likened the seminary's policy to the military's "Don't Ask, Don't Tell, Don't Pursue."

Tucker then pondered whether passing in the seminary context could not actually be seen as a cousin to civil disobedience. Both the passer and the public protester start from the same premise: *I know what the rule says. I know what the boundary conditions are. I know I don't fulfill the boundary conditions. I think the boundary conditions are wrong, morally wrong, or irrelevant to the opportunity that they are barring me from.* In a classic act of civil disobedience, the point of the public protest is to provoke a confrontation: *Here I am. Do what you have to do.* The ultimate goal is to galvanize change, even if change is not immediately forthcoming. Passing also seeks change, as it seeks opportunity in the present. It seeks the chance to fulfill a personal aspiration, perhaps a selfish one, and the change it effects in the process—a de facto change—may only be understood later, perhaps much later, when the passer discloses what he or she has done, or, as in Anatole Broyard's case, when someone else makes the disclosure.

In the instance of the seminary, Tucker said, what's at stake is the personal sacrifice of a calling ("a *calling!*") and the conviction that an unjust law is barring a worthy individual from answering that call. Whether the decision to pass is acceptable or not, he thinks, "boils down to the question of how compelling is the personal aspiration involved."

Speaking for himself, Tucker said he personally would not hesitate to pass if he felt an oppressive and unfair system was blocking him from attending rabbinical school, or even law school for that matter—two aspirations that are utterly worthy, in his view at least, aspirations with "real *gravitas.*" He would pass rather than protest because passing would enable him to meet his personal aspiration in the here and now, and because the credentials and status conferred on clergy would put him in a stronger position to act against the injustice. Passing, in that sense, becomes a course of political action.

Alter's motivation was personal, but it included his desire to serve his beloved religious denominational community. Tucker sees a cogent distinction between a personal aspiration like that of Joel Alter, one that gives a person the standing and the power to be an agent of change, and the personal aspiration that is only a personal aspiration.

Anthony Appiah easily empathizes with a case such as Alter's, in which a person with the talent and devotion for a given vocation would be unjustly barred from joining ranks should his full story be known. It is another case where he thinks it makes sense to "break bad laws" and avoid being punished for doing so. "It's a case where the identity you think of as your true identity carries a cost that it ought not to carry." Unlike Tucker, neither Appiah nor Sissela Bok would equate Alter's passing with an act of civil disobedience because passing is covert, never a public performance, and in Alter's case the action is not directed against a state. Both subscribe to John Rawls's definition of civil disobedience as a "public, nonviolent, conscientious yet political act contrary to law usually done with the aim of bringing about a change in the law or policies of the government," one that is "engaged in openly with fair notice; it is not covert or secretive." Civil disobedience, Rawls wrote, is comparable to a public speech, in which profound, tightly held convictions are expressed directly and out loud.

In Bok's view the civil disobedience argument is no more than a kind of rationalization in this case, "a good excuse for breaking the rules. That is why people look for these explanations," she said. By way of example she said it reminded her of the difference between being very public about not paying one's taxes to protest the military, which is civil disobedience, and secretly or covertly not paying one's taxes, which is tax cheating, "no matter how noble the intent claimed." Still, this does not supercede Alter's right to privacy in such a case, as in Bok's earlier example. But Appiah said he could certainly see this kind of passing as a sort of resistance. It brought to mind Frederick Douglass's pronouncement that ultimately injustices will be removed by the resistance of those who are subjected to them. "In the end," Appiah added, "you need people from the relevant group to speak out publicly from the outside, as well as people changing things quietly from the inside."

THE DAY AFTER ALTER MET WITH RABBI LEBEAU, the dean sent him an e-mail saying how pleased he was that they had talked. The dean also mentioned that when he arrived at his office that morning, he found on his desk the English diploma of one Rabbi Joel Alter. Apparently, only the Hebrew version had been signed before the two men met on Sunday. Lebeau told Alter that he signed the second document without compunction, but also with much love and friendship.

"That is exactly what my heart needed to hear," Alter said, for it helped put behind him "those terrible feelings of being a fraud, that I had no business there, and again, this terrible anxiety that gay people walk around with, *You love me when I'm straight*," he said. "To go through five years of this very formative experience and to try to believe that my being called 'Rabbi' has any legitimacy to it—that was hard. That was very hard to believe. Very hard to settle into."

In the May 2002 issue of the seminary magazine, Rabbi LeBeau, still vice chancellor of the seminary and dean once again, was quoted as saying of rabbinical students, "Regardless of where they are spiritually or academically when they begin their training, they must emerge having synthesized the three prongs critical to anyone who hopes to succeed in the rabbinate: crafting a professional vision, understanding one's connection to God, and making an unequivocal commitment to the halakhic practices required of Conservative Jews. It's not an easy transformation."

Soon after his day school hiring, Alter made a point of coming out to key members of the school's administration. He has since advanced through the ranks to become chair of the school's Bible Department. He is, as always, very well liked. Gradually and without fanfare or repercussion over the past six years, he has come out to members of the faculty one by one and has made his circumstances known to students and parents in an indirect way. In November 2000, he addressed a student assembly at a secular private school in nearby Washington, D.C., at the request of that school's gay and lesbian organization. At the time, he spoke about his journey and the ways in which he has reconciled his homosexuality with his Judaism. The following June, he was quoted in his own school's student newspaper with a general remark about gay and lesbian issues. The report notes in passing that Alter had brought his partner to a school prom.

Things go well. Alter said he cannot imagine a better work atmosphere and intends never again to be in a position where he would have to pass. In the Conservative movement there are still plenty of places where that would be necessary, and he accepts the limitations that being openly gay places on his professional opportunities. Still, the opportunities for advancement in his field are there.

As to Rabbi Lebeau's three prongs, yes, Alter has a professional vision. More problematic are his relationship to God and halakhic observance, which are closely tied. "One of my lingering frustrations about being a gay student at the seminary was that I could never ask in my voice, in my case, the questions that I needed to ask. I needed for other people to ask them for me or I needed to ask them in the abstract. I could never say *I'm gay. What do I do with that?*

"I think like a lot of people in the Conservative movement, my theology is largely Reconstructionist," he said, "My understanding of God is nontraditional. My relationship with God is something that is not fully understood, though I don't know for whom it is. It's something I worry about, but something I feel increasingly comfortable with. What remains very fuzzy is the line of authority and the bindingness between the God I believe in and the Halakha I observe."

In an earlier conversation, he said some of his ambivalence about Jewish observance and the obligatory nature of Halakha is probably complicated by his being gay, and the willingness it necessitates in him to say, *Eh! This is who I am. This is what it needs to be.* The Leviticus passage is not an injunction that can concern him. It does not stop him. It probably bleeds into his attitude, but it does not get in his way.

And in his speech to those high school students, he said, "Even as I contemplated dropping out of my rabbinical program almost every single day for five years, I also knew that within a few years, perhaps a few decades, my tradition will affirm legally what is already in practice, thank God, in families, synagogues, schools, and organizations around the world. I can tolerate that wait, because I know my tradition will get there. In the meantime, I am living my life as I feel I must, with full affirmation of my Jewishness as a gay man."

There were developments on the gay front in the Conservative movement during the winter of 2003. Judy Yudoff, president of the Conservative movement's main lay organization, called for renewed discussion among the membership about the status of gays and lesbians. Early reports in the Jewish press suggested that for the first time in a decade, those in the movement leadership on both sides of the issue might be gearing up to consider the matter once again. Alter backed Yudoff's call with an essay of his own, privately distributed to colleagues by way of a forum of Conservative rabbis in which he participates. He also passed it along to friends who in turn shared it with groups of their own. In it, he offers "what I hope is a helpful path into our discussion of homosexuality." The essay makes no personal references; Alter sticks only to the issues.

"Homosexuality," he writes, "whatever its origin, is constitutional to the gay person. It is a fixture in human society. It is demonstrably not unloving, corrosive, or unhealthy. On the contrary. That it is biologically non-procreative is hardly a reason to deny the companionship a union offers. Further, gay and lesbian couples can and do raise children. Unless we validate homosexual behavior and invoke God's blessing on its expression in marriage, we cannot expect homosexuals to embrace Judaism. . . . Once our movement comes to terms with the broader issue of the validity and dignity of gay and lesbian relationships, ordaining gay and lesbian rabbis and cantors will follow as a matter of course."

Alter's peace of mind is the promised attainment of the post-passing phase that sociologist Erving Goffman so aptly describes. By disclosing voluntarily, he writes, the passer transforms himself radically from an "individual with an uneasy social situation to manage, from that of a discreditable person to that of a discredited one." In this sense, being "discredited" is on the credit side. Passing, to Goffman, is the turning point in the moral career of the stigmatized person. But the passer who discloses voluntarily moves beyond passing and "unlearns concealment." This phase of the moral career, Goffman writes, is the "final, mature, well-adjusted one—a state of grace . . . "

⁓

THE FOCUS OF GOFFMAN'S WIDER ANALYSIS is how people "manage" stigmas of all kinds, from blindness, mental illness, and physical deformity to issues of background and sexual orientation, what he also refers to as "spoiled identity." Passing, of course, is one of the most common management strategies. Among the studies Goffman cites is the one by Drake and Cayton that identified a natural cycle of black-for-white passing in the first half of the twentieth century, the progression from inadvertent passing to passing for fun to passing part-time or full-time to passing all the way or breaking the cycle at any point. David Matthews's story certainly follows the pattern. But the cycle does not quite apply to Alter's gay-for-straight passing experience. It would be fair to say that Alter passed inadvertently in the years before his admission to JTS, and that he passed both part-time and full-time both during seminary and for many years thereafter. But at no point was there anything even remotely fun about it.

⁓

IF THE EXPERIENCE OF PASSING had become too horrendous, Joel Alter had alternatives that would have allowed him to come close to fulfilling his ambitions. This he readily admits. He could have sought ordination as either a Reconstructionist or a Reform rabbi, which would have eliminated much of his anguish. True, switching movement allegiance in this way would have required compromises he chose not to make. But the Reform and Reconstructionist movements are equally mainstream avenues of Jewish expression, and either would have allowed him to function as a full-fledged member of the clergy without having had to encase such an important part of his life in subterfuge for an extended period of time.

There is no such recourse for gays and lesbians who elect to make careers in the military, another institution in protracted struggle with transition. Army, navy, marines, even by the turn of the new century there were no denominational alternatives for gays and lesbians who elected or felt called to national military service. The policy on homosexuals does not vary. Every gay recruit who wants to serve has no choice but to pass.

CHAPTER FIVE

Conduct Unbecoming

> He who passes can find himself called to a showdown
> by persons who have now learned of his secret and are
> about to confront him with his having been false.
> This possibility can even be formally instituted.
>   —ERVING GOFFMAN

RIGHT FROM THE START, as a lesbian with military aspirations, the Careerist had to "lie like crazy." The air force application form bluntly asked: "Are you a homosexual or bisexual? Do you intend to engage in homosexual acts?" The navy's medical entrance form was only slightly more discreet: "Do you have any homosexual tendencies?"

This was during the early 1980s, more than a decade before the military removed this impertinent line of inquiry from its official forms and documents. (Such questions briefly resurfaced on the application available on the air force reserves Website as late as 2002.) At the time, two years out of high school, she responded to the questions with the requisite chain of untruths—"No," "No," and "No." Looking back on that time, she is struck by the fact that she was not particularly aggrieved, annoyed, or angry about the need to tailor her personal story to suit the military's requirements. "It was like pot," she said. "I was going to lie about that too. I figured I just wasn't going to tell them things I didn't want them to know about me."

Her situation was, in some ways, the mirror opposite of Joel Alter's. Unlike the young rabbinical student, when the Careerist decided to cast her lot with an institution expressly hostile to homosexuals, she was not the least bit in doubt about her own sexuality. That she had resolved in her own mind by the time she received her diploma from the public high school in Deerfield Beach, Florida, just south of Boca Raton. "You could drink at eighteen at that time," she said, "and I guess something came into my head. It was like, I can do this now, and it really doesn't matter a damn what anyone else thinks. And that's when it rose to my consciousness that I really wanted to be with a woman, that I didn't have to play this silly game of dating men anymore. That I could just be me." This was not to say that she had anything against men. She enjoyed men and was popular with them. It's just that her emotional connection to women was much stronger. By the time she settled on the military as a career goal, the only challenge her sexuality presented was how to cover it up.

Immediately after high school, she was too busy having a good time hanging out with her friends to get serious about a career direction, so in between barhopping and partying, horseback riding and soccer, she worked as a lifeguard and trained as an electrician's apprentice. At twenty, she went through the application process to join the air force. Once her acceptance came through, she had every intention of joining up until her girlfriend at the time pressed her not to leave by confiding, inaccurately as it turned out, that she was suffering from a life-threatening illness.

The notion of a military future stayed with the Careerist nonetheless, in part because she felt she "needed a lot of structure because I didn't have any growing up." In 1981, at the age of twenty-two, she applied again, this time for enlistment in the U.S. Navy. Embarrassed about her earlier flip-flop, she didn't dare approach the air force a second time. The navy was her new choice. She had a navy history, after all, even was born in the naval hospital while her father, who reached the rank of chief petty officer, was stationed in Chelsea, Massachusetts. He left the family when she was only two, and in the years that followed, though his support checks came regularly, her time with him was limited. Her mother remarried and moved the children to Florida and her father ended up in Las Vegas. In her father's absence, she often idealized him, handsome, always spiff in her imagination, dressed in his starched navy whites.

AFTER TWO MONTHS OF BOOT CAMP and an extra month training to be a seaman striker, she was assigned to the USS *Canopus*, a submarine tender anchored at the Charleston Naval Weapons Station in Goose Creek, South Carolina, about twenty miles north of the navy base. With its crew of twelve hundred mostly male technicians and repair personnel, the *Canopus* had the task of tending—providing maintenance and logistical support—for nuclear attack submarines.

Every five days, she, like other crew members, "stood duty" for twenty-four hours, meaning an overnight stay in a berthing aboard ship. On other days she lived in her own apartment, which, after about a year, she began sharing with a fellow shipmate. Only her most trusted confidantes knew it, but her flat mate was also her lover. Two young navy women sharing the rent is about as unremarkable as a couple of college girls sharing the rent, so this was not a particularly risky arrangement, even under

Department of Defense Directive 1332.14, which came into effect at about the time of her enlistment. The directive left no doubt that any service person who "engaged in, has attempted to engage in, or has solicited another to engage in a homosexual act" faced discharge—honorable discharge, however, so long as there were no aggravating circumstances. Her enlistment was more than a decade old when the Clinton administration instituted its "Don't Ask, Don't Tell, Don't Pursue" policy. She enlisted when witch-hunts for homosexuals in the military were still common sport. Even so, exercising stealth and good judgment, she kept her private life reasonably private.

∿

LIKE MANY PASSERS IN THE WORKPLACE, the Careerist set up decoys. A male friend back home agreed to marry her—for the record. "The only payment to him was that I said, 'Well, if you ever need medical coverage, all you'd have to do is go find a base.' He was a really great personality, very popular with other gay men. Looked like Tom Cruise." The two never lived together as a couple, but the marriage license allowed her to produce for the record the "idea of a husband" and gave her the use of his name as spouse on official documents. "And I made up this whole conglomerate story that he was in charge of his family's business and that he had to stay down in Florida and this and that and the other," she said. "You'd be surprised how many women do the 'marriage of convenience' thing. There are really a lot of them." And this is not only true in the military.

In her case, the fact of the marriage—ostensible testament to her heterosexuality—could be "verified absolutely and it kept the questioning off my back. It would be like, *Well, why aren't you dating anyone?* and I would say, *I don't date because I'm married*." She snapped her fingers. "Boom! End of discussion."

As further cover, she cultivated a friendship in Charleston with a married heterosexual man, also in the navy, a fire technician assigned to another vessel. He was someone she saw regularly—and publicly—and they have remained good friends throughout the years. In those days, their ritual was to watch *Alf* on television every week at her place. They hung out together a lot. This was particularly useful to her because of his reputation in navy circles as an inveterate philanderer. She let folks think what they liked, a passing strategy rumored to be as common among big-time gay Wall Street investment bankers, actors, and fashion designers— bring a "beard" to the big closing dinner, marry someone of the opposite sex for show—as it is among soldiers and sailors.

The Careerist's paper marriage took a strange turn. On a visit to Florida in 1984, she and her girlfriend decided to pay a call on the husband who was, after all, a good friend of long standing. He looked unwell and asked if he could borrow a thousand dollars. The Careerist agreed, but at the time, without local checks, was unable to convince a Florida bank to give her that amount on her Charleston account. So she gave him the five hundred dollars she happened to have on hand.

Oddly, that was the last time she saw or heard from him. "And to this day, I can't find him. I have his social security number and I looked in the Social Security Death Index and it didn't pop up. I don't know what happened to him."

~

THE CAREERIST MET HER NAVY GIRLFRIEND on a Sunday in the summer of 1982 while both of them were on twenty-four-hour duty. "There was a skeleton crew on board. I saw her, and at lunch we began talking. That night I went up to her office space and talked some more. Then I asked her if she'd be interested in going out for dinner. She said yes. So it was just one of those things. After that, we dated a bit, but there was no way for anyone to tell that. People wouldn't think, *Oh my God! Those two women are talking to one another!*"

The relationship lasted nearly five years, and the Careerist never felt particularly unsafe because of it. Witch-hunts notwithstanding, most of her navy colleagues, she said, were not focused on ferreting out who might or might not be gay. You only have to be casually familiar with magazines such as the *Advocate*, and *Out*, or any of a number of gay activist websites, to know how common homosexual discharge from the military still is, and how painful and unreasonable the closeting and passing remains on the other side of "Don't Ask, Don't Tell." On an Internet message board, one former marine reported being discharged in 1999 even though he never made his homosexuality known nor, he wrote, was he ever involved in a homosexual act during his time in the corps. He was ousted because a military doctor he saw for a pre-existing ailment reported him, violating what he thought was physician–patient confidentiality.

In the Careerist's case, until the words "aggravating circumstance" took on new meaning, she had no such issues. She loved the navy and was comfortable with the setup. "It's not like people were fearful of who was sleeping next to them in the berthing space onboard ship, where quarters were really crowded," she said. "Certainly, no one ever wondered about me or anybody else. I mean, look back in history. The Roman armies—all those homosexuals—it's not like they were all groping each other. They were a very cohesive, collaborative unit of men who fought wars together. And sexual attraction? If it played a part in any of it, I don't know."

The Careerist implicitly understood that she could not abandon caution. She and her girlfriend would never dream of being physically demonstrative in public, for example. They could never—would never—hold hands or put their arms around each other's waists walking down the street. "You just didn't participate in that kind of behavior," she said. "You just—you didn't!" And in conversations over lunch and at the watercooler—"when everybody is talking about their home life—*My wife this* or *My child that*—I just didn't participate." She was young enough to have a natural excuse for exempting herself from the home-and-kiddie talk. "At the time I could get away with it," she said.

She also learned to become very selective about her choice of people to bond with, suppressing a natural inclination to be as open and social in the navy as she had been in her teens and early twenties. The best survival strategy for a military gay person, she quickly intuited, was to do good work, create an excellent reputation, limit one's social circle, and never cross anyone—never give anyone a reason to use your sexuality against you. She sensed an unstated complicity in those years because, to her eye at least, the lesbian women up and down the ranks were easy enough to pick out of a crowd if anyone had inclination to do so. And yet so many gays and lesbians were able to function in the navy without ever being singled out. "The only time homosexuality is an issue in the military," she said, "is when an issue is made of it."

Honorable people need a purifying rationale when circumstances force them into a life of lies and subterfuge, and so it was for the Careerist. She is able to justify to herself the deceitfulness military regulations imposed on her because she was directing her words and actions at an "entity," not other human beings per se. The lies and deceptions, in her words, had "greater purpose." Others I spoke to among her military friends used compartmentalization to salve the discomfort their own behavior caused them. "What I would do," one current member of the Coast Guard said, "is justify it to myself by saying, *Okay, I can lie about it at work, but I'm not going to lie about it in my family any longer. I'm going to compartmentalize it.*" This in turn allowed her to say to herself, *No I'm not a liar, but in order to survive I have to lie. It's justified now.*

Sissela Bok would classify these women's justifications, their excuses, as moral reasons for lying. As she writes, "People look for moral reasons when they are troubled, or caught short, and generally, when they need to persuade themselves or others that the usual presumption against lying is outweighed in their particular case." The reasons for these excuses, she submits, include avoiding harm and producing benefits as well as fairness and veracity. The Careerist's lies, as Bok points out in *Lying*, fall under St. Thomas Aquinas's category of "officious lies," or those designed to avoid harm and produce benefit, as opposed to "malicious lies" that have the opposite intent. They are also lies told in self-defense, as Bok writes, the lies told for the sake of avoiding harm to oneself. "Self-defensive lies," she writes, "can permeate all one does, so that life turns into 'living a lie.' Professionals involved in collective practices of deceit give up all ordinary assumptions about their own honesty and that of others. And individuals who feel obliged to 'pass' as a member of a dominant religious or racial group in order to avoid persecution deny what may be most precious to them. Political beliefs or sexual preferences unacceptable to a community compel many to a similar lifelong duplicity, denying a central part of their own identity."

At the time when the lies were required of the Careerist, she wasn't particularly exercised about having to submit to such mental contortions. She readily accepted the need to take extreme precautions to obscure the kinds of facts about her personal life that heterosexuals never have a second thought about revealing to almost anyone. At the time, as a condition of employment, actively having to pass for straight all of the time seemed no more onerous than lying on her application had. "It was like, *If I want to stay in the Navy, I have to give this up.* So I gave this up," she said. This is not to say she could have given up her sexuality—how could she? The navy wasn't the priesthood; the navy demanded no vow of chastity. What she gave up was the ability to be open about her sexual preferences, which, as Bok suggests, was bound to exact its own price.

ABOARD THE *Canopus,* she started out in the carpentry shop, "a fun little area," she said. "We had a foundry and we would do things for trade-offs, what they used to call cumshaw. For example, a guy off a sub worked in the mess hall and had a big old roll of beef rib eye or something and he'd say, 'I'll trade you this rib eye if you make me seat cushions now so I don't have to put in a purchase order to get this done. And so we'd make them for him and get a few steaks out of it. We did it all the time. It was really illegal, but we did it anyway."

Eventually she met some people from calibrations and got interested their work: calibrating pressure and temperature as well as the optical, rotational, and dimensional elements of any measuring equipment aboard ship, from tachometers and micrometers to auto-collimators. The task was highly specialized "and fascinating," she said. "I liked the close-up and precise work that it entailed." She excelled at it, starting at the rank of petty officer third class in the Fleet Mechanical Calibrations lab (FMCL). The navy sent her to Denver for three months of intensive training in precision measurement. That advanced her experience level and lined her up for transfer to the USS *Frank Cable*, where she spent two years on the U.S. Pacific Fleet "warship that fixes warships," as its Website proclaims.

Working mostly with men, she was known as "Mrs. O_2" in those days, O_2 for oxygen because her specialty was going aboard submarines to calibrate their oxygen-bank gauges, sometimes at the risk of radiation contamination. "At one point I did handle some that were potentially contaminated," she said. "It turns out they weren't, but it was close. The whole ship went into an emergency November situation and people in little zoot suits came around me and ran monitors. It was like *Silkwood*." She did two years of shore duty after the *Cable*, working in shore maintenance and then at another calibration lab. The lab was a mess—too many inexperienced people who did no more than "lick 'em and stick 'em," the practice also known as "gun-decking," meaning they would grab a roll of inspection certification stickers and paste them indiscriminately onto equipment that hadn't been properly calibrated. "I was furious," she said. "I knew that was going on because I was going behind them doing quality assurance checks and reporting my findings." In the process, she made herself extremely valuable to her superiors and garnered respect up and down the ranks. "At this point, I was a second class petty officer, and I had a really good reputation for what I was doing," she said, adding, "I wouldn't even hint at that unless I knew it to be the truth."

ON HER RETURN FROM DENVER her relationship with the girl-friend started to sour. The woman's parents had both died and she began to keep the Careerist at an emotional remove. That caused the Careerist to begin to look elsewhere for company, and by June 1985 she was dating another woman. "I was a mess," she said, "but I had fun. I was on the *Frank Cable* when I started see-ing the second girl, and it went on for about six months in the course of the already existing relationship. I was confused. But I just didn't know what kind of decision I needed to make." Even-tually, she moved into her own place. Although by this time she was with Girlfriend Two exclusively, she and Girlfriend One re-mained on good terms.

In the months ahead, however, the relationship with Girlfriend Two became problematic and the Careerist responded by creat-ing some distance. She did not foresee what would follow: a series of incidents so disturbing that when the movie *Fatal At-traction* premiered the next year, it seemed to recast her experi-ences just enough to suit heterosexual movie-going tastes.

~

SHE WAS EXPECTING A VISIT AT HOME from Girlfriend One when Girlfriend Two showed up unexpectedly on the doorstep. The Careerist told Two that she was waiting for a visitor and po-litely but firmly asked Two to leave. Two wanted to know who was coming over and the Careerist told her the truth. At that point, Two drove off in her car as asked, but no sooner had One arrived at the Careerist's apartment than Two was back, knocking at the door holding a long belt of black rubber in her hands. Two asked to use the telephone to call a car repair service. The Ca-reerist examined the two ends of the belt. "This isn't broken," she said. "It's been melted. Did you set the thing on fire? What did you do that for?" The Careerist walked out the door of her building and over to Two's car. She opened the hood. "It's your air conditioning belt," she said. "You can drive."

Two calmly got into her car and backed out of her parking place. She lined her vehicle up behind the Careerist's parked car, nosed up directly behind its rear bumper, and then rear-ended it into the drainage ditch that abuts the apartment complex parking area, cleverly landscaped to look like a narrow stream. "At that point," the Careerist recalled, "I knew I was dealing with someone who wasn't in full control of her emotional faculties. It was unfortunate too, because this woman was very good at what she did. She had extremely good evaluations throughout her naval career."

Not long after, she was having lunch with a coworker in the naval yard picnic area. Two appeared from nowhere, spoiling for a confrontation. "Who is this?" she demanded to know, eyeing the coworker. The Careerist was furious at the intrusion and tartly responded that she had lost her appetite. She dumped her food and its wrappers into a nearby garbage can, and then she and her coworker walked toward the coworker's Mazda Rx7 to return to work. But as they tried to get into vehicle, Two grabbed the Careerist and pulled at her with such force that she banged her head against the framework of the car door. "You need to stop," she told Two, thinking to herself, *Where is shore patrol when you need them?* Two lunged at her again, this time ripping the buttons off her uniform. Meantime, the coworker had managed to slip into the driver's seat and somehow the two of them managed to speed away, even though Two had jumped onto the roof of the car in an attempt to stop them.

The Careerist arrived at her office, shaken and visibly upset.

Her coworker encouraged her to tell her supervisor what had happened but limit details to the isolated fact of the assault. "I had to take action," she said. "The situation was way out of hand. I really didn't know what else to do about it." So she went to her supervisor. "I said this girl for whatever reason got really pissed off at me and accosted me at the picnic grounds." The supervisor replied, "Write her up," meaning file a report against her.

The Careerist knew there was risk in filling out an official report, but because of the violence and the stalking, she felt she had no choice. Her hope—the way she rationalized her decision to involve the navy—was that the incident could be viewed as an incident in and of itself—a battery, for whatever reason, nothing more. "I put it in that perspective," she said, and she filed a report about the violence without any further elaboration.

Several weeks later, Two came up to her and matter-of-factly announced that she planned to turn both of them in. She also confided in the master at arms aboard her ship, who in turn convinced Two to provide further details of her relationship with the Careerist. "The whole story got altered to make it sound as if I coerced her into homosexuality," the Careerist said. "And I don't know whether she did it or whether it was a manifestation of her conversation with the crew's master at arms—those people are basically the police investigators of the command.

"And then all hell breaks loose like you would not believe. This ended up turning into a yearlong investigation involving the NIS [Naval Investigative Service] people, with friends of mine being called to testify. They even looked for my husband but couldn't produce him." She said the NIS investigators tried repeatedly to provoke her into confessing to the relationship, taunting her with statements such as, *Your ex-girlfriend said she was afraid of you,* and *Anything other than the missionary position is considered sodomy*, and *Being a homosexual, you can be blackmailed.* But the Careerist gave up nothing.

"I wasn't admitting to anything," she said. "But I'm thinking, *This guy is using really stupid logic on me.* And I was not a stupid person, even though I did not have a college degree at that point. I was thinking to myself, *Right, and you've never gotten a blow job or anything? Give me a break!* I just told him that I didn't know anything about it. I knew that the best way to go about doing this was never to admit anything at all."

WHEN THE INVESTIGATION WAS COMPLETE, Two was notified of the date for her executive officer's inquiry, resulting from the report the Careerist had filed about the picnic grounds assault. Suddenly Two went UA—unauthorized absence. The search for her whereabouts even extended to the Careerist's apartment. "There's not a snowball's chance in hell I would have had her in my house then, okay?" the Careerist said. "But I let them in. They were looking in cabinets. They were looking behind the shower curtain. They were looking in the most ridiculous places. I said, 'Oh God! Do you think she's going to fit in the drawer where I stick my crackers? You've got to be shittin' me!' I'm like, *Whatever.*"

The enormous physical strain on Two was evident when she resurfaced a couple of weeks later. "She was losing weight like crazy," the Careerist said. "She's only five-one or five-two and she went from something like 110 pounds to 85 pounds. Her nerves were just frazzled—I can just see it. And she was calling my house constantly—just going crazy. I remember times when I'd walk into my house and the phone would be ringing and I'd be thinking, *This is weird.* And the movie *Fatal Attraction*—same stuff, you know?"

~

THE EXECUTIVE OFFICER'S INQUIRY was held in his office on level 04 of Two's ship. At the time the Careerist was assigned to shore duty and was under a separate command. She was sure her presence at the inquiry was required solely because she had filed the assault report. Present in the office with the two women were the executive officer, Two's immediate supervisor, the ship's lawyers, the ship's master at arms, and any witnesses who had been called, including the coworker who had witnessed the picnic assault.

Everyone stood at attention. The executive officer (XO) read the incident report, going over the details of what allegedly took place and how. "And then he started," the Careerist said. "I recall that he said, 'And this leads to the next issue.'" He asked everyone to leave the room except the Careerist, Two, the master at arms, and the attorney. "He says something like, *This is a classic case of a homosexual relationship gone awry . . .*

"I thought I'd die," she said. "I couldn't believe I was actually standing there listening to this. Then he went straight over to her [Two] and looked her straight in the face and said, 'Are you two lovers?' And she said, 'Yes.' And I'm thinking, *My career is over. I'm dead. This is the end.*"

The Careerist stood at attention, mute. "I stood at parade rest and I said nothing because I wasn't asked to speak. I wasn't part of that command. And at that point I knew it wasn't a good idea to blurt out all of the sudden, *She's a liar!* I knew I would have my time but not right then. It wasn't going to be right then."

Two was sent on to the commanding officer's mast for further action in the matter. The Careerist was too upset to even consider following any more of the proceedings. "And by that point she devolved into the psych ward at the naval hospital and that took care of it." Two was discharged.

It took another month or so for the XO's report to be forwarded to the Careerist's command. "And the next thing I know my command is serving me with paperwork saying that I was subject to a UCMJ Article blah-blah regarding homosexuality and that an administrative inquiry is being held. I said nothing," she said. "It was her word against mine. And I'm thinking, *Okay. Time to get a lawyer.*"

THE CAREERIST GOT A "FANTASTIC" ATTORNEY from JAG, the judge advocate general, who built her defense—ironically—around her personal credibility, her reputation for truthfulness, and Two's psychological condition. "My saving grace was that she ended up in the psych ward," the Careerist said. "Basically, the lawyers were saying that these are the words of a lunatic and you've got a really good petty officer here."

The administrative discharge board consisted of a commander, a lieutenant, and a warrant officer. The defense produced a parade of personal witnesses: people the Careerist had worked for and people who had worked for her; people who had known her for a long time and people who knew her slightly. "Everything that was said showed that my reputation was spotless," she said. "They talked about how truthful a person I had been the whole time I had been in the navy, what a good, loyal and dedicated navy person I was, what a good, solid worker, what a great work ethic." Asked if they knew anything about her personal life, most responded with answers such as *Didn't know her personally* or *Not to my knowledge* or *Yeah, great person* . . .

"See?" she said. "That's the thing. There were people that I knew, who I know now, that I have since told the truth to, and I've explained that because of the possibility of experiences like the administrative board, I never wanted to come out and tell them because I never wanted to have to put them in a position to have to lie for me." Because she maintained her silence on the subject for all those years, her colleagues were able to vouch for her without having to lie.

For the government's case, there were no witnesses. By that point, Girlfriend Two had been discharged and there was no one else to bring forward. Not that this situation would have saved the Careerist if the navy had wanted her out. "I've seen people thrown out on less," she said. "In the '80s, it was just a gigantic witch-hunt. There were women being chucked out for just being associated—I mean, say for example you were just you and you were associated with a lesbian. You could get chucked out. The fact that I was retained was a miracle. The lawyer prepared a terrific defense."

There were several hours of testimony and an hour of deliberation before the vote was announced: 2–1 in favor of the Careerist. "The senior officer didn't buy it at all," she said. "He thought that I was full of shit. The other two bought it and that was that. I was retained, found not guilty of the charge of homosexuality under article umpty-squat blah-blah-blah. And then I asked immediately for the proceedings to be expunged from my record, so it would not disqualify me from future promotions. So they got rid of it. They had to."

An unintended casualty of the brouhaha was Girlfriend One,

who was a reservist at the time. Undone by the pressure of the NIS inquiry, which involved her because of her friendship with the Careerist, she confided in her superior officer, who happened to be a woman she thought would be sympathetic. Instead, the officer turned Girlfriend One in. "It was awful," the Careerist said. "This was a woman with an impeccable record, like twelve or thirteen years of time in and"—she whistled faintly—"that was it. I remember saying to her, 'Why did you do it? Why did you tell? Why did you? And she's like, '*I just don't know. I just don't know. I don't know why I said it.*' You know?

"So here am I," the Careerist said, "stuck in the middle of these two women, one having this fatal attraction and the other my former girlfriend of five years standing. Both of them get booted out of the navy and I remain. I remain because I'm not wanting—I'm not wanting to let it happen."

Two years later, in 1989, the Careerist rose to the rank of petty officer first class. There was satisfaction in the accomplishment but little joy. The events of 1987 had robbed her of that. "I think on an unconscious level, it really pissed me off," she said. "After that, I had a really lackluster interest in the navy. I started to develop a real resentment toward the way of life and the policies, about the fact that I had allowed myself to be told where I was going to go, what I was going to do, what times I was going to do it, everything mandated. And the balance shifted. Once 'pro,' I was becoming 'con.' And by the time I was thirty-two, I really decided that my life was going in another direction. At that point, I really didn't know what that was, but I just knew that I needed to get out of where I was and I needed to veer off into some other direction, some kind of change."

AFTER TWO YEARS OF SHORE DUTY, the Careerist completed her eight years and ten months of active duty assigned to the destroyer tender USS *Sierra*. In March 1990, she joined the reserves, assigned once again to the *Frank Cable*, but this time only one weekend a month while she studied at the College of Charleston for her degree in business and psychology. In that time, she secured her military pension. She has since built a very successful second act in a federal government post, no longer in secret because federal policy outside the military prevents discrimination on the basis of sexual preference.

Looking back on her experience, she said the navy gave her much but took as much away. The need to lie and the trouble it caused her and those close to her are at the core of her bruised feelings. She talked about the damage that building a life around a circuitry of lies inevitably causes.

"You've got this false self going on and that false self not only corrupts that part of you where you have to present yourself to the world, but it also corrupts the relationships that you have with the people that actually do know—including your significant others—because you both have to play out this whole facade," she said. ". . . It more or less forces you not to have a true sense of what's going on. In most gay relationships, it exasperates the relationship in and of itself. There is this web of dishonesty going on throughout all of the other areas of your life and your relationship can't help but be affected. Your relationship with yourself is affected, so therefore all of your other relationships are going to be affected insofar as you are not having total honesty about who you are with everyone.

"I never thought about this when I was younger, but it becomes real—real in the sense that I'm more aware of it, now that I'm in my forties. You get older and you think, *This really angers me, and I really don't want my relationships affected like this anymore.* You know?"

THIS CHAPTER BEGAN as the story of a navy careerist who spent twenty long years hiding in plain sight because she happened to be a lesbian. Her purpose in coming forward was confession, with the hope of using truth to promote change. She wanted to report openly and in detail on how she, as a member of the armed forces, experienced the U.S. military's policy of enforced passing for gays and lesbians. The burden, her friends on active duty confirm, is no less onerous since "Don't Ask, Don't Tell" came into effect in 1993.

She was anxious to detail her experience as someone readily perceived by friends and colleagues, both above and below her, as honest, forthright, and trustworthy. And yet her career choice obliged her to engage for most of her adult life in furtive, deceptive behavior as the price of admission and continued good standing. From the safety of retirement, she had the opportunity to describe the debilitating impact of two decades of personal bifurcation, both as they affected her and, even more drastically, those in her personal circle. She wanted to discuss for the record the strain these constraints placed on an otherwise consummate professional. In the process of coming forward, she hoped to neutralize the lingering bitterness of what by all other measures was an excellent career in national service. It was a way to put those difficult feelings to positive use.

Lest you still think that passing in our culture has become nothing more than a faded emblem, a remnant and reminder of times we have moved beyond, there is more.

Aaron Belkin, a professor of political science at the University of California–Santa Barbara, first suggested that the Careerist might want to reconsider the permission she originally granted me to use her name. Belkin heads the university's Center for the Study of Sexual Minorities in the Military. On hearing the Careerist's story, he explained something the navy Careerist clearly was unaware of: that she still was under military obligation not to speak out publicly about her forbidden experiences in the navy. To speak out, he said, would open her to the perhaps remote possibility of prosecution under terms of the Uniform Code of Military Justice (UCMJ), but a possibility nonetheless. Under UCMJ regulations that govern fraternization, conduct unbecoming, and sodomy, the Careerist could in principle be hauled back to active duty for the express purpose of court-martial. That in turn could mean separation from the military—separation as distinct from retirement—and the forfeit of her pension and all other benefits earned over twenty years in military service. There is no statute of limitations.

The notion seemed preposterous, but an attorney in the navy's Judge Advocate General Command confirmed that a command wanting to conduct such a court-martial could do so. Approval, however, would have to be sought from the secretary of the navy personally, who in turn would decide if the conditions were appropriate for court martial in these courts. "Typically," wrote Lieutenant Michelle M. Pettit, assistant legal counsel in JAG's navy Personnel Command in response to a question sent by e-mail, "it must be a serious offense to warrant trial after retirement."

Would the navy Careerist's situation qualify? For her protection, that question was not asked directly. Yet two civilian experts, Elizabeth Hillman, a Rutgers law professor with a military background, and Sharra Greer, chief legal counsel of the Servicemember's Legal Defense Network (SLDN), both agreed that the chance the military would go after the Careerist for her infractions was small to nonexistent. "Politically," Hillman acknowledged, "it would be very hard to sustain the argument to prosecute. But I can't say it wouldn't happen because it has happened before." Greer said the possibility of prosecution was more of a "theoretical risk than an actual risk," but still risk enough to deter many gay, lesbian, bisexual, and transsexual military retirees from telling their stories on the record, much to the SLDN's dismay.

When the Careerist checked with legal experts, she learned that her retirement benefits were subject to her willingness to continue to abide by UCMJ regulations, even though she has long since moved on to other vocational pursuits. By accepting her retirement package—by not "separating" from the military as Hillman did after seven years of active duty in the air force—the Careerist effectively bound herself to a pact of permanent nondisclosure. As long as she was receiving benefits, her personal story would never be her own to tell without risk. She lamented, "It never in a million years occurred to me that I could end up losing my benefits into retirement."

This was her reluctant conclusion: "Someone reading this would know that I 'got over' on the navy and *could* do something if they so chose and if they so felt inclined. This is not just about someone passing herself off during a career. This is about someone who lied to a navy administrative board about this very subject and got away with it. I can't afford for some nut to decide that that's enough to come after me again and retry me or whatever, no matter how 'remote' the possibility is. . . . It's obvious to me that there are no guarantees and nothing to protect me in that most unlikely event.

"The bottom line to this is that unless there is a guarantee under the law that the military can't prosecute at all in any way, I can't afford to allow my name to be used. As much as I would love to allow myself this freedom, I must prevent my past from hurting my future."

Greer, for one, was totally sympathetic with the Careerist's decision, noting that the silence this tiny risk imposes also silences those it has affected and in turn helps the military maintain its problematic status quo. As the constitutional law scholar Tobias Barrington Wolff points out, passing has as great an impact on the institutions that rely on it as it does on the passers themselves. "One of the underappreciated aspects of 'Don't Ask, Don't Tell,' which shockingly has not been discussed in court of appeals opinions that have dealt with the policy, is the information the military is deprived of vis-à-vis its gay and lesbian soldiers," he said. "Because the military prohibits all communication about sexual identity at all times with all people, you can't go to your commanding officer or your senator [or even to an author] to explain the impact that 'Don't Ask, Don't Tell' is having on gay soldiers and urge a change in the policy. So there is institutional and political harm from passing as well."

The threat of retribution means homosexuals still have to be very guarded, Wolff said, so "even people of very good will in the military only get the party line, especially under the current administration."

Yale legal scholar Kenji Yoshino goes one further. He has described "Don't Ask, Don't Tell" as a passing policy pure and simple, one that assures gays in the military that "no longer will they be excluded for their status, but only for their self-identification or conduct. Yet," he ventured, "this shift has not improved the material or dignitary conditions of gays in the military, homosexual self-identification and homosexual conduct are sufficiently central to gay identity that burdening such acts is tantamount to burdening gay status. Indeed," he wrote, "exclusions under the new policy have skyrocketed, suggesting that the shift is the reverse of progress for gays."

~

GAY FINANCIERS obviously are not subject to religious or military law, but the atmosphere on Wall Street is known to have a similar impact. At least that is how Trevor Lewis experienced it during the years he worked for a major investment bank.

Before business school at Columbia, Lewis was an aspiring actor, gay and out since his college days at Bucknell University, starting way back in 1968. After university, he enrolled in a special acting program at Julliard and then auditioned around New York for a while. But he decided to change course and enrolled at Columbia University Business School to study for an MBA. He realized immediately that he would be wise to keep his gay life to himself. In 1979 he went to work for Drexel, Burnham, Lambert and, for the same reasons, continued to pass for the next seven years as he had passed during business school.

Lewis wore the wedding band his partner gave him on his right hand and almost always attended company functions alone, except for the really lavish closing dinners, when he would often take a woman friend—his boyfriend's sister, perhaps, or a girl he knew and liked from his acting days. Following the fad of the day, he and his partner had a celebrity voice on their answering machine, and when women he met through work would show romantic interest in him, he just ignored the signals and played dumb.

"I certainly knew that Wall Street was a very closeted environment," Lewis said. "How did I know it? I guess it was just a feeling I had because of the conservative nature of the people that I talked to. During my entire tenure as an investment banker, I never met one other banker that I knew was openly gay, or was not gay openly, but just gay. Not one. And yet I'm sure there were many because subsequently, I have met a few. But while I was working on the street, I never met one." Why don't the gays protest? "I guess it's done out of fear that not doing so is going to ruin your career and that you can't chance," he said. "Once they know, they know, and the consequences will follow. And that may signal the end of your growth, your growth track at the firm."

For Lewis, that changed in 1986. His partner was dying of AIDS. The need for time and understanding forced him to confide in his boss, who turned out to be much more accepting than Lewis imagined he might be. After the disclosure, Lewis advanced through the ranks to the level of managing director, though he thinks his homosexuality complicated and lengthened the time it took to get there. On the basis of his record alone, it should have happened sooner. When the firm collapsed, Lewis went on to start a private partnership in the early 1990s.

Current Wall Streeters say the atmosphere has loosened up somewhat, but being gay is not yet a nonissue. Wall Street is a conservative environment where the pressure to conform is great. In March 1999, a *New York* magazine cover story described in detail the many dilemmas faced by closeted investment bankers and the underground organization that serves them, the New York Bankers' Group, with a roster at the time of three hundred members, according to writer Alan Deutschman. In November 2002, the discreetly gay host of a nationally syndicated radio program urged the gay working community on Wall Street and beyond to stay in the closet at work. "I tell them it's hard enough to find a job, let alone keep one," Stephen Viscusi told Lisa Belkin of the *New York Times*. "Why muddy the waters by bringing up something that has nothing to do with your ability to perform the job? They may feel better about letting the secret out. But will they feel better when they don't get the jobs or recognition they want?" A number of Belkin's readers wrote in to express strong opposition to Viscusi's advice.

On many fronts, the workplace is becoming more tolerant, they argued, and there is evidence beyond the reaction of Belkin's readers that this is true.

CHAPTER SIX

The Jane Game

What we witness . . . is a fission, then a fusion,
of the intricate life-matter at the heart of language itself:
hope, fear, a desperate need for futurity, and a longing for
the at-once striking and intoxicating experience of freedom.

—JORIE GRAHAM

THE NAME JANE DARK EMERGED from a submission requirement in a poetry competition for the Graduate Program in Creative Writing at the University of Iowa in Iowa City. The year was 1990 or maybe 1991. "Pseudonyms only," read the instructions, and the poet got the idea to take the name Jane Dark. It came from a fascination with Jean Seberg, first as she appeared in the movie *Breathless* and then in her performance as Joan of Arc in *Saint Joan*. The French Jeanne d'Arc was then elided to Jane Dark. The poet was in Iowa, hardly half a tank of gas from Jean Seberg's birthplace. Jane Dark signed the poem but did not win the competition, and the poet filed the clever pen name away for use another time.

That other time arrived four years later, in the winter of 1995–1996. Home was a basement apartment in the hills of Berkeley. New poems were under construction, but money was short. Funds had run out from the various teaching stints and fellowships of the past couple of years, including a handsome grant from the National Endowment for the Arts. The poet was relying

on borrowed money to pay the rent. There was to be another visiting professorship at the University of Indiana at South Bend,
but not until the next fall. A winter, a spring, and a summer would
have to be weathered first.

At the time, recognition was building steadily in the rarified
world of serious verse. Since the *American Poetry Review* had
published "Blue Louise" in 1991, the poet's work had appeared
with something approaching regularity in a number of very respected venues. The Pushcart Prize committee had honored
three poems with nominations and eventually gave one a prize. In
1996, three of the poet's essays appeared in three scholarly journals, each on a poem by John Berryman, John Ashbery, and Donald Revell. Still, there was plenty of free time for indulging in
other pleasures, like bicycling, watching mindless television, and
listening to and thinking about pop music.

The poet's mother lives in Berkeley too. She is a highly admired professor of rhetoric and all things Scandinavian at Berkeley, a specialist in oral literature, orality, medieval literature and
culture, an academic who bucked convention by crossing disci-
plines into feminist theory, film history, and film and popular culture. She even wrote a horror film theory classic, *Men, Women,
and Chainsaws*. She spent six years at Harvard before her appointment at Berkeley in 1977, hence a Cambridge connection for
her Berkeley-born offspring, who remained behind in the Boston
area to finish high school, fool around for a couple of years, and
then graduate Boston University magna cum laude in English
cum campus prize for a poem from the Academy of American Poets *cum* departmental prize for scholarship. Berkeley and Boston
both felt like home.

The period from the end of 1995 to the beginning of 1996 was
particularly quiet for the poet. It also happened to be the time of

ZINE MANIA!!! Fanzines are homegrown, handcrafted, self-published underground publications with minuscule circulation, magazinelets with titles such as *Riot Grrrls, Bust,* and *resister.* They were proliferating across the country, and the poet decided to create one with a focus on the world of mainstream pop music, told in the guise of "a wise-ass teen" named—Jane Dark. Yes, wise-ass teen was the voice of choice because even at age thirty-three, that is how the poet felt when the music was on.

~

sugar high! The title was spelled adolescent style, with a lower-case *s* and a lowercase *h* and a girly exclamation point: *Jane Dark's sugar high! A Forum for Thoughts on Music.* Why the pen name? The poet explained that zine writers often use pseudo-nyms to hide the identity of the one who leaves the copy shop without paying for the use of its Xerox machines and to obscure the identity of the creator in case the creation really sucks. Unlike the first Jane Dark back in Iowa, this Jane Dark had a girly, teenish writing voice that sounded a lot like Alicia Silverstone as she appeared in *Clueless,* portraying pretty Cher Horowitz, an Emma for the 1990s. This Jane Dark upheld the "pop and teenagerdom aesthetic" but she did it as if there were proof of a Ph.D. tucked neatly into the front pocket of her black Kate Spade miniback-pack. The poet's whole idea was to mix it all together. *This Wise-Ass Teen Talks Backstreet Boys and John Ashbery Too* but in a voice that did right by the poet's "weird love of trashy pop music."

This is the voice: *My name is Jane and I used to have New Kids on the Block earrings . . .*

What joy! Immediately, Jane Dark took on "an autonomous writing personality" that did not conflict with the poetry. This mattered immensely to the poet because the poetry and the music represented two "really, extremely different" sets of personal goals.

The distinction: The poetry is experimental, not, as they say, readily accessible. "And everyone says, *Well, what's going on here? You seem to have a contradiction—or a failure to match up your aesthetics.* And it's true. But there's a tiny audience for poetry in the world. If you're quite a popular poet, you can sell seventy-five hundred copies of your book. There are only a few poets who do better than that. So, if you only talk to a million people in your poem, you have to write a poem that is going to last a couple of hundred years, and thus gives of itself slowly. And so I believe in a certain density and resistance to understanding in poetry so that it can give of itself slowly.

"If you're a pop musician and you want to talk to a million people, you can do it in a week. Your material doesn't have to last. You can do it in a way that decays very quickly. It has a completely different aesthetic."

The poetry, then, had to be kept in a separate space, not necessarily a pure space but a space that could be isolated "from all the shit in your life that makes it hard for you to think. I find that I have to think very hard and very clearly to write my poems, and the crap of the day doesn't particularly help me very often." Once, for example, shortly after Iowa, the poet rented a one-room apartment with two desks, one equipped with a PC for a day job writing summaries of legal depositions, and the other desk, "a much nicer one," with a Mac for the poems. Later on, the poet took the poetry writing out of the house and into the coffee bars of Berkeley's supermarkets.

This is what the poet said about inventing the "pleasingly autonomous" Jane: "It's hard to say she felt real to me because that completely exteriorizes her from me. I understood her to be part of me, but she felt like an autonomous agent of thought. I felt like I was able to think in different ways, and for the first time doing that zine, I was able to organize the ideas I was having about pop music in ways that I thought worked."

From the first *sugar high!*:

1995 was the year I became disillusioned with hip-hop at a national level, though here in the Bay Area, sleazy Oaktown bangers of a sort continue to make interesting music (and I'm sure this is true other places as well.) Hip-hop is perhaps the music of disillusionment itself, by which I don't mean only that it's the music of the disenfranchised—or a certain culturally evident portion thereof—but rather that its practitioners become disillusioned with it so quickly. If anything has killed, or is killing hip-hop, it's less the outsiders like Bob Dole, C. DeLores Tucker, and William "Zippy the Drug Czar" Bennett than the quasi-internal acceptance of the idea that hip-hop is a more genuine music if the players are skilled instrumentalists. The people who promulgate this line are not *like* the people who said punk rock wasn't real music because they couldn't play their instruments; they're the same people . . .

～

AT SOME POINT in the first quarter of 1996, eight hundred sheets of ordinary white legal-sized stock spewed out of Jane Dark's printer in what the printer prompt calls "landscape orientation," horizontally, two pages of black-and-white text and graphics per side. Each sheet was then hand collated and creased along the centerfold to be stapled into booklets with a gauzy, sultry mug shot of Liv Tyler, cigarette dangling out of the side of her mouth, for a cover.

The U.S. mail carried *sugar high!* to Jane Dark's far-flung friends and fellow zine writers. One went to the New York City mailing address of *resister*, a culture and literary zine with a feminist slant that Jane Dark admired (RESISTance, sisTER, get it?). "So I did this very traditional zine thing which is: You send them a copy of yours and say, *Here is my zine. If you like it, send me a copy of yours.* The great fraternity—or sorority as the case may be—of weird obsessives."

Evelyn McDonnell was *resister*'s editor and publisher (she didn't use a pen name) in collaboration with her husband at the time, Lee Foust. Edwin Torres, the bilingual poet out of the Nuyorican circle, contributed art design and some of the writing, as did Foust, who was working on his doctorate in medieval literature at New York University. His dissertation topic was the Holy Grail. A typical issue of *resister* contained a diary from the U.N. Conference on Women in Beijing; a chapter from a novel by Lynn Breedlove and her story, "Kevin Costner, You're All Wet"; McDonnell on wearing a chimp mask to her wedding; a conversation between members of two punk bands, Jean Smith of Mecca Normal and Slim Moon of Kill Rock Stars; "Nature Punk" by Nikki McClure; a punk's-eye view of music of the early part of the twentieth century; and a tampon taste test.

What Jane Dark did not know was that McDonnell had a couple of other briefs, including newly appointed rock music editor of the *Village Voice* and coeditor with Ann Powers of a new anthology that had just been released. *Rock She Wrote* is a 467-page rescue mission, both a collection of the lost writings of women on rock, pop, and rap going back to the 1960s, and a tribute to the forgotten amazons who preceded the anthology's editors in "the strange network of misfits that is the rock critic community."

In the book's introductory essay, McDonnell writes of how fanzines, once a "stronghold of nerdy white boys with big egos and big mouths," had become "the latest front in the rockcrit battle. . . . From *Bikini Kill*, to glossier, female-led publications like *B-Side* and *Ben Is Dead*, to Lisa Carver's *Rollerderby*, zines have become outlets and forums for women . . . " Later on, McDonnell told an interviewer that a fundamental shift was under way in the world of rock music criticism, away from the "authoritarian, usually male" critical voice so dominant in the field, toward voices with the range and agility to respond effectively to the many subcultures and styles then finding place in the musical world.

~

THE TASK OF OPENING *resister*'s mail often fell to Foust. At some point in the first half of 1996, he found a copy of *sugar high!* in the mailbox. Foust thought the zine was outrageous, hysterically funny, "not like journalism, which I liked. It was more like art. And I remember saying to Evelyn, 'Hey, here's something funny. You should check this out.'"

Singular and fresh, McDonnell thought, not authoritarian in the least. Here was a zine with the playful style of someone obviously knowledgeable about pop music and pop criticism, very knowledgeable, but with "*this attitude.*" The pop bent made the work unique among the many zines that regularly crowded *resister*'s mailbox, especially because most of the others devoted the bulk of their pages to "the underground stuff." On top of that, McDonnell recalled, *sugar high!* stood out because "there were so few women's voices out there." The recent release of *Rock She Wrote* makes it not much of a leap to think that as an editor, McDonnell might have had a special interest in promoting talented women writers at the time. But she was quite certain even six years later that Jane Dark's zine would have stood out just as starkly if her name had been John. *sugar high!* prompted McDonnell to take the unusual step of crossing genres, of reaching out to an underground fanzine writer in her mainstream guise. The note she sent off by mail has not survived, but it read something like this:

> *Jane,*
> *Love your zine. Would you like to write for the* Voice?
> *Evelyn McDonnell*

Try to imagine the scene in the Berkeley post office the day Evelyn McDonnell's note arrived. The poet had never been in personal contact with anyone in the world of music writing or editing. A crudely photocopied fanzine had gone out just for fun to forty odds and sods and back came a bona fide invitation to write for a bona fide big-time New York weekly freakly—the *Village Voice. THE VILLAGE VOICE!* The music section of the *VILLAGE VOICE!* The *Voice* had been a fixed entry on the poet's personal required music reading list since early adolescence.

The *Voice* hadn't set up an e-mail system yet—this was 1996—so Jane Dark accepted McDonnell's offer by return letter. The prospect of seeing Jane Dark's byline in the music pages of the *Village Voice* was thrilling and turned out to be the second piece of extraordinary news to arrive in a matter of weeks. On March 6 came congratulatory notification of receipt of the most coveted prize a young poet can win: the Walt Whitman Award from the Academy of American Poets for a first book-length collection of poems. The prize was $5,000 and a commitment from Louisiana State University Press to publish the manuscript in 1997. That, plus the note from McDonnell, "made me the luckiest—I'm lucky, very much so—I got to be a poet and I got to be a rock critic. I pretty much got to be what I wanted to be when I grow up when I grew up."

~

AT SOME POINT SOON AFTER, McDonnell got Jane Dark's permission for the *Voice* to do a little column about *sugar high!* The editor also left a telephone message on the Berkeley apartment's telephone answering machine with the offer of a specific assignment. Did Jane want to write about—*about what? What did she say? I can't make out what she's saying???!!* McDonnell's message for some reason came garbled. Friends trooped over to hear the replay again and again but no one could figure out what was being proposed. "It was comical. Here was this dream come true and I couldn't understand what was on the tape. And it turned out she was saying 'the Macarena.' *Do you want to write about the Macarena?* Eventually I puzzled it out. And of course part of the impetus for puzzling it out was not to have to call back to ask."

Well, why the reluctance to call back? Was it to limit contact, to protect the fledgling persona of Jane Dark? "I can't stop you from phrasing it that way," was the reply, "but if you knew me better—which must come into all your interviews—*adventure* is the key word here. I love a sense of game playing. In fact, my politics are based around an idea of game playing and oddness and refusing to follow rules and things like that. So I'm not sure I was protecting the persona at that point. I was like, *Wow! I could get away with it, conceivably. Wouldn't that be a kick?!*"

In the meantime, McDonnell handed her copy of *sugar high!* to Rob Brunner, the summer music department intern. "Hey, this is cool," she told him. "See if you can think of something to do with it."

Brunner looked the zine over carefully. "It was this totally unusual combination," he recalled, "a very cool put-together fanzine, very underground, which is usually geared to very obscure artists, but this was somebody who was using that medium to champion a lot of mainstream artists in an intelligent way, someone who clearly, genuinely meant what they were saying. And it was very funny, very smart, not condescending. There weren't many people who, at least in my experience at the time, were writing about mainstream music in a way that was intelligent and noncondescending."

"Plus," Brunner said, "it was completely mysterious and strange: a Xeroxed, stapled thing with really high-quality writing. When you get something like that, it just made you curious. Who is this person?"

Brunner telephoned the number in Berkeley and interviewed Jane Dark for not more than fifteen minutes. "I do very much remember thinking to myself, *This sounds like a man.* And I was thinking, *Do I ask? How do I bring this up?* And then I decided, you know, there are women who have deep voices, whatever. Who cares? I'm interested in the zine." But a few minutes into the conversation, Brunner couldn't quite contain himself and tried to pry as politely as he could. Jane Dark was quicker with the grammar.

RB: "Is Jane Dark a real name?"
JD: "Yes, it's a real name." (*It may not be my real name but it is a real name.*)

RB: "You have a deep voice."
JD: "Yes, I know."

Brunner let the subject drop for several reasons. What in-trigued him more than Jane Dark's voice was her elusiveness when it came to sharing background details. "Somewhere in my mind and in Evelyn's mind we knew that there was more to the story," Brunner recalled. "To begin with, this was obviously someone who had a life and it was not that of a fourteen-year-old girl in her bedroom. It was clear to me this was somebody who had some kind of academic background and I was trying to get a sense of what that was."

But Dark gave up nothing and Brunner the intern was too green an interviewer, too reticent to push. "Now I'm sure I'd be a lot more aggressive about getting to the bottom of it," he said six years later, then on staff at *Entertainment Weekly*. "But it wasn't presented to me as a mystery that I needed to solve. It was pre-sented as a cool fanzine that I was to write about. And I didn't want to make waves."

Brunner shared his suspicions with McDonnell but not with the readers of the *Village Voice*. His story appeared July 9, 1996, headlined "Guilty Pleasures":

A self-described proponent of "confabulated low-brow eclecti-cism," Jane Dark has for the past two years compiled a synopsis of her year in rock. Yes, *Sugar High* is Xeroxed and stapled, but it also has the ubiquitous Liv Tyler on the front and argues the mer-its of Roxette versus Ace of Base. The circulation is miniscule: this year Jane sent out 40 copies. But Sugar High's dead-on popcult observations make it worth tracking down.

Dark loves high/mass culture juxtapositions, weaving Noam

Chomsky, John Ashbery, and Walter Benjamin into discussions of the relationship between "pop" (she's irritated by rock-crit usage of "pop" as a musical, rather than a market description) and why Pearl Jam's greatness is possible only in the era of programmable CDs ("hence the awe-inspiring dunderheadedness of the band's fetishizing of vinyl at every opportunity," she writes).

Not that Dark is in the dark when it comes to underground music, as passing references to Coldie, Tricky, and Slint prove. But she prefers Trisha Yearwood, Paula Abdul, and Janet Jackson. "With cutting edge music you get a good idea of someone's individual, quirky vision," she says on the phone from her Berkeley, California, home, "but it doesn't tell me anything about the world."

Of course, that could just be an excuse. "Maybe I've built up this theoretical scaffold so I cannot feel guilty about liking crap," she says. Maybe, but *Sugar High*'s elevation of pop music is more celebration than rationalization.

~

BEFORE TOO LONG, Jane Dark telephoned the *Voice* office in New York to accept the Macarena assignment. "I just left a message in my normal voice, maybe a little bit higher, but within my normal register. I did the assignment. And this is when everything started to surprise me. I'd written a few book reviews before then, for academic journals, under my name. And when you write book reviews for academic journals, they don't really edit you in the way that commercial publications do. I was stunned. They switch your *which* to *that* and often they do it wrong. And you say, 'Can you switch it back to *which* please?' And that's pretty much it. So I didn't know what editing meant. She said she was going to call back and edit me and I said okay. And I decided—I don't know how consciously—that I would be Jane."

A visiting friend helped further the ruse. "The phone call came and I knew it was going to be Evelyn and I said, 'Answer the phone, and then call out for me.' And so he answered the phone and said, 'Hold on, please,' and shouted, 'Jaaaay-neeee!!' And I picked up.

"I talked pretty much in my normal voice. I'd spoken to another friend, a novelist who has written for some magazines. He's queer and he's interested in social relationships of gender—transgender issues in particular. And he said, 'You know, just tell them your name is Jane and talk in your normal voice. It's the *Village Voice*. They're not going to gender-challenge you.' And I thought, *That's probably true.* So I did, and she didn't."

The low voice did not escape McDonnell, but her reaction to it was much like Brunner's. "We had already realized that whatever this person was doing, this is how they wanted it to be," she said. "So when I edited Jane, I was pretty sure it was a guy. I've known people in different stages of their gender evolution and usually the voice is pretty telltale. A lot of transsexuals have very male voices, especially if they're preop—so, you know, whatever. Her persona was there. I was premiering this writer. And I was focused on getting an interesting piece, which I think it was."

An excerpt from Jane Dark's writing debut, as it appeared in the *Village Voice*, August 1996:

Of course, pop culture is always about wanting the incorporeal; voice on the radio, flicker on the TV. Given this, dance crazes are hyperpop, because they drag this sad, electric desire out of the bedrooms and into the streets. They get meaning from the massive number of busy bodies gathered together (it's only a phenomenon if the numbers are phenomenal, and nothing exceeds like excess), but the bodies never, you know, get busy. It's a lonely business, this dance craze thing. When you do the Macarena you get all the partners you ever dreamed of, with only one catch: no touching. This was true of the Bus Stop and the Twist before it—and it is neatly matched by the current outburst of scheduled "YMCA" voguing at ballgames. But the formula is pure Hula Hoop: shake your love like James Brown, but only within a whirling circle of suburban plastic inviolability. And of course, exactly this mix of sexual insinuation and absolute denial explains the whole Regis and Kathie Lee thing.

FOR WHATEVER REASON, nearly a year passed before Jane Dark's byline appeared again in the *Village Voice*, "maybe because they didn't ask, maybe because I didn't know about pitching. Maybe because I didn't feel like pressing my Jane luck that much further."

Maybe. At almost the same time as the Macarena piece appeared, the *American Poetry Review* published four new poems by a poet named Joshua Clover. There was not likely to be much cross-over audience, but the accompanying author's note revealed that Clover, in addition to winning the 1996 Walt Whitman prize, was a staff writer for the pop zine *sugar high!*

Cute. Clover pushed his "Jane luck" far enough to join an e-mail circle of rock writers from around the country, a "world unto themselves. They're all freelancers. They orbit around a fairly important music critic named Chuck Eddy, who's now the music editor of the *Village Voice* but then was simply a contributor to a lot of places. After the *Village Voice* published the thing about *sugar high!* I got a bunch of requests from people whom I didn't know saying, *Here's a dollar for mailing.* (It had to be over ninety-three cents in stamps or money—that's the zine tradition.) And I sent copies out to all of them. Little did I know that half the people were in this orbiting underworld of amateur rock criticism, all surrounding Chuck Eddy. And they would send me letters. Frank Kogan was one of them. He put out a famous zine called *Why Music Sucks*, a really great zine in its time. There were like twenty-five people in the group, Don Allred, various people like that. So then this person knows that person and you e-mail this person, and so on.

"My sense of propriety is actually much greater than any of theirs—they were way more punk-rock-zine-y than I was, even though they didn't have zines for the most part. They were like, *Hey, you want Bob Christgau's e-mail address? Here it is!* I would never have done that. It was an interesting induction. And in my interactions, I was uniformly a girl. A couple of them seemed interested in that; a couple of them were indifferent."

Clover said that at one point Chuck Eddy himself "sent out a group dispatch about how he had encountered a bunch of good critics recently and they were all girls and this seemed like a thing that was going on."

THERE WERE TWO OTHER PRESUMED WOMEN in the circle besides Jane Dark. Sara Sherr was one of them, a youngish writer out of Philadelphia who, as girls are wont to do, pursued a separate e-mail friendship with Jane Dark "under the hypothesis," Clover was sure, "that I was a girl."

"This is the year I was living in Indiana," Clover recalled. "I knew no one there. I was lonely and I sat home and I e-mailed. Sara would ask me girl-bonding questions like, *What's your favorite kind of boot?* And I would be like, *Doc Martens* because that works for everyone and it was true. So I tried to answer everything honestly without ever giving away the Jane Game. There would be little things that clearly seemed like feminized gestures. *Oh, if you ever come to Philadelphia, we'll go drink kangaroos*, you know, some female-identified mixed drink. I don't know what a kangaroo is to this day."

Clover went on, "The funny thing is I didn't really try to propagate it. Periodically, I would send Chuck e-mails about baseball, which I'm quite interested in statistically even if I don't really care who wins or loses. He always responded. He never said, *What's a girl doing knowing batting averages from the Detroit Tigers in 1968?*"

Sherr simply accepted at face value that Jane Dark was a woman. "With the Internet, you have to take a leap of faith," she said. "Everybody does a little bit of posing. You can reveal what you want to about yourself. You can say, *I'm a giraffe* and believe it as much as you can. That's what makes it interesting."

Indeed, as early as 1995, MIT professor Sherry Turkle had already written expansively about human interface with computers, especially the way the Internet had provided a variety of new ways for people to project their ideas and fantasies, enabling them to create an endless numbers of different personas who are deliberate about leaping over the "RL"—real-life—boundaries of race, ethnicity, class, sexuality, and gender.

Turkle's book, *Life on the Screen: Identity in the Age of the Internet*, describes in detail the ways this "culture of simulation" affects us as well as the larger cultural context that makes the effect possible. From advanced scientific fields of research to the patterns of everyday life, she writes, the boundaries between the real and the virtual and the animate and the inanimate are eroding, as are the boundaries between "the unitary and the multiple self." In her research, Turkle interviewed, encountered, and posed as an array of fluid, shape-shifting characters in the machine-generated world of cyberspace, limited only by the powers of imagination. (It can get this complex: A man who introduces himself in cyberspace as a woman who is a lesbian posing as straight and frigid). Whether such encounters take place in chat rooms or netsex encounters, on listservs or in e-mail exchanges, or in those elaborate fantasy-game constructs, they can change one's relationship to one's own identity. What people hope, Turkle writes, is that the encounters "will change their ways of thinking or will affect their social and emotional lives." Both on the Internet and on the printed page, Jane Dark served this function for Joshua Clover as well as for those who encountered Jane Dark by way of her published writing or her e-mail exchanges, not to mention her disembodied voice over the telephone.

Rhetorically, Turkle asks, "Is it an expression of an identity crisis of the sort we traditionally associate with adolescence? Or are we watching the slow emergence of a new, more multiple style of thinking about the mind?"

~

AND WHAT OF A "new more multiple style of thinking" about the body? It is a side trip worth taking, especially now that the subject is being offered for popular perusal through such vehicles as Jane Anderson's 2003 television movie *Normal*, about a husband of twenty-five years who decides to become a woman, and novelist Amy Bloom's 2002 work of nonfiction, *Normal: Transsexual CEOs, Cross-dressing Cops* and *Hermaphrodites with Attitude*. I happened on a short essay on the website of Forge, which bills itself as a social support group for "female-to-male transsexuals and transgenderists, butches, drag kings; gender queers and radicals; gender outlaws; people assigned female at birth, raised girl-Ý woman with fairly unambiguous female bodies at some point in their lives with masculine self-identification." The essay, titled "Not Passing at the Pool," described the agony of one Jay Allen Sennett at a public swimming pool before taking off a T-shirt worn to hide an ample bosom. Off came the shirt in trepidation, but to Sennett's relief, surprise, and amusement, no one at poolside seemed to react or care.

Sennett, it turns out, is an independent filmmaker from Ypsilanti, Michigan, who was born female, came out as a lesbian in the mid-1980s, and then came out again as a man about a decade later, still with "a body that would be read as female."

In the beginning of the transition to male, Sennett made a serious effort to pass as male, accepting, as most people do, the idea that gender is fixed and immutable, that it resides in the body. "So I sort of leaped into that and started hormones in 1996 to lower my voice, to grow facial hair, to have the features of masculinity," Sennett recalled. "And it became apparent to me that passing was not acceptable for me. In that realm, born in one kind of body wanting to be in another kind of body, passing felt like a test that I was doomed to fail."

Sennett spent the ensuing years "claiming that space of being a man without reference to my body. I say I am a man with a past as a woman. I'm still taking hormones because I think some of the changes that would happen if I stopped I wouldn't be comfortable with. I would probably have some redistribution of body mass. I think it would make me look androgynous." In clothing, Sennett looks so unambiguously male that even in the old prehormone lesbian days, people invariably would react to Sennett's genetic disclosure with amazement. "Oh, no, you're not!" has been the usual response.

Psychiatrists likely would use the classification transsexual to describe Sennett, a label this self-proclaimed male adamantly rejects, along with the entire therapeutic process. "I don't agree with it and I don't need a medical model," was Sennett's rejoinder. The "psychotherapeutic medical system" is useless to Sennett because it is as deeply invested in the idea that there are only two genders and two ways to claim them as the society that spawned it.

The way Sennett lives is not passing in the way that a gay person might pass for straight or a Jewish person might pass for Gentile, or even in the more whimsically adventurous way Joshua Clover fashioned himself into Jane Dark. "That assumes, to some degree, that one is acting like what one is not," Sennett said. "In my case, and other men and women such as myself, we are acting as we are."

Members of the transgendered community can interpret their own situations as they will, Sennett said, but "I am not passing. This is who I am. I haven't had top surgery. I think I have big breasts for a guy. Trans isn't an option for me at this point, though I can claim it because the system of gender is so inculcated in all of us—including me. We are so rooted in the idea of naturalness that there's very little room for the idea or the fact of people like myself, of women becoming men. In the general audience, the idea of a transsexual is a man becoming a woman. So when I claim that space, people say, *No you're not.* I realized that this institution [the male-female either-or] was greater than any choice that I could make."

What term is appropriate to describe Sennett? Interestingly, Sennett's own clear preference is heterosexual. With a bisexual girlfriend, Sennett feels perfectly comfortable advocating for the rights of lesbians, bisexuals, gays, and the transgendered as half of what appears to be a very traditional couple. "I am a straight man," Sennett said. "Language is inadequate, especially language based on a binary [like male-female], an either-or." Where the dictionary might be working on three or four definitions of the word heterosexual, Sennett's personal lexicon lists up to eleven or twelve.

"As for me saying I'm a man with a past as a woman, my theoretical framework is very radical," said Sennett. "I don't think I was born in the wrong body. I'm inhabiting manhood from the inside out rather than from the outside in."

Clover, for one, saw Sennett's self-explanation as "a kind of acting out of Judith Butler's book, *Gender Trouble*," considered a founding text in what is known as queer theory, a book that, in the author's words, "sought to uncover the ways in which the very thinking of what is possible in gendered life is foreclosed by habitual and violent presumptions."

SARA SHERR FOUND INHABITING the rock critics' e-mail circle particularly enjoyable because she had such admiration for the work of the people who were in it, the kind that embraces a personal, emotional response to the music. From members of the group, she learned that "talking about your life can reveal a lot about the music or the artist or the effect that the music has on the audience." Still, as a woman in a male-dominated field in a male-dominated e-mail circle, the feeling of being an outsider never quite went away.

"So I was getting to know interesting people and here comes Jane Dark—another girl," Sherr recalled. "I thought it was cool to see another girl and I thought she was older and worldly—not old enough to be my mother or anything—I was like twenty-six or twenty-seven—but I'm guessing she was in her mid-thirties at that point. I'm not sure of her age anymore. She'd lived in all these interesting places and she was into all kinds of music and had really funny stories and a really great point of view and she also could be very academic, too. She sort of played both sides, you know, be a fan and be an [intellectual]. I was intimidated by her intelligence a lot, but then it also kept me on my toes."

Sherr said Jane Dark often mentioned hanging out with friends, although she never elaborated on the kinds of relationships Jane Dark had with these friends, and she never talked about her love life. "But then," said Sherr, "I didn't really ask."

"It was funny," Sherr said. "In my head, I was thinking of the cartoon *Daria* on MTV. Daria had a best friend named Jane Lane. So I'd picture Jane Dark—you know, when you're talking to someone over e-mail and you don't get to meet them, you picture them in your head—so I pictured her in my head as Jane Lane on *Daria*. Very smart. The smart best friend." At one point, Sherr remembers that one or two of the guys on the list had developed crushes on Jane Dark and devoted not a little sidebar e-mail traffic to trying to figure out what she looked like.

~

In hindsight, it is difficult to determine just how central was Clover's pose as a woman named Jane Dark to his coming success in the world of rock music writers. Would the opportunity to write professionally have come to him if he had positioned *sugar high!* as the work of a man? "That's a good question to which I think I will never know the answer," he said. "There were certainly some responses like that." To this day, it strikes him as a remarkable piece of luck that Evelyn McDonnell of *resister* was also Evelyn McDonnell of the *Village Voice*. But he thinks he might have engaged her enthusiasm anyway if he had presented himself as male, that his work was strong enough to attract serious attention even without the lip gloss pose. "If I had known I could write a piece in my own name, send it to an editor and say, *Here's my work. What do you think?* And that they would read it and say, *Sheesh! Here's someone who knows how to write as opposed to someone who really, really loves Band X*—they're dying for that—I could have probably done it all quicker."

But creating Jane Dark also enabled him to develop a very distinctive new voice in a male-dominated field, and what pulled in the attention of the cognoscenti was that smart, sassy tone with the name Jane Dark attached to it.

～

EVELYN MCDONNELL DIDN'T STAY LONG in the *Voice* job, moving on by the end of 1996. Eric Weisbard was her permanent replacement, arriving from *Spin* soon after the new year began. McDonnell chatted with Weisbard about the various writers she had worked with, and in that context she mentioned Jane Dark as one the most promising of those Weisbard didn't already know.

The *Voice* is well-known for its music criticism and Weisbard was immediately on the lookout for new voices, not just those with the ability to assess a piece of music competently, but those with a real critical edge, those whose writing demonstrates that there is a mind at work, writers who can "expand our body of thought on culture, let's say."

He no longer remembers what actually prompted him to offer

Jane Dark an assignment to write about U2's new album, *Pop*. Maybe he had seen the latest copy of *sugar high!* He might have read Jane Dark's work in another zine. Maybe it was the past summer's "Macarena" piece or McDonnell's steer. He certainly was not opposed to bringing more women music writers to the paper and Jane Dark's approach to writing about pop music was fresh, "not with an attitude of disdain, but with an intellectual take on it, and that might be the reason I suggested U2." On top of that, Weisbard found it rather exotic to be telephoning someone he didn't know in Indiana.

Jane Dark turned in her copy and the editing went much as it had gone with McDonnell for the "Macarena" piece. The big difference was that Weisbard didn't skirt the gender question.

"He's Eric Rude, which is one of his charms," Clover said. "He asked me if I was a man. I said, 'Nope.' There were many evasions, many parsings of sentences. But that was the clear, direct lie."

Weisbard acknowledged his tactlessness. *Are you a man?* Or, *Are you not a woman?* "One way or the other, I can't remember which way I asked it," he said. "But he flat-out lied."

This was the point at which the Jane Game impinged piercingly on Clover's sense of honor. "It felt awful," he said. "It didn't have much of a feeling of getting away with something, which is a main concern of lies, especially when you're a kid and you're doing bad stuff. Actually, I didn't feel morally problematic in the slightest about passing myself off as a woman. But I still feel morally problematic about lying in and of itself. I don't believe in it. I don't do it much. I imagine most people fancy themselves honest. So do I. Extremely so. So I felt lousy about that."

IN PERSON, Joshua Clover is Olive Oyl tall and Olive Oyl thin. He seems to favor form-fitting knit shirts that enunciate the elongation of his slight physique. Favored accessories are jaunty red bandannas and a delicate little dangly pierced earring worn in the lobe of each ear. His hair is prematurely white. In a room full of strange but savvy new company, everyone thought he was gay. Told that he already had privately volunteered that he was not, no one believed it.

"To be forthcoming is one thing," he had offered at the point at which he matter-of-factly disclosed that he was straight. "I don't think there's much of a call to volunteer information unless you're trying to enter into a relationship with someone which involves the volunteering of information," like, for example, the relationship between interviewer and willing interview subject. "But I do think you owe the truth to anybody who asks."

"If I were writing your book, I would need to know urgently if I were gay or straight. It bears on the subject. I would argue that it is an important part of trying to assemble my psychological experience in doing this, and that my psychological experience would be part of what you're writing about. Could you compel me to answer? No, of course not. But would you want to know? Yes. Would you hope that I would tell the truth? Yes. Would I feel obligated to tell the truth? Yes. Would I be allowed to say *I'm not going to tell you*? Of course. But one of the reasons people owe each other the truth is that the more stuff you *know know*—instead of having to hedge around and not know, not talk about—the more fascinating the world gets." The question was put directly and again Clover said he was straight.

No fan of therapists, Clover talked over with his friends the remorse he felt over lying to Weisbard and they responded with reassurance. Why was he sweating this? Were jobs or lives being lost because Joshua Clover lied to Eric Weisbard about his gender? Had calling himself Jane Dark in print done anyone any harm? They really didn't think there was anything for him to get worked up over, least of all a lie to someone who asked an awfully rude question.

Anthony Appiah had an opinion about Jane Dark's lie as well. "I have some sympathy with the person who doesn't just say, *You shouldn't have asked me that.* That usually gives it away. I have some sympathy with the person who just says to himself, *I don't have to tell you the truth*, but out loud says, 'No.'

"Everyone has some point at which they think that, all things considered, it's not that in those circumstances lying isn't wrong, it's just that telling the truth would be so much worse. *I am the SS. Do you have any Jews in your cellar?* Does anyone think the right answer is yes, if it's true?" Appiah went on, "But I do think there is a separate issue with identity questions. If you are asked directly to reveal your deepest sense of who you are, it's particularly difficult not to tell the truth. This is especially true in the free world, in the modern world, because we have this idea that you have the right to express your identity in the social world. And that's one of the things that's wrong with situations that force people to pass."

~

JANE DARK'S REVIEW of the U2 album appeared in the *Voice* on March 11, 1997, just as trade reviews of Joshua Clover's first book of poetry, *Madonna Anno Domini*, began to circulate. "Reading this collection," said the reviewer in *Publishers Weekly*, "is akin to channel-surfing a possessed television on which CNN shows horror films and Court TV embraces magical realism."

A poem from Clover's Whitman Prize–winning book:

Orchid

Seen in the south of that country's south, near the wavefront of total
war: indolent orchid, windowbox auto-da-fe, the year's acedia. The
flower was not about anything & nobody in the house to watch—not
the simplest thing, 12 hours of sun, summer's cool closure. I see you are
curious so let me tell you it was not a museum but a house. Flower in
the flowerbox, ear in the air's cyan arc, mantic green wire. Almost fall
& cool between the mountains & the master war—walking, walking . . .
Because I am not history I can return "at will" to the house like a
museum—the clothed idea of it, each of us passing, minds delinquent
panic-bulbs, the flower about nothing (we were not attached to the
beginning or to the end, diving nothing, the autumn out there beyond
the museum-house still we could not come to the boundary of the funny
war, secret heliotropes, orchid in the orchid box, God in abeyance—

—JOSHUA CLOVER

Two months later, May 5, 1997, Joshua Clover flew to New
York City from South Bend for the annual dinner of the Academy
of American poets at the J. Pierpont Morgan Library. There he
accepted the Walt Whitman Prize from John Ashbery, who was
standing in for Jorie Graham. Graham had written the citation
praising Clover's manuscript as "a poetic manifesto—as well as a
prayer book—for the millennial generation" and Clover himself as
"a physicist of syllables, a mesmerizing singer of near-apocalyptic
lullabies, a rememberer, a forgetter, a reinventer, a destroyer—a
philosopher of disappearances, an architect of mutabilities—this
poet actually sees the new world we are emerging into—from the
fission of subatomic matter to its cataclysmic effects on the
deserts of both our planet and our inner lives."

For Clover, such praise was monumentally gratifying, a cause for elation, but the event itself, he said, "creeped me out." Famous people intimidate him, so his reaction during the evening was to hide from Adrienne Rich and Charles Wright, who were seated with him, and turn his attention toward two youngish people also at the table, with whom he felt more comfortable. One, he recalled, was Robert Polito, a novelist and New School professor whose work Clover admired, and the other was a woman novelist. "And somehow we got to talking about music—probably because I was wearing my Hole T-shirt. Hole is one of my favorite bands. And this was notable because most poets don't show up to these fancy dinners wearing Hole T-shirts. But I was doing my thing, being Rock Boy."

Polito mentioned that he had recently completed a long Bob Dylan review, and then Rock Boy let drop that he too wrote music reviews. As soon as the words came out of his mouth, he realized he was not going to be able to back them up. "There are no music reviews by Joshua Clover in the universe," he said. "So I quickly hedged. I was like, *Well, I do it under a false name.* I didn't say what the name was or that it was a woman or anything like that.

"And I didn't know how tight the world was, how interconnected. It didn't occur to me that any of these people might *know* someone who worked at the *Village Voice*. But of course everyone knows everyone. New York, the writing, the literary journals; they're all interconnected." In fact, the woman novelist, René Steinke, turned out to be the fiancée of Craig Marks, the executive editor of *Spin*, the magazine Weisbard had so recently left.

"The Hole T-shirt must have been the giveaway," Clover surmised, "because I had an ex-girlfriend who had been in the band Hole but isn't anymore. And Craig Marks used to go out with Courtney Love, who's the head of Hole. There were too many chains, too much evidence."

Weisbard said the real tip-off was Clover's mentioning the U2 review to Steinke. After the evening she happened to say something to Weisbard and his partner, the same Ann Powers who coedited *Rock She Wrote* with Evelyn McDonnell, about the prize-winning poet who writes rock criticism whom she had met at the academy dinner. "And so," Weisbard said, "We were like, *All right! Ha! So he's busted!*"

⇛

WEISBARD COULDN'T WAIT to telephone Jane Dark. "Look," he said, "I've got to ask you. Are you a poet named Joshua Clover?"

And Clover didn't hesitate to reply. "What could I say? I said, 'Yes, I am.' And I apologized profusely. I felt awful about it." Weisbard was not sure why. He saw no need for an apology and couldn't quite fathom Clover's remorse. "He didn't get it at all," Clover said. "And I was like, *Well, because I lied to you. You're the one I lied to.* And he's like, *No big deal* and immediately offered me another assignment." If the roles had been reversed, if Weisbard was the one writing as Jane Dark and lied to Clover about who he was, Clover said he never would have spoken to the man again. "I had lied to him about *who I am*," Clover said. "But when I tell him the truth about who I am, it doesn't matter. I like to drive tanks down Main Street and he doesn't care as long as I deliver good copy for his section."

Naturally, Weisbard prefers writers to refrain from lying to him, "and it can be a real problem if, say, they say they're going to turn in a piece and they don't turn it in. That's the kind of lying that actually could rupture a relationship." He certainly would not be sanguine with a writer who turned out to be impersonating an actual individual. Equally unforgivable would be a writer who passed off the work of another writer as his or her own, the kinds of plagiaristic accusations that all writers dread.

And what of pseudonyms with undisclosed identities behind them? "I don't really care if the person is using an invented name," Weisbard said. "It didn't bug me." There have been pen names as long as there has been a world of letters and the identities behind the pen names have been kept secret as often as not. In pop culture, Weisbard mentioned punk rocker Richard Hell, who has the pen name Theresa Sanders, and the work of the pop fabulist Camden Joy, real name Tom Adelman, who has adopted writing personas such as a duty nurse or a fifty-year-old heroin addict. Shades of the female-to-male Georges, Elliot and Sand, and, to name just one other, Fernando Pessoa, the Portuguese poet who wrote not in pseudonyms but in heteronyms. His oeuvre contains prodigious work in his own name and in the names of three imaginary poets with distinct styles of poetry.

And what about the gender-crossing? "Gender-fuck is so inbred in popular culture that a certain fluidity already applies," Weisbard said. "In the contemporary age, you don't challenge a person saying they're male or female. People have a right to claim whatever gender identity they want to claim. You just learn not to make assumptions about people, but when in doubt, you go with the assumptions they make about themselves."

The name Jane Dark, he said, reminded him of a character in Thomas Pynchon's work, and Pynchon is one of Clover's favorite writers. "I think there's a certain way that the name Jane Dark positioned Joshua as a character and maybe gave him access to a writing voice that his own name wouldn't necessarily have given him access to."

An upside to the disclosure that Jane Dark was Joshua Clover was that Clover turned out to be so intriguing. As someone with "a developed intellectual life," he inspired more confidence in Weisbard as his editor. There is a huge difference, Weisbard explained, between a poet moonlighting as a fanzine writer and a big-time professional rock critic. Weisbard's editorial involvement with Jane Dark's transition into the world of professional music writing "started, in a way, with the discovery of who he was. There was a basis," Weisbard said. "It was worth pursuing."

"In the end," he said, "It didn't really matter what he was or how he portrayed himself. The lie just didn't feel personal. I had put him on the spot by asking him in the first conversation, before we hardly had any relationship, *What's the deal here?* He had lied. Fine. It just didn't matter that much to me. From the perspective of an editor presenting words in print to readers, who also don't know anything about the person, the only question is, *Can this person write in a marked prose voice?*"

FROM WEISBARD'S PERSPECTIVE, Joshua Clover's gender swapping is far less intriguing than the ability he exhibits to shift back and forth between the disparate roles of obscure experimental poet and mainstream pop music critic. "If you look at the comments that are made about his poetry," Weisbard went on, "it's like, *Welcome to the next poetry.* Here is 'a mesmerizing singer of near apocalyptic lullabies.' That quality which gives an aura under his own name and under his own wacky photograph is not so different from what he's doing in his music writing."

Clover is someone Weisbard sees as truly well versed in high culture and low culture, "a master of the high–low divide." And that divide is far more important than the gender divide to understanding Clover's work as a poet and as a music critic. "It's really the heart of his writing," in Weisbard's view.

With the many other divides Clover has been agile at crossing, the "gender thing," Weisbard said, "only takes it further. He likes being somebody who's both really into hardcore hip-hop and has a path that includes having been a Dead Head. There are like six or seven categories of music that he tries to maintain a position in—country music—fairly mainstream country music; a certain type of female singer/songwriter like Amy Mann and Tori Amos; dance music, hip-hop."

Lots of people cross gender lines, and that in itself does not make a writer interesting. "The fact that Jane Dark was a prize-winning poet," Weisbard said, "*that* was interesting. That was more interesting than the simple fact that Jane Dark was actually a man."

But didn't the revelation also mean the loss to *Voice* readers of a distinctive critical voice that happened to belong to a woman? "Well," said Weisbard, "if you wanted to be really cynical, I suppose you could say it wasn't completely lost so long as he was writing under the name Jane Dark in the *Village Voice.*"

Listserv commenter on the work of a woman rock critic:
Plus it's catty in a way that only a female could pull off.
Response from Frank Kogan: Have you ever read Jane Dark?

In Sherry Turkle's words, censuring deviation was a lot easier back in the days when we thought about identities as unitary, solid, and easy to recognize. Our acceptance of the concept of "a more fluid sense of self . . . makes it easier to accept the array of our (and others') inconsistent personae—perhaps with humor, perhaps with irony. We do not feel compelled to rank or judge the elements of our multiplicity. We do not feel compelled to exclude what does not fit in."

Once Clover had admitted that he was Jane Dark, Weisbard asked him what he wanted to do about the byline, and Clover responded, "I'll stay Jane Dark."

∿

AS THE YEARS PASSED Jane Dark continued to write rock criticism for the *Voice. sugar high!* became a column carried by the Minneapolis *City Pages* and then by other freaklies, including the *Voice.* Chuck Eddy replaced Eric Weisbard as *Voice* music editor, and at about the same time, Joshua Clover simultaneously started writing book reviews for the *Voice Literary Supplement* under the name Joshua Clover. ("If I could do book reviews under the name Jane Dark, I absolutely would. But that would be wrong. I publish books and you can't seem to be hiding from a response to your criticism.") He also started writing under regular contract for *Spin* until he quit in 2001 to move to Paris. At first, his reviews in *Spin* appeared under the Jane Dark franchise, but, against his better judgment and at the editor's urging, Jane switched from one week to the next to Joshua Clover. (He might have to deal with artists and the people at record labels, the editor told him, "and you can't walk into someone's office and say, *Hi! My name's Jane!* Look at you!") A few readers noticed and wondered in letters to the editor what had become of Jane Dark. Other than that, there was little reaction.

Back at the *Voice,* Jane Dark and Joshua Clover coexist peacefully, though Jane Dark has been known to sound off in a letter to the editor about matters such as the ad placement next to a Joshua Clover book review, and there was the time around the

Columbine shooting when Clover got incensed over the *Voice* cover story on the subject, objecting vehemently to its take on the cultural significance of the Colorado rampage. He opposed positioning geeky but still very privileged white, middle-class teenage boys as "the next hot marginalized community" and thought the *Voice* should give forum to another point of view.

"I found this outrageous," Clover said. "I still do. I mean I think that it sucks to be a high school nerd who is picked on. I myself was in that position in junior high school. By high school I had gone on to a special school for geeks. So I wasn't unsympathetic to how unpleasant it is to get picked on, not unsympathetic at all. But the comparisons that were being made, I found invidious. I don't imagine that I'll ever get close to getting everything I want out of my life. But as an educated, middle-class, white male, I have access to everything I could possibly desire. So did those kids. And the attempt for them to take over the discourse of the marginalized struck me as a political tragedy. I found it painful. Not just ironic—straight, white, middle-class males demanding equal rights—but gross. And that's what I said." And the byline he signed to the commentary? Jane Dark.

"I was aware that it would vex the Jane issue more than usual," he said. "And at this point everyone at the *Voice* had known I was Joshua Clover for two years." The piece precipitated more mail than any of his rock pieces or book reviews had ever garnered. It even held the reader-response record at the *Voice* for a time. And many of the letters to the editor about his piece, he said, were "notably gender-marked. A bunch of them started out, *You bitch!*"

In May 1997, about a year and a half after Jane Dark's creation, news of the ruse ripped through the rock critic community at the speed of a splitting seam. It caused only a blip of interest and some curiosity, but no one seemed to care very much. Clover heard secondhand that some people in rock critic circles were miffed that he had passed himself off as a woman, that he had somehow taken advantage of "an unspoken affirmative action." "I'm certain there were people who felt like it was weird, and maybe not okay," Clover said. "But no one's told me about it that much."

At the time, he said, a lot of people seemed to want to know if he was gay or straight "and perhaps I was being overly analytic or curious, but I started to wonder about it myself. It became sort of an issue." As to his comfort as a straight man with inhabiting a woman's identity, even if only in print, he did not think this was the least bit noteworthy, then or now. "That's the part I just don't get," he said. "You spend a year in Indiana and you're reminded that it's an issue, but mostly it doesn't even occur to me. I was born in Berkeley."

Sara Sherr stopped e-mailing Jane Dark, as did other members of the rock critic's e-mail circle. "Once the game was given away," Clover said, "I didn't get any responses from that group. And I suspect it's because they felt like they'd been taken and didn't want to be in that position with me. This is a guess. Let's say if they were annoyed that I'd done that, it was more worth it to them simply not to mention it."

Actually, Sherr said, she was so convinced that Jane Dark was a woman that when she was told otherwise, she thought it was a joke. "Like did they mean she was really butchy? Did she have a lot of facial hair or something?" Later on, she noticed in *Spin* that Jane Dark started writing for the magazine and then disappeared and a Joshua Clover started appearing in her stead. And then it became known that Jane Dark and Joshua Clover were one and the same. "I didn't feel betrayed or anything," she said. "There are times when I wish I wasn't writing as a woman—where I could just play around with my gender and my writing and have people judge my writing based on the writing itself, not who it is coming from. I felt amused. And I kind of admired her. I say *her* because that's who I thought of her as. I admired her for pulling one over on everyone."

After the Jane Game was over, Joshua Clover continued to use the byline Jane Dark, and continues to do so, but his sense of Jane as "an autonomous writer, a thinker, an individual, ended and ended immediately.

"At some level my imagination of Jane involved Jane as perceived by the world," the world, in this case, being the world of rock music insiders. "The basic rule you learn in the introduction to sociology is, as I recall, *I am who I think you think I am.* It was a magic bubble based on a set of fantasies and mistruths. And as soon as one thing popped, it was popped. That was that."

The loss of the autonomous Jane paralleled his development as a professional writer of music criticism for commercial venues. "The need to cut out extraneous and even particularly stylized stuff is often pressing," he said. "And a lot of Jane was stylized, extraneous personality stuff. So that sort of fell by the wayside, and I ended up sounding more like myself, like Joshua when he's ranting about music. The narrative autonomy was really over, and this was the beginning of the sorrowful phase of my journalism career which continues to this day."

For Clover, the idea of "the reader," an audience for his work, a public, beyond the editor who assigned the piece and the copy editor who processes it, remains an abstraction. "I would hardly deny that I'm rhetorical," Clover said. "I want to persuade people of things urgently. But I don't make much of a distinction between persuading three people and persuading fifty thousand people." It had not really occurred to him nor did he think it mattered that to the average *Voice* reader, Jane Dark to this day is still just Jane Dark.

More compelling to him than the notion of an audience beyond his editors was the still startling fact that someone actually was willing to pay him to write about pop music, that what started out as whim, as a lark, actually could provide him with professional outlets for his thoughts and opinions about music and income to boot. As opportunities in the world of music writing piled up, it wasn't long before he started to see Jane Dark as his money gig. "This is what I learned from Jane, and moreover from poetry," he said, "that these larks become our lives."

"In the end, I don't think I'm officially guilty because I never meant to get away with anything," he said. "But just the fact that some people think I did makes me feel lousy."

JOSHUA CLOVER HAD TO BE CONVINCED that his Jane Game actually qualified as passing because his story felt so frivolous. He associates passing with necessity, with the dire. In the jargon du jour, the word *passing* evokes for him the desperation of the "marginalized" in their pursuit of well-being. If it's passing, it ought to be for safety, survival, or justice. Passers flee the slave master or the Nazis, like the Jewish mother of the writer Helen Fremont, who dressed herself up as a young male Italian soldier to escape Nazi Poland, crossing Europe to get to Italy. Once safely in the United States, she and her Jewish husband immediately reinvented themselves as Catholics, never sharing their past with their children. Fremont and her sister only ferreted out these facts as adults, literally acting as sleuths against their parents' wishes, an experience she recounts movingly in her book, *After Long Silence*.

Equally in keeping with this notion of passing are the decisions of Joel Alter and the navy Careerist. They passed to sate reasonable, even urgent vocational ambitions, to pursue earnest goals that two formidable institutions unjustly put off-limits. No less worthy are the actions of David Matthews and Vivian Sanchez, whose passing sought to slip under the otherwise impenetrable walls of prejudice and preconception. As sexual, racial, and or ethnic minorities, all of these people passed to elude danger or discrimination or to find welcome where they never should have been barred in the first place. In every case the exclusion they would have faced had they come clean about their personal stories—and the exclusion the young teacher did in fact experience when she revealed that she was not black—is simply not supportable, at least not in our time.

Clover had no such difficulties. "I am neither marginalized nor oppressed," he said. "I have access to anything a middle-class, white, articulate, educated male could get, which is the world." He mentions more than once his discomfort with the amount of "social power" life has dealt him, a power he says, "I don't like having and I don't want." (His smile is a rather provocative testament to this. For a white, middle-class child of professional American parents, he has remarkably crooked teeth.) In fact, one of Clover's struggles in creating Jane Dark was whether he had inadvertently crossed a line he should not have crossed. By forfeiting the power afforded him by the name and intellectual and artistic standing of Joshua Clover, by adopting his girly teenage pose, had he somehow misused the meager recognition women rock writers had just begun to gain for themselves? "That's a tough one," he said. "And clearly, that was one of the things I was trying to puzzle out during the whole episode."

Passing is not always about desperation and safety, although those still are the stories that tear at our hearts. But there is no question that the Jane Game is passing too, what I call a kind of good-guy adventuring. It is distinct from the adventuring of con artists and hucksters, like the real-life adolescent poseur and larcenist Frank W. Abagnale, portrayed by Leonardo di Caprio in *Catch Me If You Can*. Such characters are beyond the scope of this book because of the harm their actions cause to others. They share with the good guys the fact that they pass for curiosity or kicks, experimentation or thrill, but the good guys never swindle or imperil the innocent. Their actions are never nefarious. Some may be undercover operatives, passing for the sake of investigation, infiltration, discovery or exposé, and there is room for argument in some other forum on which side of this divide to put the spies and private eyes. Adventure passers in the good-guy column can include investigative journalists and undercover law enforcers exposing wrongdoing. And whatever the impetus for the behavior, adventures in passing may or may not turn out to be a source of conflict for passers or for those who encounter their stories later on or along the way.

Barbara Ehrenreich's recent expedition into a number of minimum-wage jobs for her book *Nickled and Dimed* illustrates this kind of passing, as does Ted Conover's turn as a prison guard for *Newjack: Guarding Sing-Sing*. Both of these follow in the tradition of the classic white-for-black passing exposés *Black Like Me* and Grace Halsell's *Soul Sister,* or even George Orwell's earlier adventures in class passing in *Down and Out in Paris and London.* Like Joshua Clover, these authors found themselves engaged in an extended exploration of their own "fluidity" or lack of it, even when this was not their primary purpose. The Tramp Major bellows, "Shut yer mouth!" when Orwell makes what he thinks is a natural request to wipe out a grotesquely filthy tub before he bathes in it. Griffin looks at his newly blackened face in the mirror and back stares a fierce-looking stranger. Conover realizes what the prison experience has done to him when he responds for the first time at home to his son's misbehavior with harsh words and a spank. As a waitress working for tips and minimum wage, Ehrenreich begins to see her writerly self as coming from a "distant race of people with exotic concerns and far too much time on their hands." In the act of posing as other than who they understood themselves to be, the authors run smack into themselves. In our own reactions to their reactions, we learn something about who we are as well.

~

ANOTHER THING that sets Clover's story apart from the other five main stories in this book is the way the *Village Voice* responded to his case as an institution, and Jane Dark's fellow rock music critics as a community. At least on the subject of personal gender definition, both appear to be uncommonly free of prejudice and preconception. And once again, if there is no prejudice or preconception, the need to pass evaporates. The *Voice* and the community of rock critics in this sense represent a forward-looking stance, a kind of ideal in which there is no exclusion on the basis of irrelevant criteria, at least on this score. (In Clover's case, the irrelevant criteria are the bodily parts of a marked and noteworthy new prose voice that presented itself in a woman's name.) If David Matthews, the young teacher, or Vivian Sanchez had been outed the way Jane Dark was outed, all of them surely would have faced social ostracism. Jane Dark did not. Alter never would have been allowed to become a Conservative rabbi (even his compassionate dean would have had to adhere to policy, as Gordon Tucker had done before him), and the navy Careerist would have forfeited her retirement benefits. Clover faced no such consequences when his she turned out to be a he.

Believe it or not, this very modern, very evolved stance has an ancient precedent in the Bible, in the book of Esther. Ahasuerus, the Persian king ("Let beautiful young virgins be sought out for Your Majesty"), lavishes favors on Esther and chooses her to become his new queen once he has thrown out the old one. Esther takes the advice of her Uncle Mordecai and does not disclose to the king or any of his aides that she is a Jew, believing it will eliminate her from competition. She continues the ruse for quite some time, deciding never to disclose because Haman, the king's closest adviser, is anti-Semitic in his policies. At a certain point, however, she must step forward. Haman has issued an edict that puts every Jew in the land under threat of death and has a scaffold erected with a noose for Mordecai's neck. Mordecai implores Esther to intercede on his behalf and on behalf of all the Jews. She is their only hope. But she knows that by seeking the king's help in this way, she will reveal her deception. Still, she accepts her destiny and decides she has no choice but to take the risk, knowing full well it may mean her life.

"And if it pleases Your Majesty," she pleads, "let my life be granted me as my wish, and my people as my request. For we have been sold, my people and I, to be destroyed, massacred, and exterminated." Not only does Ahasuerus grant her plea but he orders Haman's execution by hanging on the scaffold built for Esther's uncle and then elevates Mordecai to Haman's powerful post.

Standing ovation to Esther. But what is more interesting in this connection is that at no point in the exchange between Ahasuerus and his queen does her deception come up. The king never calls her on it. Like *Voice* editor Eric Weisbard, he doesn't give a damn. Esther's decision to pass appears to be of no consequence to him. Did love conquer his anti-Semitism or was Esther's Jewishness irrelevant all along? Ahasuerus, it seems to me, had no particular interest in the Jews one way or the other. The authority he gave to Haman was not about the king's anti-Semitism; the king didn't seem to have any. He was just delegating authority in a general way to someone who did. Once the evil Haman was out of the way, out went the impact of an unjust policy, and with it the perceived need to pass.

~

E-MAIL FROM JOSHUA CLOVER in response to a question, June 8, 2001:

My father is indeed Jewish. My mother is Protestant, though both are pretty agnostic in their observances, and I was indeed originally named Kaplan. Did we cover this? Relevant to the topic at hand. There have been one or two suggestions that in changing my name, I was denying my Jewish heritage. I don't really believe this. It just occurred to me that I like my mom so much more than my dad that I would rather be identified thereto. And I also have always admired her early commitment to feminism, which led her to be among the earliest wave of divorcees recouping their maiden names.

CHAPTER SEVEN

Passing Notes,
Passing Tones

> Every profound spirit needs a mask; even more,
> around every profound spirit a mask grows continually,
> owing to the constantly false, namely *shallow*, interpretation
> of every word, every step, every sign of life he gives.
> —FRIEDRICH NIETZSCHE

IN THE SPRING OF 2003, David Matthews is working on a new screenplay, still waiting for his big break. The young teacher is happily married and close to completing her Ph.D. Vivian Sanchez and her fiancé plan to wed sometime in 2004 in a Jewish ceremony, not in a synagogue but in a banquet hall. She hopes to find a rabbi to officiate, one who performs mixed marriages. Joel Alter is getting ready to start a new job, a promotion, as director of Judaic studies at a new Jewish high school in Baltimore. He is also gearing up to engage—openly this time—with any renewed debate over the "gay issue." The navy Careerist is with a terrific new partner, still excelling in her work. And Joshua Clover and Jane Dark are still writing for the *Village Voice*. Clover also has seen fit to add various other bylines to his retinue of writing personas for other publications. The postpassing "state of grace" Erving Goffman described, indeed.

I found a formulation to describe passing that adds significantly to *Webster's* "to gain acceptance as a member of a group by
assuming an identity with it in denial of one's ancestry, background," or even my own "presenting oneself as other than who
one understands oneself to be." It was in the dictionary, a page or
so beyond the full column devoted to the word pass itself, as the
entry for the musical term passing note or passing tone. A passing
note is not part of a composition's harmonic scheme, but one the
composer introduces to ornament the work or allow for a
smoother transition from one tone or chord to another. Passing, I
think, can also be described as a kind of human ornamentation or
embellishment, an elaboration on a life story. Like a passing note,
it is sometimes a dissonant interjection against the prevailing har-
mony, but one with the purpose of smoothing a path of transition
to a new and desired position or location. With people, the idea
of a dissonant smoothing for a path of transition applies to both
the passers and the institutions, environments, or social settings
whose unjust exclusionary practices the passers seek to avoid.

Dissonant, remember, is not necessarily a pejorative term, and
neither is passing. As an action, it might be dissonant, but that
doesn't make it bad. The military, with its "Don't Ask, Don't
Tell" policy, actually enforces the need to pass on the homosexuals in its ranks, so passers in that situation can hardly be criticized
for following orders. And yet in the cases we have examined
where passing was not so directly imposed, the decision to do so
does not seem more objectionable. Passing may not be considered an act of valor, but I think some of the passing stories in this
book have a courageous cast.

Yet passing often involves secrecy and deception. Helen Fremont, whose Jewish parents passed as Catholics, picked up the
parental pattern of secrecy in her own life, waiting years to reveal

herself to them as a lesbian. I spoke to her at length about her experience as a "passing survivor," about what it means to live with other people's secrets and lies and then with one's own. Had there been openness about the past, she told me, hers would have been a very different family. The energy it took to keep the secret has mightily affected all of their lives.

"When you have a secret," she said, "you have a wall between people. You have the people who are in on a secret and then you have the people who don't know the secret—whatever benevolent, altruistic reasons are in support of keeping that person outside. For my entire life, I grew up with a wall between my parents and me. I never knew who they were and I always knew that I was excluded. All that stuff has been subtle, but potent. You start feeling that even though these are people who love you and who would give their lives for you, something is not making sense. And that something not making sense is in the reflection they're giving me of who I am and what's important. It created barriers that are, I think, insurmountable, and that starts to make you feel crazy." Joel Alter spoke about the ordeal that living a double life during seminary was for him, as did Vivian Sanchez, as did the navy Careerist, who reflected on how the subterfuge in her professional life infected all of her relationships, even those in which she had plenty of latitude to be most truly herself.

HOW WRONG IS THE LIE that eliminates bigotry as an obstacle? Legal scholar Tobias Barrington Wolff best expressed the conundrum that passing to bypass injustice presents. "It is a means of navigating between norms of expectations, on the one hand, and desires, on the other," he said. "You pass in order to obtain that which you want in defiance of that which would deny it to you. The moral status of passing thus depends on two questions, first, the morality of the norms that you seek to circumvent and, second, the morality of engaging in deception, whatever the circumstances. When a repressive norm is unjust—a ban on interracial marriages, for example, crafted to enforce a racial hierarchy with roots in the slave system—is the moral response to defy it openly, and thereby open oneself to the danger of persecution, or to utilize passing as a means of circumventing and subverting the norm, thereby obtaining some personal benefit and, perhaps, contributing to the erosion of an unjust rule? Not a question with a simple answer."

Passing is commonly regarded as a way of perpetuating a problematic status quo because the passer, by slipping through an oppressive system, helps keep that system in place. On the occasion of her fortieth birthday, philosophy professor Claudia Mills thought expansively on the ethics of passing, from a starting point of whether she "owed" the information about her advancing age to anyone else and if so, to whom. Her conclusion was that outside of our most intimate relationships, none of us has any particular obligation to present a "true" self to anyone else. Her one exception was in the case of oppressed groups, who she thinks have a special obligation to work to fight oppression directly "rather than simply minimizing the costs to oneself" by passing.

I think that makes more sense in the abstract than it does for someone like Joel Alter living his one unrepeatable life. His situation during seminary makes the notion of passing as a form of social resistance more appealing. Even if Alter's initial motivation to pass was self-serving, a means of fulfilling personal ambitions, it also served the common good. Passing put Alter in a position to promote change from within an institution he loved and believed in. By passing throughout seminary and in the years following graduation, he gained the credentials he needed to operate in a position of authority within mainstream Conservative Jewish life. In his passing guise, he was able to bring an alternative perspective into an institution that would have barred him had he not successfully passed. His now disclosed (and hopefully grandfathered) gay presence, by its very nature, along with his accruing seniority within the Conservative rabbinate, has an impact on everyone in his religious sphere, especially if and when the Conservative movement reconsiders the injunctions that would have kept Alter from the work he does so well.

New York Times literary critic Anatole Broyard provides a similar illustration of passing's social benefit, but from the perspective of someone who did not disclose publicly during his lifetime. By passing, Broyard's intention was to subvert a culture that insisted on marking him as a brilliant *black* literary figure, rather than as a brilliant literary figure full stop. Passing enabled him to attain the unmarked stature he sought in the world of letters. That plus his talent allowed him to function from a position of power in ways that most likely would otherwise have been denied him. Passing allowed his unique set of gifts and sensibilities to come to widespread mainstream attention without the encumbrance of an identity that could easily have proved problematic had he revealed it. We can safely venture that Broyard was able to accomplish more cross-culturally in his lifetime by not widely disclosing his blackness than he would have if he had disclosed it. Now that we know, his career fully discredits color as a criterion for exclusion in his field. There was no need to view Broyard, an eminent literary critic, racially, just as there is no need to view any critic through the lens of his or her heritage or upbringing. Passing allowed him to transcend that limitation. In this way, he provided the institutions in which he functioned with a new way to think about qualifications for the job, even though the only apparent social agenda in Broyard's intent was to escape someone else's.

As a form of social action, passing is work reserved for the special team. Because of its very nature, it can never be a mass approach. And it is not for the impatient.

~

HOW MUCH OF WHAT WE THINK WE KNOW or are told about another person's identity do we need to be able to rely on? Passing with intent to break the law, to cause harm to other people, is unacceptable. But what if the law itself is the problem? Tobias Barrington Wolff's allusion to the *Loving v. Virginia* case is pertinent. Shortly before they were arrested, the Lovings were in effect passing as legally married in the state of Virginia under laws that codified oppressive social mores that the Supreme Court eventually invalidated. Doesn't it make you wonder which of the social mores that guide us now will eventually end up in the legal scrap yard alongside those old racial integrity laws? How long, for example, before the enforced passing imposed on gay men and women by the military's "Don't Ask, Don't Tell" policy, with its continuing impact on retirees like the navy Careerist, will be seen as embarrassingly wrongheaded?

Amid all this talk of acceptable shape-shifting and fluidity, there are times when we must be able to rely on fixed cultural identities, on how an individual represents him- or herself. In family court in New York City, Judge Jody Adams encounters these issues every day. As the law now stands, certain obligations defined by law, such as those involving marriage and reproduction, actually depend on gender identification (regrettable as that may be, she said) and require, for example, that a male who says he is a male actually be a male. When court matters involve children, there are obligations concerning visitation, financial aid, and custodial rights that cannot be fulfilled if an identity has been falsified. "Yet," Adams was quick to add, "we are still left with the fundamental question of who assigns that fixed cultural identity."

And beyond that, how fixed is fixed? Eric Lane, an expert in public policy law, cited two instances where once legally fixed cultural identities have started to shift, for example, the mother as undisputedly preferred principal caregiver to a child. "Fathers now have a larger voice," he said, "and there are ongoing discussions of grandparents' rights and the rights of partners who are not married." The fixed cultural definition of family is also changing. In the matter of New York's rent-control laws, the state's highest court, drawing on the dictionary definition of family, extended its meaning to include relationships beyond those of blood and legal ties to include an understanding of family as a functional unit. This in turn has made it possible for surviving unmarried life partners whose names do not appear on the rent-controlled leases of apartments in which they live, to remain in their homes under the same rent-control provisions after the partner-leaseholder's death.

Encounters with passing have a way of sharpening perspective on who we are now and on who we are becoming, slipping in an often harsh rebuke to elements of society that might need a good kick into the future. The phenomenon of passing shows how destructive it is to categorize human beings on the basis of irrelevant criteria for the purpose of excluding them. But it also sheds light on what criteria may actually be relevant for this purpose. Yes, passing stories can deepen our appreciation for the wonders of human mutability and self-invention, even as they expose where the limits are as well as where they ought and ought not to be. In the ought-not camp, for example, there is no need for equivocation about excluding the would-be surgeon or pilot who seeks the role without training or a license.

Passing also makes us think about selecting or ascribing a single identity when a mixed background "legitimates" a number of options. Again, it makes us wonder what exactly makes an identity authentic, or if and how authenticity matters. Who says I am obliged to be what you think I am? Or what I think you think I am? Or even what I think I am but sincerely wish I weren't?

Passing also helps us see how far we have to go in being mindful of the destructiveness of the disparaging use of stereotypes. It also points up those too frequent instances when minorities or individuals from oppressed or "nondefault" groups feel called on to reveal or hide their orientation or background in the way David Matthews and Vivian Sanchez felt obliged to do.

~

TOGETHER, the stories collected here suggest that the modes of passing have not changed much over the years, even though our collective reaction to passing may be starting to change a great deal. The specter of life-threatening persecution, as in the case of Helen Fremont's parents, is the most extreme and empathy-inducing impetus for the decision to pass. Joshua Clover explained that the term *passing* in his imagination is always related to dire circumstances. In situations of life-threatening danger we are willing to overlook the unsavory machinations that acts of passing can require. But less dramatic passing scenarios, like David Matthews's or Vivian Sanchez's, or even an incident as seemingly trivial as the young teacher's, can also elicit a deeply compassionate response.

What we rarely see any longer is the old Peola factor, the *GASP!* moment of high drama that the traditional treatment of passing in novels and films has accustomed us to expect: a moment of unmasking to trigger shock, accusation, revulsion, or at least a mean and knowing snicker on the part of those who have been fooled by a passing ruse. In the traditional narratives, the exposed passer is subjected to disgrace, loss of position, shunning, and sometimes jail or even slaughter. Small-town Nebraskan Brandon Teena was raped and killed in 1993 for not disclosing a female past. Think of Julie's forced exile in Edna Ferber's novel *Showboat* (1926) after her blackness was exposed, or how Freddy viciously smacks, beats, and rejects the Peola character, Sarah Jane, on discovering that she is black in the Douglas Sirk version of *Imitation of Life* (1959). Thirty-three years later, in *The Crying Game*, Fergus, passing as Jimmy, doubles over and vomits when he learns that his new love interest, the hairdresser called Dil, is not a woman after all. There is no missing the message.

Few passing stories end tragically anymore, and even those that do, like Brandon Teena's, have a new denouement, a different kind of coda. Raping and retching are the exception, not the norm. Collectively we are more likely to respond like music editor Eric Weisbard or even Queen Esther's Persian king. It is not the passers who incur the wrath of the enlightened; it is their enemies. As in the stories of Joel Alter and the navy Careerist, draconian laws and regulations may still be on the books, but clearly opinion is growing that they should not be. Condemnation now falls less on the passer and more on the individuals and institutions whose policies, attitudes, or practices made the deception necessary in the first place. By the standards of the 1920s and 1950s, Peola or Sarah Jane or Julie faced shame, dispossession, and exile after being exposed. In Nella Larsen's *Passing*, Clare

Kendry experienced an untimely death. Back when those stories were written, even as audiences sympathized with these women, they also judged them severely for the pain and trouble they caused others. Not so by 1992 for Dil in the *The Crying Game*. The hairdresser's pose elicits shock from the audience, to be sure, but not anger. Even Fergus, the prospective lover Dil has totally duped, quickly moves beyond his rage and comes around.

In the real-life case of Brandon Teena, it is not Teena's deception but Teena's tormentors who raise our ire, executioners who perpetrated a violent crime spurred by ignorance and hate. Yet in the aftermath of the tragedy, as the documentary of the case showed, even the women Teena deceived in order to date them were without rancor. The same is true of three of the five "widows" of Billy Tipton, the cross-dressing Spokane jazz musician who at death was discovered to be a woman. In interviews with Tipton's biographer, Diane Wood Middlebrook, these women expressed some embarrassment but no hostility. What these stories may signal is that boundaries have started to loosen, even if they are far from disappearing. Black-for-white passing offers the best context for measuring how attitudes shift because it has persisted for so long. Certainly black-for-white passing is no longer the "matter of great moral import" W. E. B. Du Bois described in 1929, but neither is it yet the "petty, silly matter of no real importance which another generation will comprehend with great difficulty" that he prophesied at the time.

ALL OF THE INSTANCES OF PASSING described in this book grew out of specific vocational, religious, or social aims. For some of the individuals who shared their stories, I imagine the experience of talking about these events for publication was a little like standing outside their own lives, and, like Orwell or Griffin or Halsell or Conover or Ehrenreich, acting as if the motivation had been to write about the experiences all along. Some, in the process, have let the facts of their stories expose lingering social ills. Others tell us more about the nature of identity and how much of that touted fluidity we as a society are prepared to allow. Still others lay bare the confusion, the desires at cross-purposes, and the pain people continue to experience along the old passing road.

Endnotes

INTRODUCTION: PASSING THEN, PASSING NOW

3   "ideal questioners" Werner Sollors, *Neither Black Nor White Yet Both: Thematic Explorations of Interracial Literature* (New York: Oxford University Press, 1997), p. 245.

4   Americanism *passing* Sollors, *Neither Black Nor White*, p. 147.

5   "My superiors" Unsigned. "Una Vita Divisa." *Corriere della serra*, November 22, 2002.

5   self-proclaimed military heroes B. G. Burkett and Glenna Whitley, *Stolen Valor: How the Vietnam Generation Was Robbed of Its Heroes and Its History* (Dallas: Verity, 1998).

8   act of creating . . . the seen and the not seen. Elaine Ginsberg, ed., *Passing and the Fictions of Identity* (Durham, N.C.: Duke University Press, 1996), pp. 1–2.

CHAPTER ONE: NOT SOME SOCIAL AGENDA STRUGGLE

11   "If the jinnee . . . a Jew'." James Weldon Johnson, *Along This Way: The Autobiography of James Weldon Johnson* (1933; New York: DaCapo, 2000), p. 136.

12   "postmodern sense." All David Matthews quotes and paraphrased recollections are from an interview by the author, June 14, 2001, in New York City, and numerous subsequent telephone and e-mail conversations through March 2003.

13   felt entitled to be told See Werner Sollors, *Neither Black Nor White Yet*

Both: Thematic Explorations of Interracial Literature (Cambridge, Mass.: Harvard University Press, 1997), p. 249, citing William Javier Nelson on the "hypodescent" society of the United States in which the child of a higher-caste and a lower-caste parent is assigned the lower parent's status. "For an XY, X cannot be an ethnic option but only a 'disguise.' According to the rules of passing, an XY is considered immutably and permanently a Y who is therefore merely 'passing for' or 'masquerading as' what he or she is 'not really': an X."

13   **In Virginia,** Code of Virginia (1849), article 9, p. 458, as cited in Lillian H. McGuire, *Uprooted and Transplanted: From Africa to America, Focus on African-Americans in Essex County, Virginia* (New York: Vantage, 1999), p. 16. See also Randall Kennedy, *Interracial Intimacies: Sex, Marriage Identity, and Adoption* (New York: Pantheon, 2003), on racial classification, particularly pp. 223–228; also on passing, pp. 281–338. From 1910 to 1924 Virginia's laws made a 15 percent black heritage enough for classification as Negro. The one-drop rule came into effect with the 1924 racial integrity laws.

14   **identities he can so ably "perform."** From Les Back and John Solomos, eds., *Theories of Race and Racism* (New York: Routledge, 2000), chap. 41; K. Anthony Appiah, "Racial Identity and Racial Identification," pp. 608–609. See also Kayta Gibel Azoulay, *Black, Jewish, and Interrracial: It's Not the Color of Your Skin but the Race of Your Kin, and Other Myths of Identity* (Durham, N.C.: Duke University Press, 1997), pp. 3, 14–15, 92.

14   **a natural cycle** St. Clair Drake and Horace R. Cayton, *Black Metropolis: A Study of Negro Life in a Northern City* (Chicago: University of Chicago Press, 1993), pp. 159–171. Erving Goffman, *Stigma: Notes on the Management of Spoiled Identity* (New York: Simon & Schuster, 1963), p. 79, cites the Drake and Cayton work on passing.

15   **not "firmly anchored emotionally"** Drake and Cayton, *Black Metropolis*, p. 166.

15   **did not admit black in-state** The University of Maryland journalism school was founded in 1945 but would not have welcomed Ralph Matthews as a student. See Laws of Maryland (1937), chapter 506, additions to article 49B of the Annotated Code of Maryland, 1935 supplement, title "Interracial Commission" and subtitled "Negro Scholarships." No. 5 reads: "Whenever any bona fide Negro resident and citizen of this State,

possessing the qualifications of health, character, ability and preparatory education required for admission to the University of Maryland, desires to obtain an education not provided for either in Morgan College or Princess Anne College, he may make application for a scholarship provided by the funds mentioned in the foregoing section [$30,000], so that he may obtain aid to enable him to attend a college or university where equal educational facilities can be provided and furnished, whether or not such an agency or institution is operated by the State or under some other arrangement, and whether or not such facilities are located in Maryland or elsewhere." This followed Thurgood Marshall's successful Supreme Court appeal on behalf of Donald Murray, an Amherst graduate who was denied admission to the University of Maryland law school because he was black. Maryland's board of regents suggested he consider Howard University as an alternative. The scholarship fund was increased after the Murray case to head off further attempts to integrate white universities. (See University of Maryland Board of Regents minutes, April 22, 1935, courtesy of Anne S.K. Turkos, University archivist, University of Maryland, with research assistance from Sarah Bronson.)

15   coverage of . . . Malcolm X and Fidel Castro See story collected in Rosemari Mealy, *Fidel and Malcolm X* (Melbourne: Ocean, 1993), pp. 32–62, esp. 41–44.

19   "David's trapeze act. . . . come from?" Ralph Matthews, interview by author, University Park, Maryland, March 9, 2002. All quotations from and paraphrases of Ralph Matthews's words come from this interview unless otherwise indicated.

22   "This is one of . . . probably the best thing to do." Anthony Appiah, interview by author, New York City, January 22, 2003.

24   rigorous religious scrutiny. In the Conservative and Orthodox Jewish traditions, Jewish identification stems solely from the mother. The father's religious background or lack of it is of no consequence in the determination of Jewish identity. The Reform and Reconstructionist movements accept patrilineal descent as well. All of the denominations accept conversion as a valid means of entry.

24   it's immutable. From an outsider's perspective, Jews, for the longest time, had their own private racial classification, as have the Irish, the Italians, and numerous other distinctive ethnic groups. Reference to the "Jewish"

or "Semitic" race," the "Irish race," or the "Italian race" once was standard and uttered as a pejorative as often as not. Now all three groups are collapsed into the white category but always include their ethnic baggage tags. These ethnic origins still matter in the way these groups identify themselves and in the way other people identify them back. See works such as Noel Ignatiev, *How the Irish Became White* (New York: Routledge, 1995); Karen Brodkin, *How Jews Became White Folks and What That Says About Race in America* (New Brunswick, N.J.: Rutgers University Press, 1994); David A.J. Richards, *Italian American: The Racializing of an Ethnic Identity* (New York: New York University Press, 1999); Michael Rogin, *Black Face, White Noise: Jewish Immigrants in the Hollywood Melting Pot* (Berkeley: University of California Press, 1998); and Susan Gubar, *Racechanges: White Skin, Black Face in American Culture* (New York: Oxford University Press, 1997).

24 **"Israel, even when sinning"** Avi Weinstein is the director of the Joseph Meyerhoff Center for Jewish Learning at Hillel, the national Jewish campus organization (and my brother). His reference to the Babylonian Talmud, Sanhedrin 49A, refers to a Jew who flagrantly desecrates Jewish law, a Jew who does not live as a Jew. In terms of the faith, he would be considered a pagan. But if he decided to live as a Jew, there is no formal conversion or reentry process involved.

25 **"Broyard passed . . . opt in."** Henry Louis Gates Jr., "White Like Me," *New Yorker,* June 17, 1996, pp. 66–68, collected in *Thirteen Ways of Looking at a Black Man* (New York: Random House, 1997), pp. 180–214.

25 **ill-considered attempts to define blackness** As late as 1984 in Louisiana, anyone who was one-thirty-second black was designated "colored." This came to light in the case of a white woman who discovered that she was classified as "colored" on her birth certificate. The Louisiana legislature unanimously decided to repeal that law. *Jane Doe v. State of Louisiana,* through the Department of Health and Human Resources, Office of Vital Statistics and Registrar of Vital Statistics, 479 So. 2d 372 (1985). Walter Benn Michaels uses the Susie Phipps case to discuss race as a social rather than a biological concept. On rehearing the case, the Louisiana court reminded the appellants that the idea of race could not be forfeited because of the importance of accumulating "racial data" for "planning and monitoring public health programs, affirmative action and other anti-

discrimination measures" (*Jane Doe,* p. 374). Walter Benn Michaels, "The No Drop Rule," in *Identities,* ed. Kwame Anthony Appiah and Henry Louis Gates Jr. (Chicago: University of Chicago Press, 1995), pp. 401–412. (From *Critical Inquiry,* Summer 1994).

27   **"blurs the carefully marked . . . deconstruct one another."** See Linda Schlossberg's introduction in Linda Schlossberg and Maria Carla Sanchez, *Passing: Identity and Interpretation in Sexuality, Race, and Religion* (New York: New York University Press, 2001), p. 2.

28   **lecture circuit** See Thomas Lennon, producer, "Jefferson's Blood," *Frontline,* May 2, 2000; Shannon Lanier and Jane Feldman *Jefferson's Children* (New York: Random House, 2000); Stephanie Slepian, "Family Ties? Descendants of Thomas Jefferson Gather for an Unconventional Reunion," *J-post.* New York University Department of Journalism, Spring 2000. journalism.nyu.edu/pubzone/race_class/race.htm. This website describes the lecture circuit program of Hemings descendants Julia Jefferson Westerinin, who lives as a white, and Shay Banks-Young, who lives as a black.

28   **"marks us as visible in the world."** Sander Gilman, *Making the Body Beautiful* (Princeton, N.J.: Princeton University Press, 1999), p. 331. Gilman's subject is passing in the framework of aesthetic surgery, but his general observations about passing still apply. He comments in an op-ed piece in the *New York Times,* December 21, 2002, about a television program called *Extreme Makeover* in which three contestants selected from thousands of applicants underwent aesthetic surgery for the cameras. "For more than 100 years," he writes, "we have slowly been asserting our right to shape ourselves. This is the great promise of self-transformation inherent in modern life. We can move to new homes, change our jobs, alter our names and become something very different from what our parents and grandparents were. Changing how we are seen can also change how we see ourselves. 'Extreme Makeover' is just another name for life in the 21st century."

28   **"passing as human."** Gilman, *Making the Body Beautiful,* p. 331.

29   **The artist Adrien Piper** In Elaine K. Ginsberg, *Passing and the Fictions of Identity* (Durham, N.C.: Duke University Press, 1996). Also, Adrien M.S. Piper, "Passing for White, Passing for Black," p. 244.

32   **buying into . . . oppressive social order** Nella Larsen, *Passing* (New York: Penguin, 1997). See Thadious M. Davis, introduction, p. ix.

32   **passing . . . racism embedded** David S. Vine, numerous exchanges, March 2002 and beyond. My sincere thanks to David for his incisive comments all along the way.

33   **"Jewish chameleon"** In Schlossberg and Sanchez, *Passing.* See Itzkovitz, "Passing Like Me," p. 45.

33   **"dated emblem . . . modern context."** Larsen, *Passing,* p. xxiii.

33   **condemned . . . fictional predecessors** See Sollors, *Neither Black Nor White,* p. 259. "In the whole portfolio of stories of social transformations that are available, black-white racial passing constitutes an exception in that it is condemned or even punished in societies that otherwise idealize, applaud, condone, or at least express amused ambivalence toward mobility."

33   **websites** www.webcom.com/~intvoice/point.html. There is even a discussion category (active since March 1996) entitled Passing for Black? www.myshoes.com includes a promotional headline: "Passing for White? Passing for Black? Who Am I? Where Do I Belong?" It is hosted by a clinical psychologist named Juanita Brooks.

34   **riveting theater** See Brooke Kroeger, *Fannie: The Talent for Success of Writer Fannie Hurst* (New York: Times Books/Random House, 1999), pp. 205–214. In film, *Imitation of Life* is the one of the classic examples. The basic plot of the Fannie Hurst novel goes like this: In the 1920s and 1930s, two young widows, one black, one white, join forces to form one household to support their infant daughters. The white woman takes on the role of breadwinner and the black, as caregiver. The women become partners in a very successful business venture based on the black woman's family recipe. All the while, the black woman's very white-appearing daughter decides to pass "all the way" to claim the privileges she has grown up with and naturally feels entitled to, the same privileges the white members of her own household so effortlessly enjoy. In doing so, she emotionally crushes Delilah, her beloved, self-sacrificing Aunt Jemima of a mother. "This was the first popular Faust in black tradition, the bargain with the Devil over the cultural soul," Gates writes in his memoir. "Talk about a cautionary tale." Henry Louis Gates Jr., *Colored People* (New York: Vintage, 1994), p. 16. The story line shifts in the 1959 Douglas Sirk-Ross Hunter version of the film. Lana Turner plays an actress and Hattie McDonald is housekeeper and nanny to the two children. The racial sub-

plot, with variations, remains. In the James Weldon Johnson novel, *Autobiography of an Ex-Coloured Man*, the imperceptible blackness of the narrator, once revealed, forces him to endure all manner of undeserved hardship and ruined opportunity, even as the combination of his heritage and musical gifts open him to rich new cultural experiences and quests. Ultimately he decides to pass, mostly because he can. By passing, he reinvents himself as a successful white businessman. When he reveals his origins to his beloved, she leaves him but then has a change of heart and returns. (This is a point of crucial relevance to every passing story: deceit in the most intimate of relationships never works.) They marry, have children, and find happiness, but she dies young. He ceases to socialize, devotes himself almost exclusively to his children, and vows never to marry again. He is at peace with his choice. "My love for my children makes me glad that I am what I am and keeps me from desiring to be otherwise," he says in conclusion, "and yet, when I sometimes open a little box in which I still keep my fast yellowing manuscripts, the only tangible remnants of a vanished dream, a dead ambition, a sacrificed talent, I cannot repress the thought that, after all, I have chosen the lesser part, that I have sold my birthright for a mess of pottage." James Weldon Johnson, *The Autobiography of an Ex-Coloured Man* (1902; New York: Vintage, 1989), p. 211. Like the Johnson novel, Nella Larsen's *Passing* was never made into a film, but it has been published in numerous classic editions. It recounts the struggle of a privileged black woman named Irene Redfield, society matron and physician's wife, with the attempts of a childhood acquaintance to insinuate herself into Irene's adult life. Clare Kendry is the cold, calculating daughter of a well-liked but drunken mulatto janitor and a black mother who died when she was small. In womanhood, with her "ivory skin" and "pale gold hair," Clare has become the glamorous, wealthy, white wife of a virulent racist. The novel is set in the elite circles of the Harlem Renaissance, so most of its examination of passing has to do with the way passing plays out black to white. But Larsen also explores some of passing's more universal aspects: passing for convenience, passing as a passionate civic activist, not out of commitment to the cause but because it helps secure Irene's social standing. Larsen also examines the spouses who pass as attentive and faithful even as they stray, as well as the dramatic consequences of a deceit exposed—for the passer, for the deceived and for the passer's offspring. The arc of the story follows the traditional formula. The exposure of Clare Kendry's passing provokes shock, revulsion, and murderous rage on the part of the betrayed husband and then her own tragic demise. Larsen's personal story is telling in this last regard. She was the daughter of a Danish mother and a West Indian father who distanced themselves from her to become white. Under Larsen's name in the Harry Ransom Center repository of copyright information, her entry reads: "Larsen had no children, left no identification of her extended family, and her only sibling, now deceased, denied knowledge of her existence." Two other well-known treatments of the theme of passing from the same era are Walter White, *Flight*, and Jesse Fauset, *Plum Bun*. For a thorough treatment of black-for-white passing literature, see Sollors, *Neither Black Nor White*, pp. 246–284.

34   **black-for-white passing revelations** Thadious Davis points this out in her introduction to the 1997 Penguin edition of Larsen's *Passing*, pp. xxiv–xxv. I am also grateful for insights she shared with me in conversation.

34   **memoirs** Carol Channing, *Just Lucky I Guess* (New York: Simon & Schuster, 2002), pp. 8–9.

34   **Broyard . . . Williams** Larsen, *Passing*. Davis, introduction, p. xxiv. See also Henry Louis Gates Jr., *Thirteen Ways of Looking at a Black Man* (New York: Random House, 1997), pp. 180–214, "The Passing of Anatole Broyard."

35   **"White Like Me"** For a fuller examination of literary and film treatment of the subject of black for white or white for black passing, see Sollors, *Neither Black Nor White*, pp. 244–287.

35   **sketches** The 1984 sketch was entitled "White Like Me," a takeoff on white novelist John Howard Griffin's 1960 *Black Like Me* in which Griffin dyed his skin to pose as a black person in the Deep South and write about his experiences. Nine years later, Grace Halsell, a white woman, performed a similar investigation in Mississippi and Harlem by turning herself black. Her book was called *Soul Sister*. Murphy's sketch also recalls Langston Hughes's satire of *Imitation of Life* for the Harlem Suitcase Theater in the 1930s in which he reversed the roles of the two protagonists, so that the white mammy figure was seen pandering to her black employer. It was titled "Limitation of Life."

37   "of great moral import. . . . difficulty." W. E. B. Du Bois, review of Nella Larsen's *Passing*, *Crisis*, July 1929, p. 223.

37   **Professor Griff, Chuck D** Both Chuck D and Richard "Professor" Griff were Nation of Islam members who publicly endorsed the Black Muslim leader Louis Farrakhan. Chuck D, who later claimed to support only Farrakhan's views on black self-sufficiency, rapped about him in "Bring the Noise." The Griff controversy exploded after he gave an interview to the *Washington Times* on May 22, 1989 (picked up by the *Village Voice* three weeks later) in which he said, "The Jews were wicked and we can prove this." He held them responsible for the "majority of the wickedness that goes on across the globe." He had previously made anti-Semitic remarks on stage. Chuck D reacted by firing Griff from the group, brought him back, and then broke up the group entirely. Thanks to Caroline Binham for research assistance.

37   "**Elvis was a hero . . . no stamps**" Lyrics from "Fight the Power" by Public Enemy, written by Carlton Ridehour, Hank Shocklee, Keith Shocklee, and Eric Sadler. Copyright © 1989 by Terrordome Music.

39   **protesting the . . . Audubon** Here the reference is to the unsuccessful protests of the early 1990s against a Columbia University biotech facility planned for the site of the Audubon Ballroom and San Juan Theater complex in the Washington Heights neighborhood of New York City. The Audubon Ballroom was the site of the Malcolm X assassination in 1965, and was also an important meeting place for black and Latino leaders such as Marcus Garvey and Pedro Albizu Campos. The Save The Audubon Coalition (STAC), joined by some two hundred Columbia students, argued that besides robbing the neighborhood of its cultural heritage, Columbia University was guilty of environmental racism, claiming the lab would pose a risk to residents. See Karen Carillo, "Activists Tell of Their Efforts to Save the Audubon," *Amsterdam News*, March 6, 1993, p. 3.

CHAPTER TWO: PASSING, VIRGINIA

43   "**Tell me, sir, . . . man acts.**" Herman Melville, *The Confidence Man* (New York: Oxford University Press, 1989), p. 41.

44   "**I love to talk about myself.**" E-mail message from teacher to author, December 13, 2000.

45   **picture her heavy . . . a day.**" All information about the teacher, unless otherwise indicated, is from an interview by the author, June 27, 2001, and subsequent e-mail and telephone exchanges through March 2003.

49   **public schools . . . Essex County.** Lillian H. McGuire, *Uprooted and Transplanted: From Africa to America, Focus on African-Americans in Essex County, Virginia* (New York: Vantage, 1999), pp. 82–89, 101–107.

49   **Civil Rights Act of 1964** See McGuire, *Uprooted and Transplanted,* pp. 192–210. On May 17, 1954, the U.S. Supreme Court unanimously declared, "Separate educational facilities for the races are inherently unequal and unconstitutional" and violated the "equal protection" clause of the Fourteenth Amendment. The court concluded, "To separate them [black children] from others of similar age and qualifications, solely because of their race, generates a feeling of inferiority that may affect their hearts and minds in a way unlikely ever to be undone." The case was initiated in 1951 when a fourth grader, Linda Brown of Topeka, Kansas, wanted to attend a white public school near her home instead of the black school, which was much farther away. In the Civil Rights Act of 1964, Congress authorized the U.S. attorney general to bring school desegregation suits in certain circumstances. It empowered the Commission of Education to give technical and financial assistance to desegregated schools and it gave the Department of Health, Education, and Welfare the power to withhold federal funds from school districts that did not desegregate. Sometime after the 1964 Civil Rights Act, under pressure from the county's black leaders and state legal representatives, school officials of Essex County began formulating plans to desegregate, starting with a "freedom of choice" policy dated April 1, 1966, which offered a thirty-day, choose-your-own school period for the upcoming school year. That policy remained in effect for three years. As black students began to enroll in the previously all-white schools, several "white flight" private schools were established. By 1971 the newly desegregated Essex High School was built. The former Tappahannock High School (white) became the desegregated Tappahannock Elementary School and the former Essex County High School (black) became the desegregated Essex Intermediate School.

49   **period of desegregation** James B. Slaughter mentioned the integration of the movie house in a telephone interview from his office in Washington, D.C., July 8, 2002. Lillian H. McGuire mentioned the cashiers in an interview by the author in Tappahannock, Virginia, March 11, 2002.

49   **annual civil rights audits.** Essex County Schools Superintendent Phillip Iovino used the term "civil rights audits" in an interview by the author in Tappahannock, Virginia, March 11, 2002. Subsequently Bethann Canada, director of the Office of Information Technology of the Virginia Department of Education, read from a statement about the audits that federal regulations require school divisions to "maintain racial and ethnic data to meet the requirements of the regulations on non-discrimination under programs receiving federal assistance through the Department of Education effectuation of Title VI of the Civil Rights Act of 1964." The purpose, she said, is to determine "the extent to which members of minority groups benefit from and participate in federally assisted programs." In addition to compiling statistics about racial and ethnic breakdowns of students, they keep track of gender, physical handicaps, crime rates at schools, promotion rates, graduation rates, career plans, and so on. The point is to determine how successfully members of different minority groups are maneuvering through the school system. The federal government defines the categories. Canada was interviewed by Sarah Bronson by telephone on July 11, 2002.

50   **one of the few . . . starting teachers** George Towns and librarian LaVerne Hayes, interview by author, Essex County Intermediate School, March 8, 2002. Both remembered the teacher well.

51   **Central Point . . . Passing** Robert A. Pratt, "Crossing the Color Line: A Historical Assessment and Personal Narrative of *Loving v. Virginia*." *Howard University Law Review*, Winter 1998, 41; How L.J. 229; David Margolick, "A Mixed Marriage's 25th Anniversary of Legality," *New York Times*, June 12, 1992, B20, 3.

52   **integrated Essex County Intermediate.** McGuire, *Uprooted and Transplanted*, pp. 203–207, esp. 205. The new high school got a white principal and the principal of the defunct black high school took charge of the new middle school. A succession of black principals followed him in the post until 1985, when the serving principal suddenly died of a heart attack and the school board decided to replace him with a white woman. Mass meetings, protests, "the greatest black confrontation" with the board since the battles over desegregation followed. After one term the board, having honored the white principal's contract, replaced her with an African American, Russell Jarrett, who was serving his fourth year in the post when the young teacher joined the faculty.

53 **board of supervisors** James B. Slaughter, e-mail to author, July 13, 2002. Slaughter's book is called *Settlers, Southerners, Americans: The History of Essex County, Va.* (1985).

53 **"distinctly Southern . . . overwhelmed them."** Slaughter, *Settlers, Southerners, Americans*, p. v.

53 **"letting the chips fall."** James B. "Jimmy" Slaughter, telephone interview by author, July 8, 2002.

54 **"soiling the illustrious gentry."** Slaughter, telephone interview by author, July 8, 2002.

54 **free Negroes in antebellum Essex County** McGuire, *Uprooted and Transplanted*, pp. 17, 213–226, citing "A Register of Free Negroes in Essex County, 1810–1843 and 1843–1861," Essex County Courthouse, Tappahannock, Va., the Library of Virginia, Richmond, Va., microfilm reel no. 91.

54 ***Loving v. Virginia*** Margolick, "Mixed Marriage's 25th Anniversary."

54 **"a judicial recognition . . . choice of mates."** Nash, quoted in Margolick, "A Mixed Marriage's 25th Anniversary."

54 **"is a story of unambiguous triumph . . . choices people make."** Randall Kennedy, "How Are We Doing with Loving? Race, Law, and Intermarriage," *Boston University Law Review*, October 1997. 77 B.U. L. Rev. 815.

55 **Racial Integrity Act of 1924.** See Robert A. Pratt, "Crossing the Color Line: A Historical Assessment and Personal Narrative of *Loving v. Virginia*," *Howard University Law Review*, Winter 1998. 41How L.J. 229. The Racial Integrity Act of 1924 defined a white person as having "no trace whatsoever of any blood other than Caucasian" and required all Virginians to register their racial identities with a local registrar and the state registrar of vital statistics. The slightest trace of nonwhite ancestry effectively disqualified a person from marrying someone the state considered to be white. There was one exception that honored "the desire of all to recognize as an integral and honored part of the white race" the descendants of John Rolfe and Pocahontas. Pratt cites An Act to Preserve Racial Integrity, 1924, ch. 371, 1, 5, Va. Acts, and Wadlington Walter, "The Loving Case: Virginia's Anti-miscegenation Statute in Historical Perspective," 52, Va. L. Rev. 1189, 1189 n.1 (1966). See also Kennedy, "Racial Passing." Frank R. Strong Law Forum lecture, *Ohio State Law Journal* 62, no. 3 (2001): 1145–1193.

55 **"And but for the interference . . . races to mix."** See *Loving v. Commonwealth*, 147 S.E.2d 78 (1966) as cited in Pratt.

56 **Loving's car** Pratt, "Crossing the Color Line."

56 **Fourteenth Amendment.** *Loving,* 388 U.S. at 3.

57 **"both low class."** Margolick, "Mixed Marriage's 25th Anniversary."

57 **"Caroline County."** Lillian H. McGuire, interview by author, Tappahannock, Virginia, March 11, 2002; James B. Slaughter, telephone interview by author, July 8, 2002.

58 **"touchiness about delving into it."** Robert A. Pratt, telephone interview by author, July 8, 2002.

58 **"There's been plenty mingling . . . don't have to pass anymore."** Simeon Booker, "The Couple That Rocked the Courts," *Ebony,* September 1967, pp. 78–86.

62 **mixed-marriage rates nationally.** Phillip W.D. Martin, "Devoutly Dividing Us: Opponents of Interracial Marriage Say God Is on Their Side," *Boston Globe,* November 7, 1999; Kennedy, "How Are We Doing with Loving?" citing Douglas Besharov and Timothy S. Sullivan, "One Flesh," *New Democrat,* July-August 1996, p. 19.

63 **"The ultimate test . . . *being* black."** Elaine K. Ginsburg, *The Fictions of Identity* (Durham, N.C.: Duke University Press, 1996). Adrien M.S. Piper, "Passing for White, Passing for Black," p. 253.

64 **"People have ways to identify black . . . good enough."** See Drake and Cayton, *Black Metropolis,* p. 164.

CHAPTER THREE: THAT'S NOT ME

65 **"Whiteness in Latino communities . . . colonizing projects."** Maria Carla Sanchez, "Whiteness Invisible: Early Mexican American Writing and the Color of Literary History," in Linda Schlossberg and Maria Carla Sanchez, *Passing: Identity and Interpretation in Sexuality, Race, and Religion* (New York: New York University Press), pp. 64–91. Through Mexican literature, Sanchez explores the idea of whiteness and class in Mexican culture.

65 **traces her ancestry to Spain.** All information and quotations about and from Vivian Sanchez come from interviews by the author and e-mail exchanges between July 11, 2001, and March 2003.

75 **Anthony Appiah explained . . . betraying the self.** Anthony Appiah, interview by author, New York City, January 22, 2003.

79   **Hector Bianciotti** Jason Weiss, "All Roads Lead to Paris," *Hopscotch*, Winter 2000, pp. 28–36.

CHAPTER FOUR: LEVITICUS 18:22

93   **"I can define . . . that matter."** Charles Taylor, *The Ethics of Authenticity* (Cambridge, Mass.: Harvard University Press, 1991) p. 40.

94   **"chain of generations"** Quotes from Joel Alter come from his speech to students at the Sidwell Friends School, November 29, 2000, and from an interview with the author, April 12, 2001, and subsequent e-mail exchanges and telephone conversations through March 2003, unless otherwise indicated.

95   **first woman rabbi** Press reports at the time said Eilberg was a thirty-one-year old Talmud student who had entered rabbinical school the preceding fall with enough transfer credits from the JTS graduate program to complete the rabbinical program by the end of that first year. Tucker led the Rabbinical Assembly's interdisciplinary commission on the status of women, established in 1977.

95   **Equal Rights Amendment** The Senate passed the ERA by a vote of 84–8, following the House.

95   **Abraham Joshua Heschel** Susannah Heschel, "Abraham Joshua Heschel," *Tikkun*, January-February 1998: "It was originally his idea that I apply to rabbinical school. I suppose I was surprised at his openness because he was so much older, and had been raised in a very different culture, in Chasidic Warsaw, but his responsiveness grew out of his deep commitment to justice, and to his rejection of halachic absolutism."

96   **Rabbi José Faur** José Faur, Appelant, v. The Jewish Tehological Seminary of America, Respondent, Mo. No. 609, Court of Appeals of New York 76 N.Y. 2d 706; 561 N.E.2d 888; 560 N.Y. S.2d 988; 1990 N.Y. Lexis 3024, September 11, 1990. Opinion: Motion for leave to appeal denied with one hundred dollars costs and necessary reproduction disbursements.

98   **pro-gay resolution** May 1990 resolution of the Rabbinical Assembly Convention, as published in *Proceedings of the 1990 Convention,* "Gay and Lesbian Jews," p. 39. JTS Library.

99   **with a girl, a capital crime.** From the 1997–1998 academic bulletin, as it appeared on the Jewish Theological Seminary website until the summer

of 2002. The bulletin has never included specific language on the subject of homosexuality for rabbinical school students. But for students to be in "good standing," they must "be committed to, and living, an observant Jewish life." The bulletin reminds students that "standards of personal and professional conduct and interpersonal relations are a significant part of the tradition to which we are committed." The dean, it stated, reserves the right to "deny admission, registration, readmission, or ordination" to any student determined by faculty committee to be unsuitable to the profession. Gordon Tucker explained that this would not be because of the homosexuality per se, but because the action would mean a flagrant violation of the Conservative movement's interpretation of the halakhic code. For example, a student known to violate the Jewish Sabbath week after week, with indiscriminate vehicular travel or shopping or smoking, could be asked to leave. For the 2002–2003 school year, the language in the academic bulletin appearing on the JTS website became less threatening: "While Conservative Judaism recognizes the validity of pluralism in religious expression within the boundaries delineated by the movement, the dean and the Rabbinical School faculty committee reserve the right to determine the degree of observance required of candidates and students. It is recognized that applicants may be in the course of deepening their Jewish commitments. Personal religious guidance is available from a dean or adviser to students at any time."

100　"old boy's promise . . . Some get through." Dawn Robinson Rose, telephone interview by author, March 7, 2002. Leaving Dean Tucker's office, Rose felt sure the chancellor had singled her out because of the gay speaker incident and her provocative question about homosexual women. No doubt her pro-homosexuality activism was an unwelcome development in the seminary halls. See also Rose's essay in Rebecca T. Alpert, Sue Levi Elwell, and Shirley Idelson, *Lesbian Rabbis: The First Generation* (New Brunswick, N.J.: Rutgers University Press, 2001), pp. 217–225.

100　"On the one side . . . permanently compromised." Dawn Robinson Rose, "Notes from the Underground," in Alpert et al., *Lesbian Rabbis,* p. 220.

101　affirmed gay ordination "Rabbinate to Admit Gay Clergy: Delegates to Seattle Reform Judaism Meeting Vote Official Acceptance." *Seattle Post-Intelligencer,* June 26, 1990, A1.

103   **"I have to become a rabbi."** Joel Alter, essay in his application to Jewish
       Theological Seminary, Fall 1990. Alter's application essays state his inter-
       est in being a Jewish educator rather than a pulpit rabbi.

104   **"the invisibility of it."** By the definition Sissela Bok sets out in her classic
       work, *Lying: Moral Choice in Public and Private Life* (New York: Vintage,
       1999), Alter's action didn't feel like a lie because it wasn't one. A lie, she
       writes, is "any intentionally deceptive message which is *stated* [her em-
       phasis]. Such statements are most often made verbally or in writing, but
       can of course also be conveyed via smoke signals, Morse code, sign lan-
       guage and the like" (p. 13). *Webster's Collegiate Dictionary* follows Bok in
       first defining the noun lie as "a false statement made with deliberate intent
       to deceive; a falsehood" but for the second definition offers, "something
       intended or serving to convey a false impression; imposture."

104   **gay piece out of the package** Ski Hunter, Colleen Shannon, Jo Knox, and
       James I. Martin, *Lesbian, Gay, and Bisexual Youths and Adults: Knowledge
       for Human Services Practice* (Thousand Oaks, Calif.: Sage, 1998), p. 86,
       citing C. de Monteflores, "Notes on the Management of Difference," in
       T. Stein and C. Cohen, eds., *Contemporary Perspectives in Psychotherapy
       with Lesbians and Gay Men* (New York: Plenum, 1986), pp. 73–101.

105   **seek admittance or acceptance.** Hunter et al., *Lesbian, Gay, and Bisexual
       Youths and Adults*, p. 86, citing C. de Monteflores, "Notes on the Manage-
       ment of Difference," pp. 73–101.

105   **deception** Again, Bok, in *Lying*, writes, "When we undertake to deceive
       others intentionally, we communicate messages meant to mislead them,
       meant to make them believe what we ourselves do not believe. We can do
       so through gesture, through disguise, by means of action or inaction, even
       through silence" (p. 13).

105   **right to privacy** Bok, *Lying*, pp. xxxiv, 150–151; Bok, telephone interview
       by author, February 6, 2003.

107   **"undomesticated. . . . the norm."** All quotes from Gordon Tucker (un-
       less otherwise specified) are taken from interviews by author, New York
       City, December 10, 2001; White Plains, New York, January 3, 2002, and
       subsequent telephone conversations through July 2002.

107   **"powder keg in all denominations."** Paul Wilkes, "The Hands That
       Would Shape Our Souls," *Atlantic Monthly*, December 1990, p. 59. Alter
       remembers the way Tucker was quoted in the article as saying, "If a per-

son is a practicing homosexual, they are making a choice and the choice entails not being a rabbi." In a telephone interview with the author on June 21, 2002, Tucker explained that the quotation was not a statement of his personal opinion but reflected a longer statement of the seminary's policy at the time.

108 **dissertation** Tucker's dissertation is dated 1979 and titled: "The Enumeration Reducibilities: A Study of the E-Degrees of Sets of Natural Numbers and Their Constituent S-Degrees."

109 **turn to the committee for counsel** See faqs.org/faqs/judaism/FAQ/03-Torah-Halacha/section-53.html.

109 *responsa* The committee solicits these opinions, usually from Law Committee members but also from selected members of the larger Rabbinical Assembly. The rabbinic and nonvoting lay members debate the papers and then decide which ones to accept or reject. According to the current Law Committee secretary, David Fine, any paper that garners six or more votes becomes an official opinion. If only one paper is accepted, it becomes *the* official opinion. If several papers garner the six needed votes, each becomes an official position, even when they represent opposing points of view. Final authority rests with local rabbis except in cases of a binding decision, of which there have only been three. For a Law Committee opinion to become binding as Conservative movement policy, it would have to garner an 80 percent majority in the Law Committee and then be sent on to the entire Rabbinical Assembly, where it would have to pass by majority vote.

110 **official opinion** The Committee on Jewish Law and Standards of the Conservative Movement, *Responsa 1991–2000* (New York: The Rabbinical Assembly, 2002), p. x.

110 **"my welcome-to-JTS year."** The Law Committee met to debate the homosexuality issue December 11, 1991, February 5, 1992, and March 25, 1992.

111 **entire arsenal of subterfuges** Hunter et al., *Lesbian, Gay, and Bisexual Youths and Adults,* p. 87.

111 **locker-room machismo** As of 2002, the following retired major-league athletes had come out as gay: Dave Kopay, a running back who played for the National Football League Detroit Lions, Green Bay Packers, New Orleans Saints, San Francisco 49ers, and Washington Redskins, came out in

December 1975, three years after his retirement. Glen Burke, a former Los Angeles Dodgers outfielder acknowledged his homosexuality in 1979. He died of AIDS complications in 1995. Roy Simmons, a former New York Giants and Redskins offensive guard, came out during a 1992 television appearance. Two Washington Redskins, all-pro tight end Jerry Smith and fullback Ray McDonald were outed, Smith posthumously by Kopay after Smith died of AIDS in 1986. McDonald was arrested in 1968 for having sex with another man in a park. Billy Bean, who played for the Tigers, the Dodgers, and the San Diego Padres before retiring in 1995, came out in 1999 and has written a book about his experiences. In 2001 the editor of *Out* magazine, Brendan Lemon, caused a stir when he wrote that he was dating a major-league baseball player but did not name him. A year later, in the June-July 2002 issue of *Details* magazine, Mets manager Bobby Valentine is quoted as saying that baseball is "probably ready for an openly gay player. The players are a diverse enough group now that I think they could handle it." Soon after Valentine's comment was printed, a gossip column in the *New York Post* reported persistent rumors that an unnamed New York Mets star seen frequently with models was actually gay. This prompted all-star catcher Mike Piazza to hold a news conference May 21, 2002, to announce preemptively that he was not gay. But he also said, "in this day and age, it's irrelevant. I don't think it would be a problem at all" to have gay members on the team." Added Valentine, "We are all big boys. We can handle it." See Peter Bowles and Robert Kahn, "Straight Talk from Piazza: I'm Not Gay," *Newsday*, May 22, 2002, A6. See Dan Raley, "Kopay No Regrets: Twenty-five Years after Disclosing He Was Gay, He Remains a Pioneer," *Seattle Post-Intelligencer*, December 5, 2000, C1. In the fall of 2002, the Public Theater in New York featured a play entitled *Take Me Out* that tells the story of a major-league baseball superstar who comes out of the closet, upsetting his team and the sport in general. The play did well enough to go to Broadway (Walter Kerr Theater) in the spring of 2003 and went on to win the Tony Award for best play of that year.

111   **the seminary experience** See Jane Calem Rosen, "Rabbinical School Changed Their Lives," *JTS Magazine*, Winter 2000, jtsa.edu/news/jtsmag/9.2/rcs.shtml.

113   **plight of the gay seminarian.** "It is clear to us that you, as leaders of the Conservative Movement, are insufficiently informed regarding the social

and psychological effects (on both Homosexuals and Heterosexuals) of your policies and attitudes toward Homosexuals in the Movement. How could it be otherwise? Most Homosexual Jews who choose to remain in the Movement are, of necessity, incognito. Those who do not wish to live like that generally leave our community. Thus, you have been engulfed in a silence which has been detrimental to us all. . . ." Quoted by permission of Dawn Rose, "Open Letter to the Law Committee of the RA," undated (Fall 1991).

114   **first studies to indicate a biological basis for homosexuality** Sharon Begley with David Gelman, "What Causes People to Be Homosexual: A Study Pinpoints a Difference in the Brain," *Newsweek*, September 9, 1991, p. 52, citing the technical journal *Science*, September 1991; and Thomas H. Maugh II, "Survey of Identical Twins Links Biological Factors with Being Gay," *Los Angeles Times*, December 15, 1991, p. A43, citing a new study by researchers at Boston University and Northwestern University, reported the same day in the *Archives of General Psychiatry*.

115   **"old lefty from way back."** All Sue Fendrick quotations from interview by author, Boston, June 26, 2001.

118   **the most pro-gay position paper** The pro-gay *responsum* was put forward by Rabbi Bradley Shavit-Artson, a young California rabbi who occasioned the debate by preparing a paper entitled "Gay and Lesbian Jews: A Teshuva." He argued his case on historical grounds. The Law Committee opposed the paper, 19–1 with three abstentions. In effect, Shavit-Artson wrote that in biblical times, there was no way to envision a loving monogamous relationship between two people of the same sex and now there was, necessitating reconsideration of the abomination restrictions. Tucker thought the defense was creative with a certain amount of merit, but he objected to Shavit-Artson's decision to pose the argument in historical terms. If any contradictory evidence were to emerge, Tucker reasoned, the position could be easily overturned. Tucker's sense was that the argument should be framed on compassionate moral grounds, in the way other arguments have been advanced in the interest of relieving unintentional suffering. "You can trace in Jewish legal history the emergence of the point of view . . . that people ought not to be punished for things their parents did or things they, in a sense, inherited from their parents or things they haven't chosen," Tucker explained. "You can trace that. You

can see how that develops, in biblical times and certainly in postbiblical times. So there are arguments to be made in this way." As a parallel, he cited the Conservative movement's position on women whose husbands abandon them without first handing them an official divorce decree, called a *get*. Under Jewish law, a woman cannot remarry without one. "Why," asked Tucker, "has the rabbinic community for hundreds of years expressed enormous empathy and gone through all sorts of agony to relieve the plight of the abandoned woman who is in a position that the Law creates for her as a result of something she didn't choose?" These days in such cases, the Conservative movement invokes a marital nullification loophole that dates back to Talmudic times to save these women from being "sacrificed on the altar of the majesty of the Law." So, he asked, why not apply the same logic to the situation of people who are constitutionally not oriented to marry someone of the opposite sex? "And what are you going to do? Get them into marriage? I mean, we talked about this a little bit. You get them into marriages and you're punishing the spouse in a horrendous way. You're just compounding the problem."

118   **upheld the status quo** See Committee on Jewish Law and Standards, *Responsa 1991–2000*, pp. 612–729, which includes all the *responsa*, dissents, and concurrences produced during the debate except for the rejected paper of Bradley Shavit-Artson.

118   **"Consensus Statement of Homosexuality"** Printed circular, undated, on Rabbinical Assembly letterhead (March 1992). The total vote for the consensus statement was 19–3 with one abstention. See also Committee on Jewish Law and Standards, *Responsa 1991–2000* (New York: The Rabbinical Assembly, 2002), p. 612.

121   **"If those who preceded us were as angels . . . believed it passionately."** From Gordon Tucker, "Tribute at Memorial Service for Rabbi Gerson D. Cohen, 18 Elul 5752—September 16, 1992," typescript. Courtesy of Rabbi Tucker.

122   **substance abuse . . . bouts of ill health.** Hunter et al., *Lesbian, Gay, and Bisexual Youths and Adults*, pp. 84–85, cites studies by S. E. Brooks 1991; M. Hall 1986; and H. C. Triandis, L. L. Kurowski, and M. Gelfand, 1994.

122   **"retains his standing as someone who relates honorably."** Erving Goffman, *Stigma: Notes on the Management of Spoiled Identity* (New York: Simon & Schuster, 1963), p. 95.

122   the list Joel Alter, telephone interview by author, June 16, 2002.

122   burden of silence Joel Alter, letter to author, June 17, 2002.

122   his parents' sake Joel Alter, letter to author, June 17, 2002.

125   "unsafe." Joel Alter, telephone interview by author, June 16, 2002.

126   *Tikkun* Rabbi Yaakov Levado, "Gayness and God," *Tikkun*, September-October 1993, widely reprinted on gay Jewish interest websites. The author, it later emerged, was Rabbi Steve Greenberg, who has been active in attempts to gain acceptance for gay Orthodox Jews. See also *Trembling Before G-d*, Sandi Dubowski's documentary that examines a number of Orthodox gays and lesbians wrestling with their religious beliefs.

126   "The ash heap of history . . . anarchy." Ismar Schorsch, "Marching to the Wrong Drummer," *Conservative Judaism*, Summer 1993, pp. 14–19. Revised version of his address to the Rabbinical Assembly Convention in Los Angeles, March 23, 1993.

126   commission on human sexuality Rabbi Elliot N. Dorff, "Jewish Norms for Sexual Behavior: A Responsum Embodying a Proposal," in *Responsa 1991–2000*, pp. 691–711. The Law Committee vote on this paper was eight in favor, eight opposed with seven abstentions. Tucker voted in favor.

126   the issue so deeply divided Judith Plaskow, "Burning in Hell, Conservative Movement Style," *Tikkun*, May 1993, pp. 49–50. Nadine Joseph, "Rabbi's Ethics Examined as Kirschner Gets Teaching Post," *Jewish Bulletin*, May 28, 1993, p. 4. Joseph reports that Rabbi Joel Roth resigned as dean over allegations unrelated to the gay debate.

126   the prohibitions of Leviticus 18:22 should be overturned Gordon Tucker, "Two Views: Homosexuality and Halachic Judaism." Tucker provides the Conservative view and Rabbi Barry Freundel, the Orthodox view in *Moment*, June 1993, pp. 40–43.

126   Rabbi Sacks-Rosen "Gay Rabbi Gets Respect on Coast," *Forward*, April 16, 1999.

127   His notes from those remarks . . . Joel Alter, letter to author, June 17, 2002, including his speech notes.

130   "act in self-defense and lie" From Benay Lappe, "Saying No in the Name of a Higher Yes," in *Lesbian Rabbis*, pp. 197–216. Lappe was a lesbian activist before her admission to the rabbinical school who went undercover immediately upon arrival. To survive, she imagined herself a "hidden Jew, forced to hide my identity in order to protect myself from those who would

unjustly persecute me merely because of who I was." And yet, she wrote, a sense of guilt and shame had overtaken her, encouraged by the years of silence and the seminary's atmosphere. It eroded her self-confidence and her trust in her own perceptions. "Without realizing it," she wrote, "I started, not to believe exactly, but to be spiritually infiltrated by the heterosexist assumptions of the seminary and the tradition it conveyed in its own image. I began to lose the sharpness of my political and analytical voice. It was nearly impossible to keep my lesbian head above water, so to speak, with such an enormous tide of homophobia and sexism washing over me every day." She even began choosing as her regular prayer station the back pew of the seminary synagogue, with everyone's back to her, in order to minimize contact with her peers. "Standing in a room surrounded by people who I knew certainly would do everything in their power to see that I got kicked out of school if they knew who I really was, was hardly conducive to prayer," she wrote. Of her confrontation with the dean, she wrote, "it was now time to see whether I would listen to that voice deep inside me that said, 'Lying is wrong,' or instead act in self-defense and lie in order to do what was right. I sat there in the frozen but eerily calm silence of the proverbial deer-in-the-headlights for what was at least a full minute as I mentally fast-forwarded through each of the possible responses I could have given and their resulting outcomes." "The answer to the central question," she finally told him, "is no." She left the dean's office and went to see her study partner and closest seminary friend. "For the first time that evening, I could let the feelings come, and I started to cry. I was scared. I was hurt. I was ashamed. Somewhere deep down, I know I was also angry, but I couldn't feel the anger, so full of shame was I at my own lying. I could only think of what I myself had just done, not what the dean had just done to me."

131   **a cousin to civil disobedience.** Linda Schlossberg, in her introduction to *Passing* (p. 3), describes passing as a "form of passive resistance, one that protects the gay subject from hostile interpretations."

133   **"break bad laws . . . ought not to carry."** Anthony Appiah, interview by author, New York City, January 22, 2003.

133   **"a public, nonviolent . . . not covert or secretive."** John Rawls, *A Theory of Justice* (Cambridge, Mass.: Harvard University Press, 1999), pp. 320–321.

133   **"no matter how noble the intent claimed."** Sissela Bok, telephone interview by author, February 6, 2003.

135 **"not an easy transformation."** Jane Calem Rosen, "How Rabbinical School Changed Their Lives," *JTS*, May 2002, p. 6.

135 **school prom.** Josh Dugan, "The Closet Door Stands Ajar," *Lion's Tale,* June 7, 2001, reports: "Alter, who last year brought his then partner to prom."

136 **"affirmation of my Jewishness as a gay man."** Alter addressed the gay and lesbian organization of the Sidwell Friends School, Washington D.C., November 29, 2000.

137 **reports in the Jewish press** See Deborah Nussbaum Cohen, "A New Consensus for Gays? Wave of Opposition to Conservative Movement Ban Putting Issue Back on the Agenda," *Jewish Week*, December 27, 2002; Joe Berkofsky, "Conservative Movement Asked to Reconsider Its Stance on Gays," Jewish Telegraphic Agency, March 4, 2003; A Day of Learning: Sexual Orientation and the Conservative Movement took place on March 5, 2003, at the Jewish Theological Seminary (Los Angeles) (GLBT Jews Forum, February 27, 2003).

137 **"Homosexuality . . . will follow as a matter of course."** Joel A. Alter, "On Gays and Lesbians in the Conservative Movement," January 2003. Unpublished.

138 **"a state of grace . . ."** Erving Goffman, *Stigma: Notes on the Management of Spoiled Identity* (New York: Touchstone/Simon & Schuster, 1986), pp. 100–101.

138 **Among the studies Goffman cites** Goffman, *Stigma*, p. 79, citing "A Rose by Any Other Name," in St. Clair Drake and Horace R. Cayton, *Black Metropolis: A Study of Negro Life in a Northern City* (Chicago: University of Chicago Press, 1993), pp. 159–171.

Chapter Five: Conduct Unbecoming

141 **"He who passes . . . formally instituted."** Erving Goffman, *Stigma: The Management of Spoiled Identity* (New York: Touchstone/Simon & Schuster, 1986), p. 85.

141 **"lie like crazy."** The Careerist, interview by author, Arlington, Virginia, March 8, 2001; Charleston, South Carolina, March 2002; and subsequent telephone and e-mail exchanges through March 2003.

141 **website** Air force reserves 1987 recruitment form, obsolete since 1993 but reported in use by the Servicemen's Legal Defense Network, which spot-

ted it on the air force reserve website (SLDN, Second Quarter Report, 2002).

143 **submarine tender** Submarine tenders furnish maintenance and logistic support for nuclear attack submarines. They are the largest of the active auxiliaries and carry crews made up largely of technicians and repair personnel.

144 **honorable discharge** Rhonda Evans, "U.S. Military Policies Concerning Homosexuals: Development, Implementation, and Outcome," Center for the Study of Sexual Minorities in the Military, University of California–Santa Barbara, November 2001, p. 13.

144 **passers in the workplace** Annette Friskopp and Sharon Silverstein, *Straight Jobs, Gay Lives: Gay and Lesbian Professionals, the Harvard Business School, and the American Workplace* (New York: Touchstone, 1995), pp. 175–190.

146 **physician-patient confidentiality.** See www.planetout.com/people/ features/2000/05/military/harassment. Report by Nathan Shrider.

147 **do good work, create an excellent reputation . . .** "For most women, the heterosexual presumption seems to last a lifetime unless they actively challenge it." Friskopp and Silverstein, *Straight Jobs, Gay Lives*, p. 176.

148 **"People look for moral reasons . . . particular case."** Bok, *Lying*, pp. 75–79.

148 **"self-defensive lies . . . own identity."** Bok, *Lying*, p. 79, confirmed in Bok, interview by author, February 6, 2003.

150 **"the warship that fixes warships"** www.cable.navy.mil.

161 **"Typically . . . serious offense . . . warrant trial after retirement."** Lieutenant Michelle Pettit, Assistant Legal Counsel, U.S. Navy Personnel Command, JAGC, e-mail response to author query, November 14, 2002.

162 **"has happened before."** Elizabeth Hillman, assistant professor of law, Rutgers University Law School at Camden, New Jersey, telephone interview by author, October 7, 2002; **"theoretical risk than an actual risk"** Sharra Greer, chief legal counsel of the Servicemembers' Legal Defense Network, telephone interview by author, October 16, 2002. Both cited the case of retired Rear Admiral Selden G. Hooper, who was brought back from retirement to be sentenced to dismissal May 7, 1957, on a morals charge. Hooper challenged the court-martial's jurisdiction. On September 26, 1958, the U.S. Court of Military Appeals upheld the sentence of

dismissal. At the time, Chief Justice Robert E. Quinn said retired officers "form a vital segment of our national defense. The salaries they receive are not solely recompense for past services, but a means devised by Congress to assure their availability and preparedness in future contingencies. This preparedness depends as much upon their continued responsiveness to discipline and upon their continued state of physical health" (*New York Times* (UPI), September 27, 1958, sec. 8, p. 1).

163 **"even people of very good will . . . current administration."** Tobias Barrington Wolff, University of California–Davis, telephone interview by author, October 5, 2002. See also Tobias Barrington Wolff, "Compelled Affirmations, Free Speech, and the U.S. Military's Don't Ask, Don't Tell Policy," *Brooklyn Law Review,* Winter 1997.

164 **"no longer will they be excluded . . . progress for gays."** Kenji Yoshino, "Covering," *Yale Law Journal,* 111 Yale L.J. 9, January 2002, p. 769.

164 **major investment bank.** Trevor Lewis, interview by author, New York City, January 23, 2001.

165 *New York* **magazine cover story** Alan Deutschman, "Wall Street's Secret Society: Gay Men and Lesbians Are Hiding in Plain Sight All Over the Financial Industry. Why Are They Living a Fifties Life in the Nineties?" *New York* magazine, March 29, 1999, pp. 26–33.

166 **"I tell them it's hard enough to find a job . . . they want?"** Lisa Belkin, "At Work, How Far to Leave the Closet," *New York Times,* November 10, 2002, sec. 10, p. 1. See also the vociferous response from her readers to Viscusi's advice. Lisa Belkin, "Some Outspoken Opinions on Coming Out," *New York Times,* November 24, 2002, sec. 10, p. 1.

CHAPTER SIX: THE JANE GAME

167 **"What we witness . . . experience of freedom."** Jorie Graham in the *Boston Review,* 1997. See bostonreview.mit.edu/BR19.1/clover.html.

167 **Seberg's birthplace** Seberg was born in Marshalltown, Iowa.

172 *resister*'s **editor** McDonnell's vision for the zine was for it to move beyond the reinforcement of "identity niches," which so much of underground writing was about, and bring those voices together in one publication. "*resister,*" she once explained, "is stepping into the breach of faith between the omissions of the mass media and the myopia of the sub-

culture set." From "Zine Creators on Creating Zines," www.ac.wwu. edu/~pamhard/238sp02zineqts.htm, quoting Evelyn McDonnell on the creation of *resister*.

172 *Rock She Wrote* Evelyn McDonnell and Ann Powers, *Rock She Wrote: Women Write About Rock, Pop, and Rap* (New York: Cooper Square, 1999), p. 1. See also Evelyn McDonnell, "The Feminine Critique," *Village Voice Rock & Roll Quarterly*, Fall 1992, collected in McDonnell and Powers, *Rock She Wrote*. The piece was the initial inspiration for the anthology. At the time, McDonnell was the music editor of the *San Francisco Weekly* and Powers was writing for the publication.

173 "stronghold of nerdy white boys . . . for women" McDonnell and Powers, *Rock She Wrote*, p. 21.

173 "authoritarian, usually male" voice Scott Puckett, "Rewriting the Rock Criticism Canon: New Anthology Highlights Women's Contributions to Genre," *Daily Aztec*, October 10, 1996.

173 "Hey, here's something funny . . . check this out." Lee Foust, telephone interview by author, July 17, 2001, and in person by author, Florence, Italy, July 30, 2001.

173 *"this attitude."* Evelyn McDonnell, interview by author, Miami, May 21, 2001. All quotations stem from this interview unless otherwise specified.

175 prize was $5,000 Academy of American Poets, press release, March 6, 1996. "The Walt Whitman Award, established in 1975, makes possible the publication of a poet's first full-length collection. The competition is judged by a distinguished poet, and the winning manuscript is published by a prominent literary publishing house." www.poets.org/academy/news/pr960506.cfm.

175 Dark's permission First, McDonnell said she made sure that Jane Dark would not object to the crossover publicity. The protocol in the underground world of fanzines is to get permission to tout the work in an establishment venue. From an underground perspective, The *Voice*, even with its alternative press sensibilities, is way mainstream.

176 "it was completely mysterious . . . Who is this person?" Rob Brunner, interview by author, New York City, May 3, 2001. All quotations stem from this interview if not otherwise specified.

177 "A self-described proponent . . . than rationalization." Rob Brunner, "Guilty Pleasures," *Village Voice*, July 9, 1996.

179 "The phone call came . . . So I did, and she didn't." Joshua Clover, in-

terview by author, New York City, and subsequent e-mail exchanges, March 30, 2001, and e-mail and telephone exchanges through March 2003. All quotations from Clover except as otherwise indicated are from these exchanges.

179 **"Of course, pop culture . . . Regis and Kathie Lee thing."** Jane Dark, "The Popular Crowd," *Village Voice*, August 20, 1996, p. 59.

180 **published four new poems** Joshua Clover, *American Poetry Review*, July–August 1996, p. 16. The poems are entitled "Bathtub panopticon," "Royal," "Analysis of bathtub panopticon, or Hybrids of indexes and cosmologies," and "El periferico, or Sleep."

182 *Doc Martens* Sherr remembers that the exchange was about shoes and that the answer was "sneakers," but you get the drift.

182 *kangaroos* A kangaroo is one and a half ounces of vodka, three-quarters of an ounce of dry vermouth, and a lemon peel twist. Thanks to Rebekah Brilliant.

182 **"With the Internet . . . makes it interesting."** Sara Sherr, telephone interview by author, July 10, 2001. All quotations are from that interview and subsequent e-mail exchanges.

182 **"culture of simulation"** Sherry Turkle, *Life on the Screen: Identity in the Age of the Internet* (New York: Touchstone, 1995), p. 10.

183 **"will change their ways of thinking . . . emotional lives."** Turkle, *Life on the Screen*, p. 26.

184 **Sennett** Jay Allen Sennett, telephone interview by author, October 7, 2002, and subsequent e-mail exchanges.

186 **"sought to uncover . . . violent presumptions."** Judith Butler, *Gender Trouble* (New York: Routledge, 1999), p. viii.

188 **she mentioned Jane Dark** Eric Weisbard, interview by author, Brooklyn, New York, June 19, 2001. All quotations from Weisbard stem from this conversation unless otherwise noted.

191 **"akin to channel-surfing . . . magical realism."** Dulcy Brainard, "Madonna Anno Domini," *Publishers Weekly*, March 31, 1997, p. 70.

192 **Orchid** Joshua Clover, *Madonna Anno Domini: Poems* (Baton Rouge: Louisiana State University Press, 1997). Reprinted by permission of the author.

192 **"a poetic manifesto . . . inner lives."** Jorie Graham, Academy of American Poets, May 6, 1996. www.poets.org/academy/news/pr960506.cfm.

194 **"and it can be a real problem"** See Simon Dumenco, "The Glossies:

Would the Real Kurt Anderson . . . " *Folio Magazine,* October 4, 2002. According to the story, this actually happened in the summer of 2002 when a freelancer communicating only by e-mail sold a short essay to the magazine *Details,* having presented himself in e-mail exchanges with the editor as Anderson. *Details* issued Anderson a public apology and a private settlement followed.

195 **heteronyms** When Pessoa composed in heteronyms, literary alter egos who criticized and supported each other's works, Alberto Caeiro and Alvaros Dos Campos wrote in free verse but with very different tone, and Richard Reis wrote metrically but without rhyme.

196 **his own wacky photograph** On the Academy of American Poets website, Clover is pictured in a worn T-shirt with the word DISCIPLINE in capital letters splayed across his chest. His white hair is cropped short but in tight waves at the crown and three-blind-mice sunglasses hide his eyes. He angles his body away from the camera and the expression on his face is, well, disarmingly expressionless.

197 **response from Frank Kogan** Listserv exchange of June 3, 2002, on www.greenspun.com. Response signed by Frank Kogan.

197 **"a more fluid sense of self . . . what does not fit in."** Turkle, *Life on the Screen*, p. 262.

202 **flee the slave master or the Nazis** See Helen Fremont, *After Long Silence: A Memoir* (New York: Delacorte Press, 1999).

204 **investigative journalists and undercover** Werner Sollors, *Neither Black Nor White Yet Both: Thematic Explorations of Interracial Literature* (New York: Oxford University Press, 1997), "Typologies of Passing," pp. 250–252. For a consideration of white-for-black investigative passing narratives, see Phillip Brian Harper, *Are We Not Men? Masculine Anxiety and the Problem of African-American Identity* (New York: Oxford University Press, 1996), pp. 103–126, and esp. chap. 5, "Gender Politics and the 'Passing Fancy': Black Masculinity as Societal Problem." Gayle Wald, for example, describes *Black Like Me* as a form of colonial infiltration, "an essentializing piece of anthropological fieldwork designed to assuage liberal white guilt" in her essay, "A Most Disagreeable Mirror: Reflections on White Identity in *Black Like Me*," in Ginsberg, *Passing and the Fictions of Identity*, pp. 151–177.

205 **Tramp Major bellows** George Orwell, *Down and Out in Paris and London* (New York: Harcourt, 1933), p. 145.

205 **fierce-looking stranger** John Howard Griffin, *Black Like Me* (New York: Signet, 1996), p. 15.

205 **harsh words and a spank.** Ted Conover, *Newjack: Guarding Sing-Sing* (New York: Vintage, 2000), p. 244.

205 **"a distant race of people . . . time on their hands."** Barbara Ehrenreich, *Nickled and Dimed: On (Not) Getting By in America* (New York: Metropolitan, 2001), p. 34. Thanks for the preceding four citations to my graduate student seminar, Spring 2003.

206 **"Let beautiful young virgins . . . Majesty."** *Tanakh: The Holy Scriptures, The New JPS Translation According to the Traditional Hebrew Text* (Philadelphia: Jewish Publication Society, 1985), Esther 2:2, p. 1458.

206 **"If it pleases . . . exterminated."** Esther 7:4, p. 1464.

207 **out went the impact of an unjust policy and with it, the perceived need to pass.** Shirlee Taylor Haizlipp is the author of *The Sweeter the Juice,* a chronicle of her effort to reunite her black mother with the rest of her immediate family, that had become white. In a piece entitled "Passing" for the February-March 1999 issue of *American Heritage,* Haizlipp quotes Carla K. Bradshaw, a clinical psychologist, saying, "If an ideal world existed free from the psychology of dominance, where racial differences carried no stigma and racial purity was irrelevant, the concept of passing would have no meaning. In fact, passing of any kind loses meaning in the context of true egalitarianism." Of the Book of Esther: No wonder the story became such an important source of succor to the Marranos of the Inquisition, Jews forced into false conversion to Christianity in late medieval Spain.

Chapter Seven: Passing Notes, Passing Tones

209 **"Every profound spirit . . . sign of life he gives."** Friedrich Nietzsche, *Beyond Good and Evil,* 1886.

210 **way to define passing** *Webster's New World Dictionary of the American Language*, p. 1037.

210 **dissonant interjection** Special thanks to Marie Rolf, Ph.D., music theorist and director of graduate studies, Eastman School of Music, for help with the musical parallel.

212 **"It is a means of navigating . . . simple answer."** Tobias Barrington Wolff, e-mail and telephone interview by author, December 22, 2002.

212   **"rather than simply minimizing the costs to oneself"** Claudia Mills, "The Ethics of Pretending to Be What You Are Not," *Social Theory and Practice,* Spring 1999, pp. 29–51; telephone interview by author and e-mail exchange, December 17, 2002.

215   **"Yet, we are still left . . . fixed cultural identity."** Honorable Jody Adams, interview by author, New York City, December 31, 2001.

215   **New York's rent control laws** Eric Lane, Eric. J. Shmertz Distinguished Professor of Public Law in Public Service at Hofstra University, telephone interview by author, December 22, 2002, and subsequent e-mail exchanges. The rent control case is *Braschi v. Stahl Associates*, 543 N.E. 2d 49 (1989).

218   **Brandon Teena . . . were without rancor** The documentary was entitled *The Brandon Teena Story* (1998), written and directed by Susan Muska and Greta Olafsdottir. The feature film starring Hilary Swank, *Boys Don't Cry* (1999), was directed by Kimberly Peirce and written by Peirce and Andy Bienen.

218   **"widows" of Billy Tipton** In an interview by jerryjazzmusician.com, Middlebrook is asked if Tipton's "wives" felt embarrassed by the revelations. "Did they feel silly having to admit to you that she is going to write a book and expose how I didn't know that this guy I was married to was actually a woman?" Middlebrook replies: "Of course they were! But I wasn't the first person that had talked to them about this. They had been sought out by the journalists. I think I benefited by showing them that I am not a journalist, that I was interested in their own accounts of their own lives and how that fits into the story. The thing that was quite appealing to me about this whole story is that Billy did not make enemies, even of these women that he deceived. First of all, it was a kind of funny class issue. One has to think about the glamour of the performer. Even though this was pretty small time stuff, still a guy on the bandstand who was good looking and cool, nicely dressed and flirtatious, and he turns his eye on 'you,' you like being admired like that, by someone like Billy. He had an air of superiority over these young women—party girls—they were delighted, they were flattered by Billy's attention. They were also good-hearted women who really seemed to enjoy themselves. Billy was good to them. He had a good education, was well spoken. He was a man who had a rather superior education. . . . He made the rules in the house. He in-

sisted on his privacy. None of the women who thought of this afterward felt his requirements were abusive, or doing something fundamentally dishonest to them. It was very odd, they did not feel deceived in any way." See www.jerryjazzmusician.com/linernotes/wood.html#Billy's family life.

218 "matter of great moral import" "petty, silly matter . . . great difficulty." W. E. B. Du Bois, review of Nella Larsen, *Passing, Crisis*, July 1929, p. 223.

Bibliography

Abagnale, Frank W., with Stan Redding. *Catch Me If You Can: The Amazing True Story of the Most Extraordinary Liar in the History of Fun and Profit.* New York: Broadway, 1980.

Abel, Elizabeth, Barbara Christian, and Helene Moglen. *Female Subjects in Black and White.* Berkeley: University of California Press, 1997.

Alpert, Rebecca T., Sue Levi Elwell, and Shirley Idelson. *Lesbian Rabbis: The First Generation.* New Brunswick, N.J.: Rutgers University Press, 2001.

Anthony, Sterling. *Cookie Cutter.* New York: Ballantine, 1999.

Appiah, Kwame Anthony, and Henry Louis Gates Jr. *Identities.* Chicago: University of Chicago Press, 1995.

Appiah, Kwame Anthony, and Henry Louis Gates Jr., eds. *Critical Inquiry.* Chicago: University of Chicago Press, 1995.

Appiah, Kwame Anthony, and Amy Gutmann. *Color Conscious: The Political Morality of Race.* Princeton, N.J.: Princeton University Press, 1996.

Azoulay, Katya Gibel. *Black, Jewish, and Interracial: It's Not the Color of Your Skin but the Race of Your Kin, and Other Myths of Identity.* Durham, N.C.: Duke University Press, 1997.

Back, Les, and John Solomos. *Theories of Race and Racism: A Reader.* London: Routledge, 2000.

Baldwin, James. *Giovanni's Room.* New York: Dell, 1956.

Bay, Mia. *The White Image in the Black Mind: African-American Ideas About White People, 1830–1925.* New York: Oxford University Press, 2000.

Bakhtin, Mikhail. *Rabelais and His World.* Bloomington: Indiana University Press, 1984.

Beals, Melba Pattilo. *White Is a State of Mind.* New York: Putnam, 1999.

Beck, Gad. *An Underground Life: Memoirs of a Gay Jew in Nazi Berlin.* Madison: University of Wisconsin Press, 1999.

Becker, Ernest. *The Denial of Death.* New York: Free Press, 1997.

Berger, Maurice. *White Lies: Race and the Myth of Whiteness.* New York: Farrar, Straus and Giroux, 1999.

Bloom, Amy. *Normal: Transsexual CEOs, Crossdressing Cops, and Hermaphrodites with Attitude.* New York: Random House, 2002.

Bok, Sissela. *Lying: Moral Choice in Public and Private Life.* New York: Vintage, 1978.

———. *Secrets: On the Ethics of Concealment and Revelation.* New York: Vintage, 1989.

Bornstein, Kate. *Gender Outlaw: On Men, Women, and the Rest of Us.* New York: Routledge, 1994.

———. *My Gender Workbook.* New York: Routledge, 1998.

Boureau, Alain, and Lydia G. Cochrane. *The Myth of Pope Joan.* Chicago: University of Chicago Press, 2001.

Bowman, Elizabeth Atkins. *Dark Secret* New York: Forge, 2000.

Brodkin, Karen. *How Jews Became White Folks and What That Says About Race in America.* New Brunswick, N.J.: Rutgers University Press, 1998.

Browder, Laura. *Slippery Characters: Ethnic Impersonators and American Identity.* Chapel Hill: University of North Carolina, 2000.

Brown, Ursula M. *The Interracial Experience: Growing Up Black/White Racially Mixed in the United States.* Westport, Conn.: Praeger, 2001.

Broyard, Anatole. *Kafka Was the Rage: A Greenwich Village Memoir.* New York: Vintage, 1993.

Broyard, Bliss. *My Father, Dancing.* New York: Knopf, 1999.

Butler, Judith. *Gender Trouble: Feminism and the Subversion of Identity.* New York: Routledge, 1990.

Campbell, Jeremy. *The Liar's Tale: A History of Falsehood.* New York: Norton, 2001.

Campbell, W. Joseph *Yellow Journalism: Puncturing Myths, Defining the Legacies.* Westport, Conn.: Praeger, 2001.

Caughie, Pamela L. *Passing and Pedagogy: The Dynamics of Responsibility.* Urbana: University of Illinois Press, 1999.

Charett, Sheldon. *The Modern Identity Changer: How to Create a New Identity for Privacy and Personal Freedom.* Boulder, Colo.: Paladin, 1997.

Chesnutt, Charles W. With an introduction by Donald B. Gibson. *The House Behind the Cedars*. 1900. New York: Penguin, 1993.

Coetzee, J. M. *Disgrace*. New York: Viking, 1999.

Cohen, Patricia Cline. *The Murder of Helen Jewett: The Life and Death of a Prostitute in Nineteenth Century New York*. New York: Knopf, 1998.

Colapinto, John. *As Nature Made Him: The Boy Who Was Raised as a Girl*. New York: HarperCollins, 2000.

Cross, Donna Woolfolk. *Pope Joan: A Novel*. New York: Ballantine, 1996.

Crouch, Stanley. *The All-American Skin Game, or, The Decoy of Race: The Long and Short of It, 1990–1994*. New York: Vintage, 1995.

Dalmage, Heather M. *Tripping on the Color Line: Black-White Multiracial Families in a Racially Divided World*. New Brunswick, N.J.: Rutgers University Press, 2000.

Davis, F. James. *Who Is Black? One Nation's Definition*. 1920. University Park: Pennsylvania State University Press, 2000.

Davis, Thadious M. *Nella Larsen: Novelist of the Harlem Renaissance. A Woman's Life Unveiled*. Baton Rouge: Louisiana State University Press, 1994.

Dericotte, Toi. *The Black Notebooks*. New York: Norton, 1997.

Diamond, Elin. *Performance and Cultural Politics*. New York: Routledge, 1996.

Diderot, Denis. *Rameau's Nephew/D'Alembert's Dream*. London: Penguin Classics, 1966.

Dobbs, Michael. *Madeleine Albright: A Twentieth Century Odyssey*. New York: Holt, 1999.

Docter, Richard F. *Transvestites and Transsexuals: Toward a Theory of Cross-Gender Behavior*. New York: Plenum, 1988.

Douglas, Mary. *Purity and Danger: An Analysis of Concepts of Pollution and Taboo*. 1966. London: Routledge, 2002.

Drake, St. Clair, and Horace R. Cayton. *Black Metropolis: A Study of Negro Life in a Northern City*. Chicago: University of Chicago, 1993.

Dubner, Stephen J. *Turbulent Souls: A Catholic Son's Return to His Jewish Family*. New York: Avon, 1998.

Dyer, Richard. *White*. New York: Routledge, 1997.

Early, Gerald, ed. *Lure and Loathing: Twenty Black Intellectuals Address W.E.B. Du Bois's Dilemma of the Double-Consciousness of African-Americans*. New York: Penguin, 1993.

Ehrenreich, Barbara. *Nickled and Dimed: On (Not) Getting By in America.* New York: Metropolitan, 2001.

Eliot, George. *Daniel Deronda.* London: Wordsworth Classics, 1996.

Ellison, Ralph. *The Invisible Man.* 1947. New York: Vintage, 1995.

———. *Juneteenth.* New York: Random House, 1999.

Erdrich, Louise. *The Last Report on the Miracles at Little Horse.* New York: HarperCollins, 2001.

Eskin, Blake. *A Life in Pieces: The Making and Unmaking of Binjamin Wilkomirski.* New York: Norton, 2001.

Fausto-Sterling, Anne. *Myths of Gender: Biological Theories About Women and Men.* New York: Basic Books, 1992.

———. *Sexing the Body: Gender Politics and the Construction of Sexuality.* New York: Basic Books, 2000.

Fitzgerald, F. Scott. *The Great Gatsby.* New York: Scribner's, 1925.

———. *The Jazz Age.* New York: Scribner's, 1931.

Frankenburg, Ruth. *Displacing Whiteness: Essays in Social and Cultural Criticism.* Durham, N.C.: Duke University Press, 1997.

———. *White Women, Race Matters: The Social Construction of Whiteness.* Minneapolis: University of Minnesota Press, 1993.

Fremont, Helen. *After Long Silence.* New York: Delacorte, 1999.

Fried, Charles. *Right and Wrong.* Cambridge, Mass.: Harvard University Press, 1978.

Friedman, Lester D. *Jewish Image in American Film: 70 Years of Hollywood's Vision of Jewish Characters and Themes.* Seacaucus, N.J.: Citadel, 1987.

Friskopp, Annette, and Sharon Silverstein. *Straight Jobs, Gay Lives.* New York: Simon & Schuster, 1995.

Funderburg, Lise. *Black, White, Other: Biracial Americans Talk About Race and Identity.* New York: Morrow, 1994.

Garber, Marjorie. *Vested Interests: Cross-Dressing and Cultural Anxiety.* New York: Routledge, 1992.

Garvey, John, and Noel Ignatiev. *Race Traitor.* New York: Routledge, 1996.

Gates, Henry Louis. *Colored People.* New York: Knopf, 1994.

———. *Thirteen Ways of Looking at a Black Man.* New York: Random House, 1997.

Gilman, Sander L. Afterword to *Seeing the Insane.* Lincoln: University of Nebraska Press, 1996.

_____.*Creating Beauty to Cure the Soul: Race and Psychology in the Shaping of Aesthetic Surgery.* Durham, N.C.: Duke University Press, 1998.

_____. *Difference and Pathology: Stereotypes of Sexuality, Race, and Madness.* Ithaca, N.Y.: Cornell University Press, 1985.

_____. *Freud, Race, and Gender.* Princeton, N.J.: Princeton University Press, 1993.

_____. *The Jew's Body.* New York: Routledge, 1991.

_____. *Making the Body Beautiful: A Cultural History of Aesthetic Surgery.* Princeton, N.J.: Princeton University Press, 1999.

Gilroy, Paul. *Against Race: Imagining Political Culture Beyond the Color Line.* Cambridge, Mass.: Belknap, 2000.

Ginsberg, Elaine K. *Passing and the Fictions of Identity.* Durham, N.C.: Duke University, 1996.

Gitlin, Todd. *The Twilight of Common Dreams: Why America Is Wracked by Culture Wars.* New York: Holt, 1995.

Glazer, Nathan, and Daniel P. Moynihan. *Beyond the Melting Pot: The Negroes, Puerto Ricans, Jews, Italians, and Irish of New York City.* Cambridge, Mass.: MIT Press, 1995.

Goffman, Erving. *The Presentation of Self in Everyday Life.* New York: Anchor, 1959.

_____. *Stigma: Notes on the Management of Spoiled Identity.* New York: Touchstone/Simon & Schuster, 1963.

Goldberg, David Theo, ed. *Anatomy of Racism.* Minneapolis: University of Minnesota Press, 1990.

Gordon, Linda. *The Great Arizona Orphan Abduction.* Cambridge, Mass.: Harvard University Press, 1999.

Gossett, Thomas F. *Race: The History of an Idea in America.* New York: Oxford University Press, 1997.

Graham, Lawrence Otis. *Our Kind of People: Inside America's Black Upper Class.* New York: HarperCollins, 1999.

Gregory, Steven, and Roger Sanjek, eds. *Race.* New Brunswick, N.J.: Rutgers University Press, 1996.

Griffin, John Howard. *Black Like Me.* New York: Signet, 1962.

Gubar, Susan. *RaceChanges: White Skin, Black Face in American Culture.* New York: Oxford University Press, 1997.

Hacker, Andrew. *Two Nations: Black and White, Separate, Hostile, and Unequal.* New York: Ballantine, 1992.

Haizlip, Shirlee Taylor. *The Sweeter the Juice: A Family Memoir in Black and White.* New York: Touchstone, 1995.

Hale, Grace Elizabeth. *Making Whiteness: The Culture of Segregation in the South, 1890–1940.* New York: Vintage, 1999.

Hall, Wade. *Passing for Black: The Life and Careers of Mae Street Kidd.* Lexington: University of Kentucky Press, 1997.

Halter, Marilyn. *Shopping for Identity: The Marketing of Ethnicity.* New York: Schocken, 2000.

Hammer, Joshua. *Chosen by God: A Brother's Journey.* New York: Hyperion, 1999.

Handlin, Oscar. *The Newcomers: Negroes and Puerto Ricans in a Changing Metropolis.* Cambridge, Mass.: Harvard University Press, 1959.

Harper, Phillip Brian. *Are We Not Men? Masculine Anxiety and the Problem of African-American Identity.* New York: Oxford University Press, 1996.

———. *Framing the Margins: The Social Logic of Post-Modern Culture.* New York: Oxford University Press, 1994.

———. *Private Affairs: Critical Ventures in the Culture of Social Relations.* New York: New York University Press, 1999.

Harrington, Walt. *Crossings: A White Man's Journey into Black America.* New York: HarperCollins, 1992.

Hart, Dianne Walta. *Undocumented in L.A.: An Immigrant's Story.* Wilmington, Del.: SR Books, 1997.

Havel, Vaclav. *Living in Truth.* London: Faber & Faber, 1986.

Hecht, Anne. *Call Me Crazy.* New York: Scribner's, 2001.

Henry, Neil. *Pearl's Secret: A Black Man's Search for His White Family.* Berkeley: University of California Press, 2001.

Holquist, Michael, ed. *The Dialogic Imagination: Four Essays by M. M. Bakhtin.* Austin: University of Texas Press, 1981.

Hoover, Kenneth, with James Marcia and Kristen Parris. *The Power of Identity: Politics in a New Key.* Chatham, N.J.: Chatham House, 1997.

Huggins, Nathan Irvin. *Harlem Renaissance.* New York: Oxford University Press, 1971.

Hunter, Ski, Colleen Shannon, Jo Knox, and James I. Martin, eds. *Lesbian, Gay, and Bisexual Youths and Adults: Knowledge for Human Services Practice.* Thousand Oaks, Calif.: Sage, 1998.

Hurston, Zora Neale. *Dust Tracks on a Road.* New York: Lippincott, 1942.

———. *Jonah's Gourd Vine.* New York: Lippincott, 1934.

_____. *Their Eyes Were Watching God.* New York: Lippincott, 1937.

Ignatiev, Noel. *How the Irish Became White.* New York: Routledge, 1995.

Isaacs, Susan. *Lily White.* New York: HarperPaperbacks, 1997.

Jacobson, Matthew Frye. *Whiteness of a Different Color: European Immigrants and the Alchemy of Race.* Cambridge, Mass.: Harvard University Press, 1998.

Jacoby, Susan. *Half-Jew: A Daughter's Search for Her Family's Buried Past.* New York: Scribner's, 2000.

Jewish Law and Standards Committee of the Conservative Movement. *Responsa 1991–2000.* New York: Rabbinical Assembly, 2002.

Johnson, James Weldon. *Along This Way: The Autobiography of James Weldon Johnson.* 1933. New York: DaCapo, 2000.

_____. *Autobiography of an Ex-Coloured Man.* 1912. New York: Vintage, 1989. Reissue with new introduction by Henry Louis Gates Jr.

Johnson, Kevin R. *How Did You Get to Be Mexican: A White/Brown Man's Search for Identity.* Philadelphia: Temple University Press, 1999.

Jones, Patricia. *Passing: A Novel.* New York: Avon, 1999.

Kaplan, Amy, and Donald E. Pease, eds. *Cultures of United States Imperialism.* Durham, N.C.: Duke University Press, 1993.

Kenan, Randall. *Walking on Water: Black American Lives at the Turn of the Twenty-First Century.* New York: Knopf, 1999.

Kennedy, Randall. *Interracial Intimacies: Sex, Marriage, Identity, and Adoption.* New York: Pantheon, 2002.

Kessel, Barbara. *Suddenly Jewish: Jews Raised as Gentiles Discover Their Jewish Roots.* Hanover, N.H.: Brandeis University Press/University Press of New England, 2000.

Kull, Andrew. *The Color-Blind Constitution.* Cambridge, Mass.: Harvard University Press, 1992.

Kunzru, Hari. *The Impressionist: A Novel.* New York: Dutton, 2002.

Lanier, Shannon, and Jane Feldman. *Jefferson's Children: The Story of One American Family.* New York: Random House, 2000.

Larsen, Nella. *Passing.* Introduction by Thadious M. Davis. New York: Penguin, 1997.

_____. *Passing.* Introduction by Ntozake Shange. New York: Modern Library, 2000.

_____. *Quicksand and Passing.* Edited by Deborah McDowell. American

Women Writers Series. New Brunswick, N.J.: Rutgers University Press, 1986.

Lazarre, Jane. *Beyond the Whiteness of Whiteness: Memoir of a White Mother of Black Sons.* Durham, N.C.: Duke University Press, 1996.

Leslie, Kent Anderson. *Woman of Color, Daughter of Privilege: Amanda America Dickson, 1849–1893.* Athens: University of Georgia Press, 1995.

Lewis, Alfred Allan. *Ladies and Not-So-Gentle Women.* New York: Viking, 2000.

Lewis, David Levering. *When Harlem Was in Vogue.* New York: Oxford University Press, 1979.

Lewis, Earl, and Heidi Ardizzone. *Love on Trial: An American Scandal in Black and White.* New York: Norton, 2001.

Lipsitz, George. *The Possessive Investment in Whiteness: How White People Profit from Identity Politics.* Philadelphia: Temple University Press, 1998.

Lopez, Ian F. Haney. *White by Law: The Legal Constitution of Race.* New York: New York University Press, 1996.

Maalouf, Amin. *In the Name of Identity: Violence and the Need to Belong.* New York: Arcade, 2001.

MacDonald, Michael Patrick. *All Souls: A Family Story from Southie.* Boston: Beacon, 1999.

McBride, James. *The Color of Water.* New York: Riverhead, 1996.

McClintock, Anne. *Imperial Leather: Race, Gender, and Sexuality in the Colonial Contest.* New York: Routledge, 1995.

McCloskey, Deirdre N. *Crossing: A Memoir.* Chicago: University of Chicago Press, 1999.

McDonnell, Evelyn, and Ann Powers, eds. *Rock She Wrote: Women Write About Rock, Pop, and Rap.* New York: Cooper Square, 1999.

McGhee, Millie L. *J. Edgar Hoover: Passing for White?* Rancho Cucamonga, Calif.: Allen-Morris, 2000.

McGuire, Lillian H. *Uprooted and Transplanted: From Africa to America: Focus on African-Americans in Essex County, Virginia. Oppressions-Achievements-Contributions. The 1600s–1900s.* New York: Vantage, 1999.

Malcolmson, Scott. *One Drop of Blood: The American Misadventure of Race.* New York: Farrar, Straus and Giroux, 2000.

Manegold, Catherine. *In Glory's Shadow: Shannon Faulkner, the Citadel, and a Changing America.* New York: Knopf, 2000.

Marcus, Greil. *Lipstick Traces: A Secret History of the Twentieth Century.* Cambridge, Mass.: Harvard University Press, 1989.

————. *Mystery Train.* New York: Plume, 1997.

Maurer, David W. *The Big Con: The Story of the Confidence Man.* New York: Anchor, 1999.

Mealy, Rosemari. *Fidel and Malcolm X: Memories of a Meeting.* Melbourne: Ocean, 1993.

Melville, Herman. *The Confidence-Man.* Oxford: Oxford University Press, 1989.

Mendelsohn, Daniel. *The Elusive Embrace: Desire and the Riddle of Identity.* New York: Knopf, 1999.

Mullings, Leith. *On Our Own Terms: Race, Class, and Gender in the Lives of African American Women.* New York: Routledge, 1997.

Myrdal, Gunnar. *An American Dilemma.* Vols. 1–2, *The Negro Problem and Modern Democracy.* 1944. New Brunswick, N.J.: Transaction, 1996.

Nahai, Gina. *Sunday's Silence.* New York: Harcourt, 2001.

The National Data Book: Statistical Abstracts of the United States. 120th ed. Austin, Tex.: Hoover's Business Press, 2000.

Nestle, Joan, Clare Howell, and Riki Wilchins. *GenderQueer: Voices from Beyond the Sexual Binary.* Los Angeles: Alison, 2002.

Orwell, George. *Down and Out in Paris and London.* New York: Harvest Harcourt, 1933.

Peiss, Kathy. *Hope in a Jar: The Making of America's Beauty Culture.* New York: Owl Books/Henry Holt, 1998.

Powdermaker, Hortense. *After Freedom.* 1939. Madison: University of Wisconsin Press, 1993.

Powers, Ann. *Weird Like Us: My Bohemian America.* New York: Simon & Schuster, 2000.

Rabinow, Paul, ed. *The Foucault Reader.* New York: Pantheon, 1984.

Rawls, John. *A Theory of Justice.* 1971. Cambridge, Mass.: Belknap Press, Harvard University Press, 1999.

Reddy, Maureen T. *Crossing the Color Line: Race, Parenting and Culture.* New Brunswick, N.J.: Rutgers University Press, 1994.

Reed, Adolph, Jr. *Stirrings in the Jug: Black Politics in the Post-Segregation Era.* Minneapolis: University of Minnesota Press, 1999.

Reed, Ishmael, ed. *MultiAmerica: Essays on Cultural Wars and Cultural Peace.* New York: Penguin, 1998.

Rich, Adrienne. *Arts of the Possible*. New York: Norton, 2001.

———. *On Lies, Secrets, and Silence*. New York: Norton, 1979.

Richards, David A.J. *Italian-American: The Racializing of an Ethnic Identity*. New York: New York University Press, 1999.

Richburg, Keith B. *Out of America: A Black Man Confronts Africa*. New York: BasicBooks, 1998.

Robbins, Bruce, ed. *The Phantom Public Sphere*. Minneapolis: University of Minnesota Press, 1993.

Roediger, David R. *The Wages of Whiteness: Race and the Making of the American Working Class*. London: Verso, 1991.

Roediger, David R., ed. *Black on White: Black Writers on What It Means to Be White*. New York: Schocken, 1998.

Rogers, D. E. *White Lie: An American Tragedy*. Bryn Mawr: Buy Books on the web.com, 1998.

Rogin, Michael. *Blackface, White Noise: Jewish Immigrants in the Hollywood Melting Pot*. Berkeley: University of California Press, 1998.

Roiphe, Anne. *1185 Park Avenue*. New York: Touchstone, 1999.

Root, Maria P.P., ed. *Racially Mixed People in America*. Newbury Park, Calif.: Sage, 1992.

Rushton, J. Philippe. *Race, Evolution, and Behavior: A Life History Perspective*. Port Huron, N.Y.: Charles Darwin Research Institute, 2000.

Russell, Kathy, Midge Wilson, and Ronald Hall. *The Color Complex: The Politics of Skin Color Among African Americans*. New York: Harcourt Brace Jovanovich, 1992.

Sanchez, Maria Carla, and Linda Schlossberg, eds. *Passing: Identity and Interpretation in Sexuality, Race, and Religion*. New York: New York University Press, 2001.

Sanford, Rick. *The Boys Across the Street*. New York: Faber & Faber, 1999.

Santiago, Esmeralda. *Almost a Woman*. New York: Vintage, 1998.

———. *When I Was Puerto Rican*. New York: Vintage, 1993.

Sartre, Jean-Paul. *Anti-Semite and Jew: An Exploration of the Etiology of Hate*. 1948. New York: Schocken, 1995.

Scales-Trent, Judy. *Notes of a White Black Woman: Race, Color, Community*. University Park: Pennsylvania State University Press, 1995.

Schlesinger, Arthur M., Jr. *The Disuniting of America: Reflections on a Multicultural Society*. Rev. ed. New York: Norton, 1998.

Senna, Danzy. *Caucasia*. New York: Riverhead, 1999.

Skerry, Peter. *Counting on the Census: Race, Group Identity, and the Evasion of Politics*. Washington, D.C.: Brookings Institution, 2000.

Sleeper, Jim. *Liberal Racism*. New York: Penguin, 1997.

Smiley, Jane. *The All-True Travels and Adventures of Lidie Newton*. New York: Fawcett, Ballantine, 1998.

Smith, Dinitia. *The Illusionist*. New York: Scribner's, 1997.

Sollors, Werner. *Beyond Ethnicity: Consent and Dissent in American Culture*. New York: Oxford University Press, 1986.

———. *Neither Black Nor White yet Both: Thematic Explorations of Interracial Literature*. New York: Oxford University Press, 1997.

———. *Theories of Ethnicity: A Classical Reader*. New York: New York University, 1996.

Sollors, Werner, ed. *Interracialism: Black-White Intermarriage in American History, Literature, and Law*. London: Oxford University Press, 2000.

Spickard, Paul R. *Mixed Blood: Intermarriage and Ethnic Identity in Twentieth Century America*. Madison: University of Wisconsin Press, 1989.

Stanford, Peter. *The Legend of Pope Joan: In Search of the Truth*. New York: Berkley, 1999.

Stern, Jessica. *The Ultimate Terrorist*. Cambridge, Mass.: Harvard University Press, 1999.

Sullivan, Evelin. *The Concise Book of Lying*. New York: Farrar, Straus, Giroux, 2001.

Taylor, Charles. *The Ethics of Authenticity*. Cambridge, Mass.: Harvard University Press, 1991.

Taylor, Charles, and Amy Guttmann. *Multiculturalism: Examining the Politics of Recognition*. Princeton, N.J.: Princeton University Press, 1994.

Thernstrom, Stephan, and Abigail Thernstrom. *America in Black and White: One Nation Indivisible*. New York: Touchstone, 1997.

Trilling, Lionel. *Sincerity and Authenticity*. Cambridge, Mass.: Harvard University Press, 1971.

Turkle, Sherry. *Life on the Screen: Identity in the Age of the Internet*. New York: Simon & Schuster, 1995.

Wald, Gayle. *Crossing the Line: Racial Passing in Twentieth Century U.S. Literature and Culture*. Durham, N.C.: Duke University Press, 2000.

Walker, Rebecca. *Black, White, and Jewish: Autobiography of a Shifting Self*. New York: Riverhead, 2001.

Wall, Cheryl A. *Women of the Harlem Renaissance.* Bloomington: Indiana University Press, 1995.

Washington, Mary Helen. *Invented Lives: Narratives of Black Women, 1860–1960.* New York: Doubleday, 1987.

Waters, Mary C. *Ethnic Options: Choosing Identities in America.* Berkeley: University of California Press, 1990.

West, Nathanael. *Miss Lonelyhearts and The Day of the Locust.* New York: New Directions, 1933.

Whitley, Burkett, and Glenna Whitley. *Stolen Valor: How the Vietnam Generation Was Robbed of Its Heroes and Its History.* Dallas: Verity, 1998.

Wiegman, Robyn. *American Anatomies: Theorizing Race and Gender.* Durham, N.C.: Duke University Press, 1995.

Wilchins, Riki Anne. *Read My Lips: Sexual Subversion and the End of Gender.* Ithaca, N.Y.: Firebrand, 1997.

Wilensky, Amy S. *Passing for Normal: A Memoir of Compulsion.* New York: Broadway, 1999.

Williams, Gregory Howard. *Life on the Color Line: The True Story of a White Boy Who Discovered He Was Black.* New York: Plume, 1995.

Williamson, Joel. *New People: Miscegenation and Mulattoes in the United States.* Baton Rouge: Louisiana State University Press, 1995.

Woodward, Kathryn, ed. *Identity and Difference.* London: Sage, 1997.

SELECTED ARTICLES

Adelman, Ken. "Islam Unveiled." *Washingtonian*, November 1999, p. 31.

Bates, Karen Grigsby. "Passing: Blacks Who Go Incognito in White Society Learn Terrible Truths and Tell Dangerous Lies." www.salon.com/books/feature/1998/04/15feature.html.

Baye, Betty Winston. "In the Good Old Days of Being Colored." *Gannett News Service*, June 3, 1994.

Bethune, Brian. "Truth and Consequences: Archie Belaney's Life of Deception Brought His Cause to the World." *Maclean's*, October 4, 1999, p. 58.

Billinton, Linda. "Dressed for Excess: Female Impersonators Set the Stage for Campy Fun and Ego-Gratification." *Anchorage Daily News*, November 3, 1995, Weekend sec., p. 8.

"Black America and Tiger's Dilemma: National Leaders Praise Golfer's

Accomplishments and Debate Controversial 'Mixed Race' Issue." *Ebony*, July 1997, p. 28.

"Black Like Whom? The Whitney Museum's Political Show May Stir Up a Cultural Storm." *Newsweek*, November 14, 1994, p. 64.

"The Blurred Racial Lines of Famous Families." *Frontline*, 1998. www.pbs. org/wgbh/pages/frontline/shows/secret/famous.

Bowley, Graham. "How Grey Owl Won Over the West: Arcadia: Graham Bowley Charts the Life of an Englishman Who Fooled the Public into Believing He Was a Red Indian." *Financial Times,* December 24, 1999, p. 1.

Brody, Jennifer Devere. "Book Review: Rereading Race and Gender: When White Women Matter." *American Quarterly* 48, no. 1 (1996): 153–160.

Brown, Cecil. "Doing That Ol' Oscar Soft-Shoe: Do This Year's Crop of Oscar Nominees Perpetuate the Same Old Racial Stereotypes?" *San Francisco Examiner* magazine, March 26, 1995, p. M24.

Caputi, Jane. "'Specifying' Fannie Hurst: Langston Hughes's 'Limitations of Life,' Zora Neale Hurston's *Their Eyes Were Watching God,* and Toni Morrison's *The Bluest Eye* as 'Answers' to Hurst's *Imitation of Life*." *Black American Literature Forum*, Winter 1990.

Cardenas, Jose. "Authors: The People Behind the Books We Read: But, Gosh, You Don't Look Like a Latino." *Los Angeles Times*, November 10, 1999, E1.

Clines, Francis X. "For Gay Soldier, a Daily Barrage of Threats and Slurs." *New York Times*, December 12, 1999, p. 33.

Cose, Ellis. "Census and the Complex Issue of Race." *Society*, September 19, 1997, p. 9.

Cotter, Holland. "Art Review: Inside-Out Meditations on the Poison of Racism." *New York Times,* January 8, 1999, p. E42.

"Crossing Over: Transsexuals Come Out." *20/20*, January 19, 1996, transcript 1603–3.

Curtis, Cathy. "Art Review: 'Ciphers': Is Prejudice Only Identity Deep?" *Los Angeles Times*, January 24, 1995, p. F3.

Demchuk, David. "Unleashing the Queen: Drag Has Steadily Increased Its Public Profile Since the Rise of the Modern Day Gay Liberation Movement." *Toronto Life*, October 1994, pp. 54–60.

DeMott, Benjamin. "Passing." *New York Times*, November 2, 1997, sec. 7, p. 45.

———. "Put On a Happy Face: Masking the Differences Between Blacks and Whites." *Harper's*, September 1995.

Deutschman, Alan. "Wall Street's Secret Society: Gay Men and Lesbians Are Hiding in Plain Sight All Over the Financial Industry. Why Are They Living a Fifties Life in the Nineties?" *New York Magazine*, March 29, 1999.

Dobbs, Michael. "Double Identity: Why Madeleine Albright Can't Escape Her Past." *New Yorker*, March 29, 1999, pp. 50–57.

Dubner, Stephen J. "Choosing My Religion." *New York Times,* March 31, 1996, sec. 6, p. 36.

Edwards, Tamela M. "Family Reunion: The Revelation About Thomas Jefferson's Liaison Spotlights a Sensitive Racial Issue—Passing for White." *Time*, November 23, 1998, pp. 85–86.

Ferguson, Stuart. "TV: Masculine/Feminine." *Wall Street Journal*, July 26, 1999, p. A21.

Flitterman-Lewis, Sandy. "*Imitation(s) of Life*: The Black Woman's Double Determination As Troubling 'Other.'" *Literature and Psychology* 34, no. 4 (1988): 44–57.

Foreman, Gabrielle P. "'Reading Aright': White Slavery, Black Referents, and the Strategy of Histotextuality in *Iola Leroy*." *Yale Journal of Criticism* 10, no. 2 (1997): 327–354.

Foster, Thomas. "'Trapped by the Body'? Telepresence Technologies and Transgendered Performance in Feminist and Lesbian Rewritings of Cyberpunk Fiction." *Modern Fiction Studies* 43, no. 3 (1997): 708–742.

Fox-Alston, Jeanne. "Children's Books." *Washington Post*, February 8, 1998.

Fried, Charles. "The Evil of Lying." In *Right and Wrong*, pp. 59–69. Cambridge, Mass.: Harvard University Press, 1978.

George, Lynell. "Big Eyes for Details of Life; Author's Memoirs Explore Culture, Race, and Identity." *Los Angeles Times*, Southern California Living, Part E, p. 3, View Desk, December 14, 1998, Monday, Home Edition.

_____. "Black Women's Hair Wars Seeking Victory over Locked-in Relaxers." *Commercial Appeal*, August 30, 1998, p. F2.

_____. "Inside Story: Guessing Games, Passing, an Embarrassing Remnant of Race Politics and History . . ." *Los Angeles Times*, February 21, 1999.

Giddings, Paula. "The New Season/Art; Black Makes and the Prison of Myth." *New York Times*, September 11, 1994, sec. 2, p. 50.

Gladwell, Malcolm. "True Colors: Hair Dye and the Hidden History of Postwar America." *New Yorker*, March 22, 1999, pp. 70–81.

Goldberg, Carey. "Shunning 'He' and 'She,' They Fight for Respect." *New York Times*, September 8, 1996, sec. 1, p. 24.

Goodhue, Thomas W. "TV Review: Film Shows Basketball Became More Than Game." *Asbury Seminary News*, February 10, 1999.

Gordon, Meryl. "The Boy Can't Help It." *New York Times*, April 26, 1999, pp. 38–44.

Hackett, Regina. "Artists' Study of Racism Is Beyond the Pale: A Dramatic Display of Flawed Reasoning." *Seattle Post-Intelligencer*, April 22, 1994, What's Happening section.

Haizlip, Shirlee Taylor. "Questioning the Mysteries of Her Own Family, the Author Finds Answers That Affect Us All." *American Heritage*, February-March 1999.

Handzo, Stephen. "Imitations of Lifelessness: Sirk's Ironic Tearjerker." *BrightLights Film Journal*. www.brightlightsfilm.com/18/18—lana.html.

Harper, Phillip Brian. "Passing for What? Racial Masquerade and the Demands of Upward Mobility." *Callaloo* 21, no. 2 (1998): 381–397.

Harrison, Judy. "Queen for a Night." *Bangor Daily News*, July 26, 1997.

Hartigan, Patti. "'Brandon' Probes Crime, Both Real and Virtual." *Boston Globe*, August 5, 1998, p. C1.

Hartl, John. "Documentary Questions the Meaning of Family." *Seattle Times*, October 17, 1997, p. G4.

Haviland, Beverly. "Passing from Paranoia to Plagiarism: the Abject Authorship of Nella Larsen." *Modern Fiction Studies* 43, no. 3 (1997): 295–318.

Hill, Mike. "What Was (the White) Race? Memory, Categories, Change." *Postmodern Culture* 7, no. 2 (1997).

Hirsch, Arthur. "Ghosts of the South." *Baltimore Sun*, September 21, 1997, p. K1.

Holden, Stephen. "A Rape and Beating, Later 3 Murders and Then a Twist." *New York Times*, September 23, 1998, p. E5.

Ignatiev, Noel. "Abolitionism and 'White Studies.'" *Race Traitor*. www.postfun.com/racetraitor/features.whitestudies.html.

James, Caryn. "Black Artists Grappling with Profound Questions of Art and Race." *New York Times*, February 1, 1999, television review sec., p. 8.

Jefferson, Margo. "Books of the Times; Reflections of Endings and Family Secrets." *New York Times*, January 12, 1994, p. C19.

———. "The Lives They Lived: Ella Fitzgerald; Ella in Wonderland." *New York Times*, December 29, 1996, sec. 6, p. 41.

_____."Revisions: On Defining Race, When Only Thinking Makes It So." *New York Times*, March 22, 1999, p. E2.

_____. "Revisions: Seeing Race a Costume That Everyone Wears." *New York Times*, May 4, 1998, pp. E2–3.

_____. "Revisions: Sometimes Survival Is More Important Identity." *New York Times*, February 22, 1999, p. E2.

_____. "Seven Unsung Novels Crying to Be Filmed." *New York Times*, January 18, 1998, sec. 2, p. 1.

_____. "Tricks the Mirrors Play." *New York Times,* October 17, 1999, sec. 5, p. 98.

_____. "Vintage Glimpses of a Lost Theatrical World." *New York Times*, October 20, 1996, sec. 2, p. 1.

_____. "Wandering Jew." *Newsweek*, May 9, 1977, p. 103.

_____. "Writing About Race, Walking on Eggshells." *New York Times,* June 10, 1999, p. E1.

Jones, Lisa. "Biracial Enough? (Or, What's This About a Multiracial Category on the Census?: A Conversation)." Address presented at Common Differences conference, Wesleyan University, May 1993.

Kaplan, Carla. "Undesirable Desire: Citizenship and Romance in Modern American Fiction." *Modern Fiction Studies* 43, no. 1 (1997): 144–169.

Kleeblatt, Norman L. "Multivalent Voices: Gay and Lesbian Artists Who Are Also Jewish Search for Ways to Address Questions of Ethnicity and Sexuality in Their Work; Identity Politics." *Art in America*, December 1995, p. 29.

Koppelman, Susan. "The Naming of Katz: Who Am I? Who Am I Supposed to Be? Who Can I Be? Passing, Assimilation, and Embodiment in Fiction by Fannie Hurst, Thyra Samter Winslow, Shalom Aleichem, Jamaica Kincaid, Elliott Roosevelt, Sue Grafton, and Alice Walker, with a Few Jokes Thrown In and Various References to Other Others." *Gold in Fish* 17, typescript.

Kuchta, Todd M. "The Dyer Straits of Whiteness." *Postmodern Culture* 9, no. 1 (1998).

Kumin, Maxine. "The Metamorphosis: At 52, the Economist and Historian Donald McCloskey Decided to Become a Woman." *New York Times Book Review*, November 14, 1999, p. 10.

Lassonde, Stephen. "Family Values, 1904 Version; Everyone, including the Supreme Court, Agreed That Anything Was Better Than Being Raised by Mexicans." *New York Times Book Review*, January 9, 2000, p. 7.

Lingeman, Richard. "First Master of the Universe: In the Gilded Age, J. Pierpont Morgan Bestrode the Financial Nation Like a Colossus. Maybe Two Colossi." *New York Times Book Review*, March 28, 1999, p. 7.

Lipsyte, Robert. "Raising an Old Question About Race, and Ignoring the Real Issue." *New York Times*, November 28, 1999, sec. 8, p. 13.

Loos, Ted. "A Role Within a Role: A Girl Who Became a Boy." *New York Times*, October 3, 1999, E pt. 1, p. 10.

Loury, Glenn C. "Race and Identity in America: A Personal Perspective." *History Place*. www.historyplace.com/pointsofview/loury.htm.

Magagnini, Stephen. "Will Rejection of Labels Create New American Identity? A Race Free Consciousness." *News & Observer*, November 23, 1997. www.news-observer.com/daily/1997/11/23/qq00.html.

Maslin, Janet. "Sometimes Accepting an Identity Means Accepting a Fate, Too." *New York Times*, October 1, 1999, E pt. 1, p. 10.

McKinley, Chris, Jr. "Weighing Therapy for a Narrow Mind." *New York Times*, January 9, 2000, sec. 4, p. 5.

Mills, Claudia. "'Passing': The Ethics of Pretending to Be What You Are Not." *Social Theory and Practice*, Spring 1999, pp. 29–51.

Morrison, Benjamin. "The Life and Death of Brandon Teena." *Times-Picayune*, July 25, 1999, p. T5.

Muhammad, Larry. "Duplicity, Originality, and Questions of Race Leaven 'Cookie Cutter'; During Detroit's Mayoral Contest, a Black Detective Pursues an Artful Killer." *USA Today*, January 6, 2000, p. 6D.

Neff, Beth. "Breaking Down Racial Barriers; Feminist Says Work of Women Artists Shows Changing Culture." *South Bend Tribune*, January 22, 1999, p. D3.

Nelson, Jill. "Black, But Not Like Me; A Journalist Slouches into a Party Celebrating the Black Elite—Whatever That Is." Salon.com, February 4, 1999. archive.salon.com/books/feature/1999/02/04/feature.html.

Newitz, Annalee. "Gender Slumming." *Bad Subjects*, September 1993.

Newitz, Annalee, and Jillian Sandell. "Bisexuality and How to Use It: Toward a Coalitional Identity Politics." *Bad Subjects*, October 1994.

O'Meally, Robert G. "An Annotated Bibliography of the Works of Sterling A. Brown." *Callaloo* 21, no. 4 (1998): 822–835.

Parker, Lonnae O'Neal. "White Girl? Cousin Kim Is Passing. But Cousin Lonnae Doesn't Want to Let Her Go." *Washington Post*, August 8, 1999, p. F1.

Pattison, Mark. "Kathleen McGhee-Anderson: Movin' On Up." *Horizon*. www.horizonmag.com/8/kathleen-mcghee-anderson.htm.

Perkins, Judith. "An Ancient 'Passing' Novel: Heliodorus' *Aithiopika*. *Arethusa* 32 (1999): 197–214.

Pisares, Elizabeth H. "Passing for Asian: Filipino Americans and Filipino American Studies within Asian American Studies." Paper presented at the Association for Asian American Studies, Philadelphia, April 1, 1999.

Powers, Ann. "Queer in the Streets, Straight in the Sheets," *Village Voice*, June 29, 1993, p. 24+.

Radano, Ronald M. "Soul Texts and the Blackness of Folk." *Modernism/ Modernity* 2, no. 1 (1995): 71–95.

Rauch, Jonathan. "Boys to Men: The Paradox of Identity and the Culture of Possibility." *Los Angeles Times*, October 31, 1999, p. 4.

Reddy, Maureen T. "White, Whiter, Whitest." *Women's Review of Books*, March 1999, p. 5.

"Readings: Blacks at Harvard: A Documentary History of African-American Experience at Harvard and Radcliffe." *Frontline*. www.pbs.org/wgbh/pages/frontline/shows/secret/readings/wilsonchapter.html.

"Readings: The Gregory Family." *Frontline*. www.pbs.org/wgbh/pages/frontline/shows/secret/readings/gregory.html.

Rich, Frank. "American Pseudo." *New York Times*, December 12, 1999, sec. 6, p. 80.

Rodriguez, Roberto, and Patrisia Gonzales. "Latino Spectrum: Whitewashing of America." *Chronicle Features* (San Francisco), May 16, 1997. www.gladstone.uoregon.edu/~mecha/news/washing.html.

Roediger, David. "White Lies: Race and the Myths of Whiteness." *Village Voice*, February 23, 1999, p. 125.

Rosenbaum, Thane. "Family Secrets: The Author Was Shocked to Find Her Catholic Parents Were Jewish Holocaust Survivors." *New York Times Book Review*, March 21, 1999, p. 7.

Schiesel, Seth, and Robert L. Turner. "Is Race Obsolete? A Move to Change Racial Designations in the US Census Underscores Some Prickly Questions About Who We Are." *Boston Globe Magazine*, September 22, 1996, p. 13.

Seifert, Leslie. "Confronting Racial Stereotypes." *The Record*, November 20, 1994, p. E2.

Selby, Holly. "Art That's Designed to Get Under Our Skin; Adrian Piper Exposes Our Racial Divide in Hopes of Bridging It." *Baltimore Sun*, November 14, 1999, p. F7.

Senna, Danzy. "Passing and the Problematic of MultiRacial Pride." *Black Renaissance/Renaissance Noire*, Fall-Winter 1998.

Seymour, Gene. "The Middle of the Rainbow." *Newsday*, July 10, 1994, p. 39.

Shales, Tom. "Brandon Teena: Anatomy of a Murder." *Washington Post*, July 26, 1999, p. CO1.

Shalit, Ruth. "Today's Woman." *Lingua Franca Book Review*, Fall 1999, pp. B33–35.

Sim, Jillian A. "Fading to White: One Woman's Journey into Her Family's Past Uncovers a Story That Affects Every American." *American Heritage*, February-March 1999. www.americanheritage.com/99/feb/002/htm.

Smith, Errol. "Race and Responsibility." *Reason Magazine,* May 1993.

Span, Paula. "Kingdom of the Drag Queens; They're All Dressed Up and Now They're Going Places." *Washington Post*, March 11, 1993, p. C1.

Stacy, Greg. "Interview with the Hermaphrodite." *OC Weekly*, October 8, 1999, p. 18.

Staples, Brent. "Hey, Wait a Minute: The Real American Love Story: Why America Is a Lot Less White Than It Looks." Slate.com, October 4, 1999. slate.msn.com/id/35817.

Strickland, Daryl. "Interracial Generation: 'We Are Who We Are': Individuals of Mixed Heritage Are Tired of Being Labeled as 'Other' on Census Forms." *Seattle Times*, May 5, 1996, p. L1.

"Topics of the Times: Passing for White in Hollywood." *New York Times*, August 23, 1993, p. A14.

Watson, Rod. "So What If Traffic Stops Single Out Blacks? Think of the Happy Side of Racism." *Buffalo News,* April 2, 1998, p. 2B.

Werts, Diane. "Gutsy Lifetime Series Butts Racism Head-On." *Florida Times-Union*, October 23, 1999, p. D-5.

Wheelwright, Julie. "The Boyfriend; 'He Was a Lot of Girls' Dream Guy,' According to a Friend. There Was Just One Problem: He Wasn't a Guy." *Guardian*, February 20, 1996, p. T6.

Wilgoren, Jodi. "Elite Colleges Step Up Courting of Minorities." *New York Times*, October 25, 1999, p. A1.

Will, Ed. "Murder in a Small Town." *Denver Post* magazine, March 6, 1994, p. 10.

Williams, Gregory Howard. "It Was Time to Stop Being White and Live as Black." *Houston Chronicle*, February 12, 1995, p. 6.

Williams, Monte. "Is There a Black Upper Class?" *New York Times*, March 7, 1999, sec. 9, p. 1.

Wynter, Leon E. "'Born Again' Hispanics: Choosing What to Be." *Wall Street Journal*, November 3, 1999, p. B1.

Acknowledgments

In addition to the individuals explicitly mentioned in the text, endnotes, and bibliography, to whom I owe an enormous debt, I need to thank the following people:

- The unnamed primary subjects as well as their friends, colleagues, former colleagues, and associates. Of those not otherwise acknowledged whom I can identify, I extend special thanks to Joanne Ruffa, LaVerne Hayes, Ernestine Jackson, Molly McCabe Silverstein, George Towns, and Keiko Sono.
- For research assistance and transcription, my gratitude to Caroline Binham, Rebekah Brilliant, Sarah Bronson, Gail Dottin, and Ben Fishman, as well as to Gail Gregg and Marsha Pinson, who took it upon themselves to help keep tabs on passing stories in the media.
- For sources, good counsel, and wise critiques, I thank my colleagues, former colleagues, and students at New York University, and my indulgent family and friends, particularly Marilynn Abrams, Fiamma Arditi, Geraldine Baum, Giovanna Borradori, Bettina Bosé, Lisa Bowles, Jodi Cahn, Gioia Diliberto, Charlotte Frieze, Bill Gaskins, Alex Goren, Andrea Goren, Selina Goren, Dax Goren, Gail Gregg, Peter C. Jones, Alex Kogan, Carol Kogan, Suzanne Kogan, Brett Kroeger, Michael Lowry, Ilene Mandell, Sandro Manzo, Deobrah Margolis, Malka Margolies, Rabbi Morris Margolies, Bernadette Murray,

Michael Oreskes, Patricia O'Toole, Nell Irvin Painter, Marsha Pinson, the late Martin Pinson, Max Pinson, Luke I. Pontifell, Savine Pontifell, Candace Rondeaux, Noliwe Rooks, Lauren Sandler, Alison Smale, Paula Span, Stephanie Sandberg, Augusta Tilney, Ellen Walterscheid, Jean Washington, Joshua R. Weiner, the late and deeply missed David Weinstein, Helen Weinstein, Randy Weinstein, Ricki Weiss, and Arturo Zampaglione.

• Abundant thanks also to Peter Osnos, Lisa Kaufman, Chrisona Schmidt, Melanie Peirson Johnstone, and all the team at Public Affairs, and, as always, a special place for Philippa Brophy.

Index

PUBLICAFFAIRS is a publishing house founded in 1997. It is a tribute to the standards, values, and flair of three persons who have served as mentors to countless reporters, writers, editors, and book people of all kinds, including me.

I. F. STONE, proprietor of *I. F. Stone's Weekly,* combined a commitment to the First Amendment with entrepreneurial zeal and reporting skill and became one of the great independent journalists in American history. At the age of eighty, Izzy published *The Trial of Socrates,* which was a national bestseller. He wrote the book after he taught himself ancient Greek.

BENJAMIN C. BRADLEE was for nearly thirty years the charismatic editorial leader of *The Washington Post.* It was Ben who gave the *Post* the range and courage to pursue such historic issues as Watergate. He supported his reporters with a tenacity that made them fearless, and it is no accident that so many became authors of influential, best-selling books.

ROBERT L. BERNSTEIN, the chief executive of Random House for more than a quarter century, guided one of the nation's premier publishing houses. Bob was personally responsible for many books of political dissent and argument that challenged tyranny around the globe. He is also the founder and was the longtime chair of Human Rights Watch, one of the most respected human rights organizations in the world.

.   .   .

For fifty years, the banner of Public Affairs Press was carried by its owner Morris B. Schnapper, who published Gandhi, Nasser, Toynbee, Truman, and about 1,500 other authors. In 1983 Schnapper was described by *The Washington Post* as "a redoubtable gadfly." His legacy will endure in the books to come.

Peter Osnos, *Publisher*